Whole Language Teaching, Whole-Hearted Practice

Studies in the
Postmodern Theory of Education

Joe L. Kincheloe and Shirley R. Steinberg
General Editors

Vol. 236

PETER LANG
New York • Washington, D.C./Baltimore • Bern
Frankfurt am Main • Berlin • Brussels • Vienna • Oxford

Whole Language Teaching, Whole-Hearted Practice

LOOKING BACK, LOOKING FORWARD

EDITED BY Monica Taylor

PETER LANG
New York • Washington, D.C./Baltimore • Bern
Frankfurt am Main • Berlin • Brussels • Vienna • Oxford

Library of Congress Cataloging-in-Publication Data

Whole language teaching, whole-hearted practice:
looking back, looking forward /
edited by Monica Taylor.
p. cm. — (Counterpoints: studies in the postmodern theory of education: vol. 236)
Includes bibliographical references and index.
1. Language experience approach in education.
2. Critical pedagogy. I. Taylor, Monica.
LB1576.W4869   372.6—dc22   2006022460
ISBN-13: 978-0-8204-6310-0
ISBN-10: 0-8204-6310-8
ISSN 1058-1634

Bibliographic information published by **Die Deutsche Bibliothek**.
Die Deutsche Bibliothek lists this publication in the "Deutsche
Nationalbibliografie"; detailed bibliographic data is available
on the Internet at http://dnb.ddb.de/.

Cover design by Sophie Boorsch Appel

The paper in this book meets the guidelines for permanence and durability
of the Committee on Production Guidelines for Book Longevity
of the Council of Library Resources.

In loving memory of Rose, my grandmother and first whole language teacher.

Contents

Acknowledgments

This edited collection was created as a result of the hard work of many people. My first thanks go to my colleagues whose insightful chapters make this book unique and engaging. I have learned a tremendous amount from their experiences and know that the readers will benefit equally from this collection. Thanks to Ken and Yetta Goodman, who have been extraordinary parents, mentors, and role models to me. They inspire me to be a change agent! I owe thanks to my graduate assistant, Andy Beutel, who helped me with many of the details necessary for an edited collection. I would also like to express my appreciation to Shirley Steinberg and Joe Kincheloe who gave me the idea and the opportunity to assemble this book. Additionally, I would like to express my gratitude to Chris Myers for his guidance and support.

I would like to give special thanks to my husband, Mark, for his endless hours of patience late night and on Sunday afternoons and also for his skills as a formatter. Thanks also to my boys, Michael and Griffin, for their support and understanding as sons of a whole language mom and agitator.

CHAPTER ONE

Whole Language Teaching Is Wholehearted Activism

MONICA TAYLOR

With the current return to homogeneous tracking, standardized testing, hierarchical basal schemes, and state-approved textbook adoption lists, the political role of literacy, which whole language threatened to disrupt, has been firmly reinstated. Those teachers who are struggling to maintain their whole language perspectives must understand that in doing so they are not only defending an instructional model for literacy, but a political stance toward education. Classroom literacy can never be politically neutral. Literacy can be taught either as a tool for critical literacy or passive transmission. It can be a vehicle for posing and solving important problems or for accepting official explanations and solutions. The organization of classroom life, the way learning is assessed, and the materials and practices used for instruction may all either reinforce hierarchical systems of authority and power or demonstrate principles of democracy and justice.

Whole language must become part of a larger educational effort to transform education and society in the direction of equity and social justice…. We must begin to see ourselves not just as whole language educators, but as educational activists with clear pedagogical principles. (Altwerger & Saavedra, 1999, pp. xi-xii)

Introduction

W hy put together a book on whole language in this age of No Child Left Behind and scripted curricula like Reading First, Success for All, and Open Court (Altwerger, 2005)? Why focus on whole language teaching when many smart, well-educated parents are advocating for phonics only and unintentionally have adopted the rhetoric of fundamentalists and the far right? Why discuss the ways in which whole language teachers are facilitating critical literacy when the big business of publishers has usurped curriculum development and material selection from teachers (Poynor & Wolfe, 2005)? Why share stories of successful whole language teachers when many are too afraid to admit that they are whole language teachers? As Dudley-Marling (1999) sarcastically refers to himself: "I'm not a communist, a liberal, or a whole language teacher (and I don't beat my wife)" (p.1). Regardless of these obstacles and barriers, we need to be hopeful because (as I heard Yetta Goodman say at the 2005 Whole Language Umbrella Conference in San Diego, California) "Whole language is still alive and well."

The intention of this book is to highlight, over the course of the past thirty-five years, the complex ways in which whole language teachers have and continue to be political activists through their interactions with students, their beliefs about teaching, learning, and curriculum, their commitment to critical thinking and social justice, their collaborative engagements with other teachers, their role as leaders of change in schools and communities, and finally their activism in society. The authors in this volume were invited to contribute because their voices and stories poignantly illustrate the ways in which whole language educators have been and always will be political.

Whole language teaching is inherently political. It has been and will always be a grass-roots collective based on a teaching philosophy that values the theoretical knowledge, research, and practices of teachers as the vehicle to support the needs, strengths, and interests of the learner within the context of multiple learning communities. As Edelsky (1999) writes when she describes the politics in Ken Goodman's psycholinguistic model of reading:

> Civil rights, Woodstock, the fatal bombing in Madison, San Francisco State, police shootouts with Black Panthers, the Chicago Convention, Charles Manson, Black power, Women's power, State power, Kent State, open classrooms, Chomsky, behaviorism, My Lai, language deficits, race and generic inferiority, Tet offensive, Distar, Make Love Not War, assassinations, Where Have All the Flowers Gone, decode first make sense later, sound it out, sound it out.

> Ken Goodman's work is located in and grew out of that swirl. It gets its revolutionary flavor from what it opposed, what it supported, what it leaned on, what it transformed. It opposed racist depictions of diversity and societal hierarchies. It supported movements of minority power, for trusting ordinary people as they did ordinary things (like learn and use language)....And through transformed conceptions of reading, it transformed the school lives of millions. (p. 16)

This collection of narratives shares a glimpse of the commitment of whole language teachers both to teaching in a just, equitable, and empowering manner and to initiating change in classrooms, among teachers in schools, and in school communities.

I emphasize "glimpse" because I believe that many teachers all over the world are engaged in the types of political endeavors that the authors describe. But most whole language teachers are so busy teaching, working on curriculum, kidwatching, developing relationships with children, and acting as leaders in their schools that, as Debi Goodman explains in her chapter, they do not take the time to publicize the ways in which, through the cracks of scripted curriculum and testing, they resist surrendering their teaching beliefs and practices and engage with students in meaningful ways (Altwerger, 2005; Altwerger & Flores, 1999; Darder, 2002; Edelsky, 1999; Edelsky, 2005). I hope that this chronology of authentic narratives is a call to arms. As Church (1996) writes:

> While I believe that teachers must bring a more critical stance to their teaching, I am convinced that there is equally significant political work to be done outside the classroom. . . We know from our earlier experiences with whole language that even our less overtly political challenges to the status quo did not sit easily within the hierarchical school system. Those of us who have moved outside the classroom to positions of responsibility within that hierarchy cannot avoid taking on those bigger political issues, but I believe that we *all* need to make institutional structures, practices, and relationships the focus of our critique and projects of possibilities. We all need to see ourselves both as teachers and as leaders engaged in social change. (p. 30-31)

As whole language educators whose work has always been political, we must make transparent our often hidden subversive acts for school change. We must strategize continually to remind the world that "whole language is alive and well" in whatever town, city, state, or country where we live and work.

Below I will briefly share experiences of strengthening my own voice as a whole language teacher and activist, which will help to illustrate my intentions for the volume. I will then describe how the whole language teaching philosophy and practices constitute wholehearted activism, illuminating the strands that will be more thoroughly illustrated in the chapters that follow.

Whole Language Has Social Justice Roots

The inception of this volume occurred after a series of continuous "aha!" moments. With a background in language, literacy, and culture (I did my doctoral work with Ken and Yetta Goodman at the University of Arizona), I worked as a teacher educator in the more general arena of middle school teaching at Wagner College on Staten Island, NY, for three years, and was starting my first year at Montclair State University in curriculum and teaching. Up until that point, I would often tell people who asked that I was a literacy person in the more general arena of curriculum and teaching—as if I were an anomaly or strange. As I write this, I realize the truth is that I often find myself in strange positions and these circumstances work for me. I came into teaching through the back door—through alternate routes and some connections cultivated by my grandmother as a kindergarten teacher. I was a middle school Spanish teacher getting my Masters in English Education. I have always seemed to find my way even if I did not fit the traditional mold or follow the traditional path. I have always embraced taking risks and facing challenges.

But the more I think about this, the more I realize (and this is really the big continuous "aha!") that a background in language, literacy, and culture (or more specifically in whole language and critical literacy) is serving me well as a teacher educator in curriculum and teaching. The theoretical and research foundation that was laid during my work as a graduate student has provided extensive roots for the understanding of teaching and learning in general and social justice teaching and inquiry more specifically. I understand what Freire (1993) meant when he wrote that "it does not matter where or when it has taken place, whether it is more or less complex, education has always been a political act" (p. 127). I continually draw upon this foundation when I am working with preservice and in-service teachers of all content areas. I have used my whole language lens to think about the issues of empowerment of teachers, the need for students, teachers, families, and communities to learn in authentic and engaging ways, the ways to forge successful partnerships between schools and universities, between students, teachers, student teachers, and teacher educators, and the commitment to teach for social justice.

I realize (aha!) that the theories and beliefs about whole language teaching and learning that I studied as a doctoral student have created a theoretical foundation that supports my work with secondary preservice teachers of all content areas. My philosophy is drawn from the work of John Dewey, Louise Rosenblatt, Maxine Greene, Lev Vygotsky, Paulo Freire, Ken and Yetta Goodman, Luis Moll, Patrick Shannon, bell hooks, Deborah Britzman, Michael Apple, Cornel West, Jerry Harste, Kathy Short, Connie Weaver, Carole Edelsky, Linda Christensen, and others, as well as my own research. I work to prepare teachers drawing from the whole language beliefs and practices which shape my understanding of teaching and learning. These tenets or roots also lay the foundation for the ways in which whole language has been and always will be a grassroots, political, and wholehearted practice.

As I write this, I begin to have another "aha!" moment: perhaps not fitting the traditional mold or being "normal" has also laid a foundation for me as a whole language teacher and activist. I am willing to take risks, speak up for what I believe, and be subversive. I have learned to observe my students, listen to their voices, and be their advocate. I am not afraid.

When Shirley Steinberg approached me to organize this edited collection, I was unsure whether I could do it. My new work as a curriculum and teaching educator made me wonder if I could return to the literacy world as an insider. As I began to think about the concept of the volume—to provide a space for the voices of whole language teachers from the past, present, and future to share their navigations through treacherous political waters—I realized that this was an endeavor that was both necessary and worthwhile. As I talked further with Shirley, who was so supportive and enthusiastic, and later had multiple discussions with Yetta and Ken Goodman, who proposed a similar theme for the book, I realized again (aha!) that focusing on whole language teaching as activism was essential.

Whole Language Teaching as Wholehearted Activism

Although I believe that this volume echoes many of the concerns and critical reflections about whole language teaching for justice and equity discussed in both Edelsky's (1999) *Making Justice Our Project: Teachers Working Toward Critical Whole Language Practice* and Boran and Comber's (2001) *Critiquing Whole Language and Classroom Inquiry*, the authors in this collection illustrate the multilayered dimensions of social justice activism involved in whole language teaching. Some have criticized whole language teachers for being undemocratic or perpetuating and contributing to systems of injustice (as described by Edelsky, 1999). They also have been identified with "the white, privileged, dominant culture" (Altwerger & Saavedra, 1999). The whole language philosophy is committed to social justice teaching, and many whole language teachers (some in this volume) strive to teach from this perspective, bringing together "a range of social and cultural practices which assist students to question the truths of texts, to ask different questions about texts, and indeed to seek out conflicting texts. Students need to learn that inquiry is not simply finding right answers to old and familiar questions, but that the questions themselves and the sources investigated must also be subject to interrogation" (Boran & Comber, 2001, pp. viii-ix). But this is just one part of the picture.

The contributors to this book argue that whole language has been, is, and will always be an education movement/philosophy that is critical, pro-justice, and pro-democratic. The whole language movement is inherently democratic: the power of the philosophy resides in the ways teachers and their students, not administrators or even university professors, take ownership of their learning and teaching. As Yetta Goodman stated in an interview, "Teachers teach me a lot about what happens in classrooms. They work very hard and they know so much." Together, the authors of this volume illustrate how whole language teachers can be examined as engaged activists from multiple dimensions. These dimensions include their interactions and relationships with students, their beliefs about teaching, learning, and curriculum and the ways that they "teach against the grain" (Cochran-Smith, 1991), their commitment to social justice, their engagement with parents, their collaboration with other teachers, and their role as leaders of change in their schools, communities, professional teaching organizations, teacher education, and state and national legislation. These levels of social justice activism pervade the work of whole language teachers. Debi Goodman (1999), when discussing what it was like "growing up whole language," echoes these dimensions. The qualities that she values as a teacher are:

- A belief in myself and my ideas
- A respect for other human beings and a belief in civil rights
- An appreciation of language and learning
- An understanding of grassroots movements for change
- A respect for teachers and teaching (as an exalted profession!)
- A view of teachers as researchers
- An understanding of the power of story, parable and metaphor in expressing and coming to know complex ideas (pp. 193-194)

Whole language teachers have and will always "teach against the grain." They recognize their students as individuals and they themselves practice as individuals. As Whitmore and Goodman (1996) explain: "One unwarranted criticism of whole language has been that it looks different from teacher to teacher. That's as it should be. Each teacher is an independent professional, a decision maker who builds his or her own teaching on a common knowledge base, a common belief system, and a common set of principles" (p. 2).

Whole Language Beliefs about Language

Whole language teachers understand that "language learning is universal. All people can think symbolically and share a social need to communicate" (Whitmore & Goodman, 1996, p. 3). They believe that learning language, learning through language, and learning about language all occur at the same time (Halliday, undated). They realize that language and literacy develop through authentic engagements with real-life concerns and interests.

Whole language teachers have a broad view of what constitutes language and literacy. They accept a range of sign systems used to communicate and make meaning of the world (Harste, 2001). They encourage students to use language and literacy in a critical way to problematize the social and cultural norms that are produced and reproduced in texts. They understand that language and literacy can be politically powerful.

Whole Language Students

One of the most important principles of the whole language philosophy is the belief that all students enter the classroom with knowledge, experiences, and meaning-making tools. Whole language teachers draw upon their students' knowledge, interests, strengths, and needs to develop a curriculum that is relevant, challenging, and engaging. Learners are viewed from the perspective of their potential or strengths, with high expectations rather than from a deficit model. They trust their students as learners and invite them to take ownership of their learning.

Whole language teachers respect and accept all learners regardless of their ability, race, gender, religion, class, ethnicity, or sexual orientation. They are kidwatchers (Y. Goodman, 1985) and are determined to get to know their students and make an effort for their students to get to know them. They understand the importance of a relationship or partnership that supports learning, and they actively strive to develop democratic learning communities in their classrooms where learners and teachers learn together. They value and facilitate student collaboration.

Whole language teachers are caring, compassionate individuals who promote respect, acceptance, and understanding among their students. They are advocates for their students. They are strongly committed to democratic principles and the empowerment of their students. They model these dispositions as well as provide opportunities for students to problematize their positions in society.

Whole Language Learning, Teaching, and Curriculum

In whole language classrooms, teaching and learning involve the construction of knowledge and the making of meaning rather than the transmission of information. Learning is considered a life-long, ongoing process that occurs in a supportive collaborative environment where each student is viewed as an individual. Learners develop a zone of proximal development (Vygotsky, 1978), a range of potential learning. In democratic classrooms, students and teachers act together as learners and teachers, providing scaffolding for one another. Choice and ownership enhance learning for students. Learning in schools must be connected to the lives of students and teachers outside of schools. Because learning is viewed as a personal process, reflection, self-evaluation, and authentic assessments are utilized to understand students' growth.

Whole language teachers understand that inquiry is a natural inclination for learners. Inquiry invites students and teachers to question social and cultural norms, discover the perspectives that are often not represented, and take action towards a socially just society. Critical reflection of students and teachers leads to a rethinking of perspectives and concepts.

A whole language curriculum is whole and integrated. It is a "dual curriculum," constructing "thought and language at the same time that it builds knowledge and concepts" (Whitmore & Goodman, 1996, p. 4). The curriculum begins with the learners, with their identities, the knowledge that they bring, and the questions that they have. The curriculum emerges through the interaction of students, teachers, families, and community members when there is trust. The curriculum and materials used represent a wide spectrum of voices, including those whose perspectives often go unheard.

Whole Language Collaborative Communities

Whole language teachers invite multiple people to collaborate when it comes to enhancing the learning of their students and their own teaching. They realize the importance of building partnerships with families to support the learning of students. They value "the funds of knowledge" (Moll et al., 1992) of all families and strive to incorporate family knowledge, language, and culture into the curriculum. They draw upon families' expertise in their understanding of their children to better meet the needs of their students. They are also committed to keeping families informed about the learning experiences of their children. Whole language teachers involve families in any way that they can.

Much of what whole language teachers know about teaching and learning has emerged from their reflections on being a learner. They envision themselves as lifelong learners and therefore create multiple partnerships that enhance their own teaching. They work collaboratively with their colleagues through team teaching, teacher study groups, action research, planning, curriculum development, and professional development. They believe that the collaboration of teachers and administrators is powerful and can lead to school change and social justice.

Whole language teachers understand that teaching is political. They are savvy in the ways that they navigate the systems in which they work. They often take on leadership roles in their schools, districts, towns, and local professional organizations. They seek out ways to collaborate with teacher education programs at colleges or universities. They attend local and national professional conferences to continue developing as teachers, share their own work and research, and participate in their professional communities.

Whole language teachers are enormously committed to their profession. They are reflective practitioners who take their work seriously and to heart. Sincerely believing in the potential of their students, they spend considerable time preparing materials, observing and understanding students, discovering ways to support their individual learners, growing as professionals, and being political.

The goal for this book is to demonstrate the political tenets of the whole language movement through the eyes of teachers, teacher educators, students, and families. The narratives here voice the ways in which whole language teachers have striven and will continue to strive to empower teachers and students and to promote social justice. By examining both the history and potential future of whole language teaching, we are able to discover consistent themes across time, location, and communities. These narratives inspire us to continually strive to understand what it means to be a whole language teacher and activist. Perhaps these documented experiences will encourage you to speak up and share your own stories of being involved in this powerful grassroots educational movement.

References

Altwerger, B. (2005). The push of the pendulum. In L. Poynor & P. M. Wolfe (Eds.), *Marketing fear in America's public schools: The real war on literacy* (pp. 31-49). Mahwah, NJ: Lawrence Erlbaum Associates.

Altwerger, B. & Flores, B. (1999). Towards a critical, whole language pedagogy. In A. M. Marek & C. Edelsky (Eds.), *Reflections and connections: Essays in honor of Kenneth S. Goodman's influence on language education* (pp. 371-402). Cresskill, NJ: Hampton Press.

Altwerger, B. & Saavedra, E. R. (1999). Foreword. In C. Edelsky (Ed.), *Making justice our project: Teachers working toward critical whole language practice* (pp. vii-xii). Urbana, IL: National Council of Teachers of English.

Boran, S. & Comber, B. (2001). Introduction: The inquirers and their questions. In S. Boran & B. Comber (Eds.), *Critiquing whole language and classroom inquiry* (pp. vii-xvii). Urbana, IL: National Council of Teachers of English.

Church, S. (1996). *The future of whole language: Reconstruction or self-destruction?* Portsmouth, NH: Heinemann.

Cochran-Smith, M. (1991). Learning to teach against the grain. *Harvard Educational Review, 61*, 279-310.

Darder, A. (2002). *Reinventing Paulo Freire: A pedagogy of love.* Boulder, CO: Westview Press.

Dudley-Marling, C. (1999). I'm not a communist, a liberal, or a whole language teacher (and I don't beat my wife). *Talking Points 10*(2), 14-16.

Edelsky, C. (2005). Relatively speaking: McCarthyism and teacher-resisters. In L. Poynor & P. M. Wolfe (Eds.), *Marketing fear in America's public schools: The real war on literacy* (pp. 11-28). Mahwah, NJ: Lawrence Erlbaum Associates.

Edelsky, C. (1999). Introduction. In C. Edelsky (Ed.), *Making justice our project: Teachers working toward critical whole language practice* (pp. 1-6). Urbana, IL: National Council of Teachers of English.

— (1999). The psycholinguistic guessing game: A political-historical retrospective. In A. M. Marek & C. Edelsky (Eds.), *Reflections and connections: Essays in honor of Kenneth S. Goodman's influence on language education* (pp. 3-25). Cresskill, NJ: Hampton Press.

Freire, P. (1993). *Pedagogy of the city.* New York: Continuum.

Goodman, D. (1999). Growing up whole language. In A. M. Marek & C. Edelsky (Eds.), *Reflections and connections: Essays in honor of Kenneth S. Goodman's influence on language education* (pp. 187-210). Cresskill, NJ: Hampton Press.

Goodman, Y. M. (1985). Kidwatching: Observing children in classrooms. In A. Jaggar & M. T. Smith-Burke (Eds.), *Observing the language learner* (pp. 9-18). Newark, DE and Urbana, IL: Co-published by International Reading Association and the National Council of Teachers of English.

Halliday, M. A. K. (undated). Three aspects of children's language development: Learning language, learning through language, learning about language. In G. S. Pinnell & M. Matlin Haussler (Eds.), *Language research: Impact on educational settings.* Unpublished manuscript.

Harste, J. (2001). What education as inquiry is and isn't. In S. Boran & B. Comber (Eds.), *Critiquing whole language and classroom inquiry* (pp. 1-17). Urbana, IL: National Council of Teachers of English.

Moll, L. C., Amanti, C., Neff, D., & Gonzalez, N. (1992). Funds of knowledge for teaching: Using a qualitative approach to connect homes and classrooms. *Theory into Practice, 31,* 132-141.

Poynor, L. & Wolfe, P. M. (2005). Introduction. In L. Poynor & P. M. Wolfe (Eds.), *Marketing fear in America's public schools: The real war on literacy* (pp. 1-9). Mahwah, NJ: Lawrence Erlbaum Associates.

Vygotsky, L. S. (1978). *Mind in society.* Cambridge, MA: Harvard University Press.

Whitmore, K. F. & Goodman, K. S. (1996). Practicing what we teach: The principles that guide us. In K. F. Whitmore & K. S. Goodman (Eds.), *Whole language voices in teacher education* (pp. 1-16). York, ME: Stenhouse Publishers.

CHAPTER TWO

The Whole Language Movement in Detroit: A Teacher's Story: Part One

DEBRA GOODMAN

Reading and Writing in Community Voices

It's virtually impossible for someone to tell me and my children what we should be learning. We have to make those decisions ourselves. It has to be something that interests us and that we think is important. The idea that people can create these asinine tests, that paranoid administrators can dictate curriculum to teachers and children, is ridiculous. If I don't like something, I'm not going to be enthusiastic about it in the classroom. If it's not interesting to me and I don't think it's meaningful, I'll convey that to the kids somehow. I can't get up there and lie. So I'm constantly looking for what they're interested in and sharing what I'm interested in and trying to tie it all together in learning about life.

-Toby Kahn Curry (Interview by Y. Goodman, 1991, p. 92)

Mother Curry: The Beginnings of Whole Language in Detroit

I first met Toby Kahn Curry (now Toby Kahn Loftus) in the spring of 1982, when I was a daily substitute teacher at Burton International School, a magnet school in Detroit's center city. Toby's[1] room was crowded with both of her classes—over sixty eighth graders—and I was sent to assist on a field trip to the main library. When I got to her room, she shrugged and said, "I don't really need help, but that's fine." I took a seat as the group prepared to leave.

As a young teacher, I found middle schoolers somewhat intimidating, and I was impressed with Toby's easy rapport with this large group. She stood with her arms folded, waiting for all of their attention before she began to speak. She took no nonsense but also had tremendous patience and a sense of humor. She was "Mother Curry," and everyone was "sweetheart" and "honey."

Once the game plan for the trip was reviewed, we went down the stairs to begin the mile-long hike up Cass Avenue to Detroit's Main Library. Burton International was housed in a school building built in the early 1900s in the middle of Detroit's Cass Corridor. We walked past neglected apartment buildings, boarded houses, closed businesses, and fields of weeds sometimes used as illegal waste dumps. Community members in one or two tenement apartments, a few renovated homes, and a very few shops, restaurants, schools and churches struggled to hold together the community. Called "The Corridor" because it was a two-mile strip that connected Downtown Detroit with Detroit's Cultural Center, the neighborhood was known as one of the worst in the city. But the Cass Corridor was also a prime location for a school, just a short walk from Orchestra Hall, the downtown sights, government and courts, museums, public libraries, and the facilities of Wayne State University.

Toby later described the diverse population of students we worked with at this K-8 magnet school:

> At that time I taught in a multi-cultural, multi-lingual school in Detroit's Center City. The student population was approximately 60% African-American, 20% white European, including several Appalachian children and about 20% "other." The "other" part of our student body came from China, Pakistan, India, Nigeria, Liberia, Ghana, the Philippines, Sri Lanka, Korea and several other countries, giving us a total of eighteen different ethnic backgrounds represented in the school. I loved teaching there because of the rich cultural and ethnic diversity of the children. I learned a tremendous amount about literacy and language from my students and their families. (Curry, 1992, p. 32)

The Detroit Main Library is a beautiful three-story building with many wings of spacious reading rooms and sweeping marble staircases. Toby had the students sit at the long wooden tables near the card catalogs and explained where they might go to find information, pointing out the historic and periodic collections and the other areas of the library. She told them when we would meet back at the tables, and then she set them loose.

As we wandered through the library, checking on small groups of students here and there, I talked with Toby about her teaching. I was impressed that her eighth graders were engaged in research projects, that she had taken them to the library—rather than expecting they would find it by themselves—and that she had the trust and confidence to let them work on their own. I told Toby that she was an amazing "whole language" teacher. Toby, along with most of the 10,000 teachers in the Detroit Public Schools, had never heard of "whole language." But our dialogue had begun.

About a year later, Yetta Goodman provided an informal talk for teachers at our school. She talked about whole language, reading and writing process, and kidwatching. She provided some specific suggestions, such as dialogue journals, for exploring the whole language philosophy. After the talk Toby said she felt like she was doing everything right as a parent but everything wrong as a teacher.

At that time I was a reading specialist, housed in two tiny rooms in the basement, just off the playground so that if I opened the windows the dust was kicked in on my classroom library. Toby tried dialogue journals and dropped by to talk about how it was going. She told me about her "Fifty Book Club," where students were encouraged to read fifty (100 pages counted as a "book") trade books a year. By spring, many of the students had already read well over the fifty books. Extending her "Fifty Book Club," Toby invited her seventh graders to write letters to authors. I suggested she might enjoy reading *Dear Mr. Henshaw* (Cleary, 1983) to her class. Toby and her students loved the book and Toby came back to ask me for other suggestions to read aloud. I realized that reading aloud to middle schoolers was not a common teaching strategy. Toby, with secondary English certification, was amazed at the breadth of children's and adolescent literature available.

Traveling down from the fourth floor, Toby began to join me for our 25-minute lunch period. Every day we shared our triumphs and frustrations. Toby and I talked about writing workshop and sustained silent reading. At the same time, Toby was teaching a traditional English grammar program. She was using the social studies textbook to teach American History, and she and the other middle school teachers, as part of the school's Joplin plan, exchanged children for a traditional basal reading program. Toby came in one day and said, "I just can't do it all!" How was she supposed to do writing workshop, journals, and independent reading, and also teach Social Studies, English Grammar, and Reading?

"Why try?" I answered. I suggested that she consider using the "Fifty Book Club" as the reading program and the writing workshop as her English/Language Arts program. Excited with the possibilities, we talked over ideas for creating a curriculum (Short and Burke, 1991) for the following year. We went home and both returned the next day with the same thought: Why not focus on the social studies program, using the content themes for meaningful reading and writing experiences?

It was in these rushed lunchtime conversations that the whole language movement in Detroit was born. While our conversations focused on children and curriculum, theoretical and sociopolitical issues were evident. "Objective referenced tests" were the buzzwords of the day, and Detroit had a supplemental "reading" program with hundreds of objectives that were constantly tested. Ginn 360 was the adopted reading program for the district, and the students had two workbooks and a posttest for every textbook level. Desks were all in rows, and board work (where children copied both questions and answers) was a common learning experience. The students were tested every spring on the California Achievement Test. Fourth and seventh graders also took statewide assessments for reading and math.

I saw Toby as a whole language teacher because of the kinds of learning experiences that she was creating and because of the respectful way that she worked with middle schoolers. But I also saw Toby as a whole language teacher because of her strong beliefs about social justice and equity for the children of Detroit and because she viewed teaching as being part of a transformative social movement. Toby and I were both Detroiters who grew up in the city and chose to teach there. Toby was active in the Cass Corridor community—shopping at the food co-op, attending St. Pat's church, organizing her kids to sell items at "dally in the alley" and participating in other neighborhood events. She was active in the teachers' union and in city politics.

When a large incinerator was built near the school, she and her seventh graders sent helium balloons out of the fourth-story window. The balloons each had a card explaining that our school was near the largest incinerator in North America, and the students wanted to track where the smoke from the incinerator might go. They asked people who found the balloons to return them in the mail. Students tracked the responses on a map and shared their findings in letters to the newspaper, the city council, and the mayor.

I think of these early meetings as the beginning of a whole language movement in Detroit, because now there were two of us working together. Before we met, I was one teacher trying to be innovative behind the closed doors of my own classroom. Toby writes, "I think we need to recognize here that Debi and I didn't begin sharing and working together as the result of a system selected 'in service' meeting… Debi and I came together because we both care about kids and learning and we both sensed that we had something to offer each other" (Curry, 1986).

Toby was a veteran teacher who was well liked and accepted. She participated in a variety of school functions with a great sense of humor that seemed to come from teaching middle school. She had a respectful but open and direct approach to colleagues that was both charming and disarming. She was hardworking and well organized and was sought after for district committees and projects. Her position in the school system and the community was critical for carrying whole language forward as a teachers' movement in the Detroit schools.

The Whole Language Movement in Detroit

This is a story much lived but largely untold. In Detroit, much as in other places, small groups of teachers, parents, administrators, and teacher educators came together to develop programs and schools that built upon our understandings of how language works and how kids learn language. We were typically swimming upstream with little support or understanding from the district administration. But we continued because we believed whole language classrooms were the best places for children, and we knew they were the best places for teachers. In our desire to be learners as well as teachers, and in the face of constraints and active opposition, we banded together in teacher support groups, such as Detroit Teachers Applying Whole Language (Detroit TAWL).

The term "whole language" was created by groups of educators exploring common theoretical orientations towards language, literacy, learning, teaching, and classroom communities. "Whole language" started as a descriptor of a curriculum where learning is experiential and language is "whole", with meaning and social function intact (For detailed discussion: Harste, Woodward, & Burke, 1984; Goodman, 1986; Cambourne, 1988). Teachers began to use the term "whole language" to identify themselves as a group of educators who were exploring the possibilities of these theoretical orientations within the classroom.

Ken Goodman (1986) describes four theoretical "pillars" of whole language that teachers bring to the classroom: a theory of language, a theory of learning, a theory of teaching, and a theory of curriculum. Whole language, as a curriculum, emerges in conversation among teachers with varied backgrounds, living and teaching in different cultural settings and communities, and negotiating a curriculum with each group of students. For this reason whole language classrooms are very diverse from teacher to teacher and year to year (For example: Edelsky, Altwerger & Flores, 1991; Goodman, Hood, & Goodman, 1991).

Weaver describes the process of understanding whole language as exploring the "unity *within* the diversity." She writes: "Whole language is not a static entity but an evolving philosophy, sensitive to new knowledge and insights. It is based upon research from a variety of perspectives and disciplines—among them language acquisition and emergent literacy, psycholinguistics and sociolinguistics, cognitive and developmental psychology, anthropology, and education" (1990, pp. 4-5). Susan Austin, a Detroit whole language teacher, says, "You can't really 'box up' a whole language program. Whole language moves you away from the teachers' manuals and set curriculum" (2003, survey response).

Over the past twenty years, whole language teachers often defined and refined what whole language is in opposition to what it isn't. Whole language is often contrasted with "traditional" teaching. But when I described whole language to kindergarten teachers, they often said, "that sounds like the *traditional* kindergarten" program. We considered the erosion of "traditional" kindergartens with playhouses and finger paints, and "traditional" Detroit schools with well-stocked libraries and certified librarians. In Detroit, where the school district is over 80% African American, parents are wary of "experimental" programs and want their children to have the quality of education enjoyed by mainstream students (for example, Delpit, 1995; Ladson-Billings, 1994; Paley, 1995). As we became Detroit whole language teachers, it was important to connect whole language theory with a long tradition of progressive, student-centered, democratic classrooms and schools (Shannon, 1990).

We found Weaver's (1990) dichotomy between "transaction" and "transmission" useful. Weaver writes that "a transactional model emphasizes active learning, while the transmission model emphasizes 'repeat-after-me' and 'find-the-right-answer' kinds of behavior" (Weaver, 1991, p. 1). Ken Goodman has described reading as a dynamic transaction between a reader and text (for example, 1996). Goodman's use of the term "transaction" was informed by Rosenblatt's (1978) "transactional theory of the literary work" focusing on reading as an aesthetic transaction: the active role of the reader in experiencing text meanings.

Weaver (1990) extends the use of "transactional" to describe classrooms where children are encouraged to engage with texts, with each other, and with the teacher. In a transactional model, language learning occurs with whole, meaningful texts and "smaller parts" of language are learned within a meaningful context. Learning is the result of "complex cognitive processes," and not the behaviorist stimulus response. Errors are not discouraged, as they are signs of risk-taking and "essential parts of learning." Learners are expected to develop at their own pace rather than master the same content and to apply knowledge rather than reproduce it.

Weaver's theoretical model focuses on understandings of socio-psycholinguistic processes and teaching practices that underpin whole language theory. She describes the importance of "social interaction" and recognizes the potential of whole language to "prepare students to participate actively in a democracy" (1990, p. 15). For Detroit teachers, working in urban and inner-city settings, the relationship between whole language, in what Freire (1994) calls "liberatory" teaching, was central.

While some teachers and researchers have raised questions about whether whole language pedagogy works well in urban, inner-city settings, whole language has tended to attract teachers with concerns for equity and social justice in schools. Edelsky, Altwerger, and Flores, in a piece first published in the *Reading Teacher*, wrote:

> More and more educators are warming to a new idea of education—whole language. Those of us who want to see fundamental changes in schools—the kind of change that improves all children's educational chances, the kind that does more than simply offer a traditional curriculum in two languages rather than one, the kind that resists centralized control over teachers, that resists practices that perpetuate societal inequities, that democratizes classrooms and encourages pluralism—are, in turn, gratified by this increased popularity for a pedagogy with just those intents. (1996, p. 108)

From the beginning, becoming a whole language teacher in Detroit involved "becoming political" (Shannon, 1992). The curriculum becomes political because it involves students in thinking, meaning making, experiencing, expressing themselves, and making choices. The teacher becomes an advocate for the learner, seeking to understand and build upon what students bring to school. Toby says, "There's nothing on a standardized test that says anything about Alex getting up in February and reading a poem in front of the class, a kid who in September said he couldn't read well and thought he couldn't write because he couldn't spell. These are the incidents that I'm evaluating all the time in the classroom" (Goodman, Y., 1991, p. 92). When students and teachers negotiate the curriculum, the content evolves to include the social concerns students face in their lives outside of school. Families and communities are welcomed into the classroom as resources and co-teachers. Students become critical thinkers and problem-posers (Freire, 1994) involved in social action research.

Detroit teachers—sometimes without meaning to—found themselves becoming political activists. Curriculum and evaluation mandates such as required textbooks and testing became structural constraints on teaching and learning. Within the school, we found that "our lesson plans had better be twice as organized and twice as spelled out and our evaluation system had better be more highly documented because we're under a lot of scrutiny" (Goodman, Y., 1991, p. 82). Outside of the school we found ourselves at board meetings and state departments arguing for a pedagogy that supported learners.

In telling the story of whole language in Detroit, I define whole language, as I have always viewed it, as a social and political teachers' movement. Scholars who have greatly informed whole language teaching (such as Frank Smith or Denny Taylor) have never embraced the term whole language, in part because it is nebulous and difficult to define. In many places, such as New Zealand, where the kinds of classrooms and programs we might call whole language are widely embraced, the term becomes somewhat redundant.

Susan Church (1996) described potential problems with viewing whole language as a movement rather than a philosophy, "The problem with movements, however, is that they seem to spawn orthodoxies and surface understandings as new teachers enthusiastically become swept along" (p. xxi). I don't disagree. Around the time Church's words were published, at a Whole Language Umbrella conference in San Diego, half of the large audience walked out as Kathy Short and Carolyn Burke brilliantly discussed the difference between making a paradigm shift and what they called "window dressing": when teachers change the activities and appearance of a classroom without changing the underlying philosophy.

Edelsky, Altwerger, and Flores (1996) were "delighted with the increasing popularity" of whole language but also concerned with the potential of educational innovations in the United States to be distorted and co-opted. They wrote, "Open education was a recent casualty. It was widely distorted so that open space was substituted for openness of ideas, learning centers for learning-centeredness. The final irony is that it was judged a failure even though (because of distortions) it was never implemented on any broad scale" (p. 108).

This discussion of open classrooms prophetically describes the rise and fall of whole language in popular pedagogy. In the late '80s, by the time of the first Whole Language Umbrella conference, droves of teachers were anxious to try whole language, and publishers were publishing almost anything as a "whole language lesson" or curriculum. In recent years, the term "whole language" has become anathema, and proponents have experienced a climate of censorship reminiscent of McCarthyism.

In light of these discussions, I've always viewed the whole language teachers' *movement* as the only reason for adopting such a messy, all-purpose term to describe an extremely complex theoretical orientation towards language, learners, learning, teaching, curriculum, and schooling. The term "whole language" was created because of the need to identify ourselves with others working for whole language and for the rights of teachers, children, and families to learn language (and use language to learn) within functional, "real life" contexts and caring communities. The whole language movement has evolved and continues to be viable in the face of strong political opponents that seek to control children, families, and teachers through mandated curriculum and testing.

Whole language pedagogy builds upon a research base and shared understandings, but it evolves with teachers, parents, and students engaged in classroom practice and in dialogue within and beyond the school community.

For me, it is within and through conversation and practice that the term "whole language" came to have meaning (for example, Whitmore and Crowell, 1994). Through the process of becoming whole language teachers in Detroit, we learned to respect the learning process of teachers as well as children. As Toby stated, "I have a support group of teachers that I meet with once a month, and the knowledge I've gained in the last five years I feel really powerful from that. I've learned a lot about language and reading and how kids learn to read and write, and I can verbalize it. And I feel like I'm getting better at watching kids and learning about them, so I can help their parents understand what I am seeing" (Y. Goodman, 1991, p. 89).

In these chapters, I hope to shed insight into the complexities of the whole language movement. I want to explore how a theoretical framework evolves in dialogue among a community of teachers, how shared readings, personal histories, and conversations influence teachers' decision making and the development of curriculum. When Monica Taylor approached me to tell the "Detroit Whole Language Story," I was reluctant because I did not have the extensive time required to gather the many voices of teachers, parents, and students who were a part of this story. The whole language movement in Detroit involves many people and a multitude of perspectives. As a White teacher in a largely African American city and school system, I am especially sensitive about telling my own story without including the voices of other teachers, particularly African American teachers.

I started by saying this story is largely untold. It is largely untold because the major participants are hard-working teachers (typically parents of young children) deeply involved in their teaching and many other projects. However, I do feel this is a story that needs to be told, particularly at a time when the term "whole language" is under attack. And so I decided to accept the invitation to write the Detroit Whole Language Story in the same way busy teachers always accept invitations—the best I can. This story is constructed from my own memories, informal conversations with other participants, student samples and other saved documents, and some papers and publications that were written during the years (1982 to 1996) when I was involved in the whole language movement in Detroit.

Whole Language in Detroit: The Prequel

It could be argued that whole language was born in Detroit (See Goodman, D., 1999). In the 1960s and 1970s, Ken Goodman was a professor at Wayne State University, a mile north of Burton International, when he started exploring a socio-psycholinguistic model of reading based on miscue analysis research. Early miscue analysis data was collected in classrooms in

Detroit and Highland Park, an urban city within Detroit's borders. And many of the researchers who worked with him (such as Carolyn Burke, Dorothy Menosky, Rudine Sims, and Dorothy Watson) were teachers in these urban schools. Yetta Goodman, Carolyn Burke, and Dorothy Watson developed a form of miscue analysis, the Reading Miscue Inventory (RMI) (Goodman, Y., et al., 1987b) that provides an accessible format for classroom teachers. Yetta Goodman and Dorothy Watson were later instrumental in forming two of the first TAWL groups: Tucson TAWL and Mid-Missouri TAWL.

Since Ken and Yetta Goodman are my parents, growing up I remember language, linguistics, and literacy were part of the dinner table conversations (See Goodman, 1999). Before TAWL groups, and before "whole language" existed, there were lunch meetings at the Miscue Research Center and meetings of groups like SALE (Society for Applied Linguistics in Education). The RMI makes it possible for classroom teachers to explore the reading process by "replicating" miscue research. I was around for many of those discussions. What makes whole language unusual among progressive education movements (although similar to some of the work that went on at the Bank Street School) is the role that classroom teachers have had in research and theory construction.

In 1977, I had the opportunity to observe and assist in Vera Milz's classroom in a Detroit suburb. Vera was among the first teachers in the country to take socio-psycholinguistic theory to the classroom. Vera went to the University of Arizona to study language experience with Roach Van Allen (for example, Allen, 1965 and Allen, 1982) but ended up working closely with Ken and Yetta Goodman. What Vera and other whole language teachers did was to bring together the experiential, student-centered learning of open classrooms, a history of progressive approaches to language arts education (such as "creative writing" and "language experience," and "individualized reading") and new theoretical understandings about reading, writing, and language learning. In her classroom children were invited to send letters through the class mailboxes, author books, read in rocking chairs, browse the well-stocked classroom library, listen to stories on tape, or observe plants growing.

Vera was also one of the first of a group of teacher researchers who emerged within whole language and the writing process movement. During the year that I spent in her classroom, she observed her students becoming proficient writers and developing spelling and mechanics without formal instruction. My work with Vera, as well as another opportunity to student teach in a wonderful open classroom, provided me with the firsthand experiences to go with my developing theoretical understandings.

Co-Constructing Whole Language

In the years following our lunch meetings, Toby and I worked together to develop a Social Studies/Language Arts curriculum that grew out of dialogue with whole language theory and practice. We envisioned a curriculum that was relevant to students' lives, where students had choice and ownership, and where language learning occurred as students engaged in meaningful learning experiences.

As I've been reconstructing this history, it strikes me that very few of the references I'm citing had been written when Toby and I began our collaboration. In 1983, Donald Graves (1983) first wrote *Writing: Teachers and Children At Work* and Denny Taylor (1983) published *Family Literacy*. Our collaboration predates the classics *What's Whole in Whole Language?* (Goodman, K., 1986), *In the Middle* (Atwell, 1987), and *Joyful Learning* (Fisher, 1991, revised 1998). We were working together before Bess Altwerger and the teachers with whom she works talked about theme cycles (Edelsky, Altwerger, & Flores, 1991), and Short, Harste, and Burke (1988) described Inquiry Cycles. It was before we had heard about Cambourne's Conditions of Language Learning (1988). It was before the Whole Language Umbrella.

What I'm saying is that Toby and I "invented whole language." Of course, we were not alone. We both had theoretical frameworks building upon Dewey, Vygotsky, and Piaget. We knew the work of people like Sylvia Ashton-Warner, Vivian Paley, Bill Martin, Jr., Jonathan Kozol, and Daniel Fader. At conferences and meetings, we heard, and sometimes had chances to talk with, many influential researchers including Marie Clay, Michael Halliday, Frank Smith, Don Graves, Bess Altwerger, Carole Edelsky, Barbara Flores, Ken and Yetta Goodman, Dorothy Watson, Kathy Short, Brooks Smith, Patrick Shannon, Jerry Harste, and Carolyn Burke. We also had the opportunity to talk with whole language pioneers: teacher researchers such as Kitty Copeland, Vera Milz, Nancie Atwell, Bobbi Fisher, Shelley Harwayne, Karen Smith, Jane Baskwill, and Paulette Whitman.

We were in touch with teacher educators at Oakland University, Michigan State University, and Western Michigan University (Connie Weaver). David Bloome moved with his family to the University of Michigan in the summer of 1981, just before I met Toby. David and his family became friends as well as colleagues, and he hosted the first TAWL group meeting at his house in Detroit, bringing together people from around Southeast Michigan. David was interested in working in an urban community, and I introduced him to the Detroit Public Schools. He introduced Toby and me to ethnographic understandings of classroom communities, and the three of us worked closely together over the next several years. We began to gather a TAWL group of teachers and teacher educators from around Lower Michigan.

In inventing whole language, we were not unique. Locally situated, social constructions of whole language theory-in-practice were occurring across the country and Canada, and many of these groups informed our understandings. In *Becoming a Whole Language School: The Fair Oaks Story* (Bridges-Bird, 1989), Gloria Norton describes ten years of "working at becoming a whole language school." She describes becoming whole language teachers as an ongoing learning process; a slow process where those involved must be patient but never complacent. She says, "We always talk about trusting the child—we need to trust ourselves as well. We can't close off and think, 'Now I'm a whole language teacher.' Instead we must think of ourselves as *whole language thinkers*, always open to new ideas, always thinking, always questioning, always studying, and *always learning*" (Norton, 1999, p. 114).

Norton calls her chapter "What Does It Take to Ride a Bike," because she had heard Ken Goodman tell a story of mine, describing how I explore the learning process by asking my students how they learned to ride a bike. She uses my analogy (You have to want to, you have to practice, and you have to fall down) to describe the learning process for teachers. Norton's use of a story from a Detroit classroom illustrates the national and international conversations that were going on at that time. However, in addition to these national conversations, whole language curriculum was greatly informed by local conversations about the students with whom we were working, by the communities where we lived and taught, by the learning experiences that we tried together, and by the stories that we told ourselves about these experiences.

Toby loved to retell the story of Brea (Goodman, D., 1989) who was "on grade level" but could not seem to pass the end-of-level test for her reader. The fourth-grade teacher put her through the workbook and the skill pack exercises a second time (he didn't have her read because she'd already read the book) and she failed again. Mystified, the teacher asked me, as the reading specialist, what I thought. I asked Brea to read the end-of-level test and concluded that she did not have the schema and experiences for the concepts she was expected to understand. I suggested that Brea come to my reading/writing center during her daily reading time. Brea came to me each day for a month, and I invited her to read any text she chose. I met with her once a week for a reading conference. At the end of the month, Brea passed the end-of-level test.

These "language stories and literacy lessons" (Harste, Woodward, & Burke, 1984) helped us to continually evolve in constructing whole language theory-in-practice, to advocate for students as readers, writers, and learners, to share our understandings with colleagues, and to defend whole language beliefs and practices. I knew that as Brea used reading to experience literature and learn about the world, she would also learn to read. During conferences I talked with her about texts and pointed out the strategies she was using, helping her to view herself as a proficient reader. The change in Brea as a reader, given a learning context that supported meaning making, was dramatic—almost magical—but not surprising if you have observed language learning in meaningful contexts. Viewing Brea from a different perspective, I could advocate for her as a reader and for myself as a whole language teacher. Brea's teacher respected my "creative" approach to teaching. However, other teachers asked Toby and me what we were doing to prepare our students for their skills-driven classrooms. And the district continued to mandate a basal reading program.

I said earlier that the whole language movement in Detroit was political from the start. Shannon (1992) tells us that teaching is both "liberating and dominating":

> By teaching we can learn the connections between our lives and those of others and the relationships between those lives and the world we live in. In this way, we achieve a type of solidarity among teachers and students and a blurring of teacher and taught as we explore and help others to explore what we wish to make of this world. But by teaching, we may also control the lives of others by concentrating on the management of time, students, information, and materials. In the end, we may not realize that by doing this we too are controlled in the maze of organization without real choices about what how and why we teach. (p. 1)

Whole language teaching becomes quickly political as a classroom "theory-in-practice" (Edelsky, Altwerger, & Flores, 1996) because whole language teaching suggests a shift in the very nature of curriculum and schooling. The collaborative learning communities advocated by whole language teachers provide fertile ground for exploring connections between our lives and the world we live in. In addition, curricular decisions, such as moving from basals to literature, immediately challenge the status quo: "At the beginning (and also currently), when whole language teachers took control of their teaching, they explicitly advocated and acted to overthrow the established reading technology (basals, workbooks, commitments to publishers, packaged programs tied to tests with stakes attached, etc.). Before the advent of the now popular term "literature-based," such an action had immediate political consequences. For example, some teachers were threatened with dismissal for insubordination if they refused to use the basal reader" (Edelsky, Altwerger, & Flores, 1996, pp.110-111). In my early years of teaching, before I met Toby, I was removed from one subbing job for using individualized reading and threatened with unsatisfactory ratings for using miscue analysis and learning centers as a reading specialist.

Norton says, "One universal remains constant. Teachers need to be learners more than they need to be teachers. Whole language teachers are learners. What varied from teacher to teacher and setting to setting, like all whole language learning communities, was the content, nature, and focus of the learning experience" (1989, p. 114). In becoming whole language teachers, we were always learning, but we were learning in a sociocultural and sociopolitical context. We were exploring whole language in a climate of constraints (mandated curriculum, tests, and subtests) that subtly shifted over the next ten years. (The Michigan Educational Assessment Test, for example, shifted from multiple questions on "reading" skills and subskills to multiple questions on two long passages: one fiction and one nonfiction.) Imbedded in our growing understanding of whole language was a "clear vision of the liberatory potential in this theoretical framework" (Edelsky, Altwerger, & Flores, 1996, p. 126).

Creating a Dual Curriculum

During the first years that Toby developed a whole language curriculum with her seventh graders, I worked in a variety of positions as a creative-writing teacher, reading specialist, and humanities teacher. In 1985, I was offered the fifth-grade homeroom. Burton International used a "platoon system" from the third through eighth grades, where homeroom teachers taught Social Studies/Language Arts and students went to specialists for math and science, as well as art, music, gym, and foreign language.

Toby and I viewed social studies and literature as content areas, with reading and writing as the tools for learning. Ken Goodman describes whole language as having a "dual curriculum," focusing on both content and process. As Toby said later, "Whole language philosophy taught me that reading and writing are tools and that fragmented curriculums are a thing of the past. My students and I build thematic units of study and classroom literacy invitations founded on Detroit's curriculum requirements, but built upon our needs and interests" (Curry, 1992, p. 33).

The first thing that Toby did was to opt out of the "Joplin plan" where students in grades six through eight were ability grouped and exchanged for reading instruction. She wanted to keep her seventh graders with her for the half-day Language Arts/Social Studies block. She dropped the basal readers (not difficult for a secondary teacher) and used trade books—fiction, non-fiction, and poetry—as well as newspapers, magazines, and other texts as the reading materials for her classes. The American History books, along with a wide range of other textbooks, became part of a resource library for the class. Toby established reading and writing workshops where students had their choice of texts and topics and time for reading, writing and talking during the school day.

Initially, it was difficult for Toby to trust that students would learn language while using language to learn. The first year, Toby told me she planned to spend the first month teaching the kids "the skills" so that she could feel satisfied that they had the basics. This also made sense because the statewide test was given in October. I didn't argue with her because I knew that she needed control of the change process, and I trusted that her learning/teaching experiences would prove to her that students could learn "skills" and strategies with a focus on literature and social studies. By spring, when we went to the International Reading Association conference, Toby was complaining about all of the sessions focusing on skills instruction.

In the middle of the first "whole language" year, Toby got nervous about whether the students, especially individual students, were learning enough general history through the inquiry process. She said, "The first year I was really worried about it. I even gave them a test. I remember they were all writing about different topics in colonial America and we had webs and it was great. Then I panicked and gave them a test to see if they were really learning anything. But I made up something like thirty individual tests" (Goodman, Y. 1991, p. 88).

Toby's decision to give them individual tests, rather than a typical exam, grew out of conversations with David Bloome, who was a participant observer in Toby's classroom that year. David shared with us his ethnographic observations of Detroit classrooms and helped us to become aware of classroom culture. He was interested in relationships between families, communities, and schools. David was talking with students from immigrant families and cultural backgrounds where the families expected more "traditional" schooling. David felt the students were just beginning to accept that they would be evaluated on their own progress. He was concerned that a test might make them feel double-crossed and unprepared. Toby designed a test that had about twenty short-answer questions. But, in addition, each student was given a topic to research and report on by the end of the half day. Toby reports that the students "passed" with flying colors, "It was the last teacher-made test I gave" (Goodman, Y., 1991, p. 88).

Whole language involves a shift from teaching subject areas to teaching children and from acquiring content information to developing understandings about learning (and language and math) processes and strategies. In making this shift, it initially seems that the specific areas of study are less important than the process; the emphasis is on students learning how to be learners. As students engage in studies of literature and social science, they use a variety of semiotic systems, language functions, and forms such as oral language (interviews, discussions, presentations, debates), written language (informational reading, fiction reading, taking notes, surveys, writing reports), and graphic texts (charts, diagrams).

While whole language shifts from teaching subjects to teaching processes (thus the "writing process" approach), *content* is also critical, in part because students will not engage in learning processes if they don't have an interest in what they are learning. Toby and I found this to be particularly true for middle school students. When Toby was exploring whole language and I was still a reading specialist, we collaborated on a variety of projects. I suggested a mini-workshop on research strategies such as reading for information or taking notes. I designed a series of strategy lessons on reading for information using topics and texts I had selected.

However, the seventh graders resisted every step of the way. They wanted to know why they were reading about spiders and what the point of the activity was. Even worse, they weren't picking up on the strategies I was teaching. Toby and I discussed breaking the workshop down further into smaller strategies and more sessions. However, we decided that the lack of any relevance and function in the content of the strategy lessons and the lack of time and experiences to try out the strategies, had set the students up for failure. We had created slow learners. We decided to just throw the kids into research on their own questions. I later reflected,

> Toby and I learned not to try to get the kids ready to learn but to expect they will learn. Most of the students will start out the year not knowing how to ask questions, read for information and take notes. But they soon find that these strategies are essential in order to do research. They struggle with a question that is too broad or too specific. They eagerly ask me how they can find out information they need to know. (Goodman, Y., 1991, p. 149).

Toby and I found that students learn how to be researchers when we place them in the role of researcher. I describe our experiences in an interview:

> When we culminate a two-month family research project, my students ask each presenter process questions, as well as content questions: "How long did it take you to plan your presentation?" "How did you think of your display?" "Where did you get your information?" They gently ask the less-prepared presenters why they didn't write some notes. They want the well-prepared presenters to show them their note cards and other organizers.

> Before, when Toby and I set the agenda for learning—focusing on strategies rather than on content—the kids were confused and disinterested. When the kids are focused on an exciting learning experience, they demand strategies and information, and eagerly attend the results. At this point, a short workshop on finding information or on taking notes is appreciated, but the kids learn more from their own experiences and the opportunities to work together. (Goodman, Y., 1991, p. 149)

In these early days of whole language the focus on language and learning processes sometimes overshadowed any consideration of content. It was not so much what you learned but the learning process that was important. However, the content—the themes, topics, issues, and texts—of learning represents a critical aspect of whole language teaching, particularly for teachers concerned with equity and social justice. I remember one discussion with Ken Goodman where he reminded me that I cared deeply about content as well as process. For example, the first theme I selected for my fifth-grade classroom was "Cultures in Contact in America," because I strongly believe that students need to be aware that American history is the story of many people and cultures. While "Cultures in Contact" neutrally avoids suggesting cultural diversity necessitates conflict, the title rejects the assimilationist "melting pot" view of American history. Over the years, I moved more and more to negotiate themes, topics, and texts with my students. But I recognized that I had an important role in introducing important concepts and texts into the discussion.

Toby remembers Frank Smith saying that teachers don't teach kids to read, books teach kids to read. But teachers are the keepers of the books. This statement reminded us of the powerful role of teachers in the texts selected, the types of literacy events and learning experiences organized, and how the experiences are organized. At that time David Bloome, who was a frequent visitor to the Dewey Center, was interested in students' experiences in the classroom and often suggested that filling a classroom full of books and materials and offering "invitations" do not mean that all students have access to literacy.

In an exploration of whole language theory-in-practice, Edelsky, Altwerger, and Flores distinguished between theoretical discussions where "literature was a means for teaching reading as opposed to the whole language idea that reading is a means for learning literature" (1996, p. 124). This distinction positions the relationship of process and content in a framework of how we view learning and schooling. Altwerger points out that in the traditional integrated theme unit, for example, the topic was a vehicle for teaching social studies, reading, and math. She proposed an alternative "theme cycle" where reading, math, and social science research strategies are used as students inquire into an area of study (Edelsky, Altwerger, & Flores, 1991). Inquiry provided the potential for what Freire (1994) calls a "problem posing" curriculum. The common theme provided opportunities for collaboration and shared conversations around issues and texts.

Theme Cycles

In the typical social studies classroom, students read the research studies of others, recorded in most textbooks as factual information without any particular author. They then answer someone else's questions, often borrowing the wording of the text with little understanding or interest. We wanted to engage students in "learning how to learn" by placing them in the role of researchers: studying social studies as a social scientist, language as a linguist, and so on. We initially started with the KWL questions: What do you know? What do you want to know? What have you learned? For example, at the beginning of our study on "Cultures in Contact in America," we talked a little about culture, and I asked my fifth graders to write about the culture of their families. Patrice wrote:

Culture

By Patrice

My family is not that anything. We do eat pizza and spaghetti. We eat Chinese food. My father is from Kenya and we eat his food sometimes. But my mother is from Alabama. I'm from Royal Oak. I have some class mates that are from a different country or state.

At the end of that year, I invited the students to share something about their cultural background at a culminating presentation for parents. Patrice wrote:

My name is Patrice. My parents say I'm the best of both worlds: Africa and America. I am really an Afro-American. My mother is from Alabama and my dad comes from Kenya. When I was young, my parents sent me to Kenya to visit my grandmother so that I could learn my culture and language. Dad says I learned Kikumba, our clan's dialect, so well that I forgot English. My dad told me that he sent me to Africa to live so that I could see there is [sic] more things in the world than just technology like America has. He wanted me to see how people live in a small farming village. I saw people helping each other to plant and harvest crops and even though they were mostly poor, they would always invite people to have Chai (that's tea in my language). They like to share what they have even if it's just a little. I want to be a doctor when I grow up. I might go back to my dad's home to teach people how to be doctors, nurses, and midwives.

What I find striking about this second reflection is that Patrice's visit to her father's village occurred before she wrote, "My family is not that anything." Patrice's first piece is very sketchy and might lead to the conclusion that she has little "prior knowledge" of culture. Of course, there are many explanations: Patrice may not have a complex understanding of the term culture, and she may not have had a chance to think through the significance of culture in her family. But Patrice's reflections point to the problem of seeing knowledge as pieces of information, or facts, that a student has or doesn't have. Patrice has many rich experiences to draw from. Over the year, the learning experiences of engaging in a family history and exploring culture through literature and personal research helped Patrice to organize these early experiences into new understandings: knowledge. They may have also invited her to talk with her parents about the importance of culture within her family.

Brooks Smith, a scholar of Dewey, describes learning as a process of "perceiving, ideating, and presenting" (Goodman, K., Smith, Meredith, & Goodman, Y., 1987, p. 24). During a class I took with him, he said that probably the most important role of the teacher is in the "ideating" stage. We came to see ideating as the link between experience and knowledge as teachers invite students to engage in processes (such as thinking, talking, writing, reading, drawing, or dancing) that help them to organize perceptions and experiences into understandings.

Through Patrice's story, and similar ones, we learned not to make assumptions about students' experiences based on their initial responses to complex questions like "what do you know?" We adopted more open exploration at the beginning of a theme study, giving students a chance for "wondering and wandering" (borrowing from Eve Merriam's *Wise Woman and Her Secret* (1991)). We provide students with an opportunity to explore a topic by viewing films, sharing a read aloud, browsing through texts, and so on before asking them to consider what they know and what they want to learn.

In the book *Twenty Teachers* (Macrorie, 1984), Toby discovered I-Search, (which Macrorie later described in a book by that name). His focus on in-depth study—where students become the expert in one area—was a strong model for classroom research. However, we often found that students who had five to seven years of transmission-type instruction found inquiry-based learning somewhat uncomfortable. Asked to investigate their own questions and topics, students might come in the next day with a written report, generally copied from a book, circumventing the inquiry process. The extreme example is when one of my fifth graders brought in two pages copied from the encyclopedia on "Slavs" in response to her question: What about slaves? Toby describes a similar experience with a group of sixth graders:

> The sixth-grade curriculum is geography so I told them to pick any country in the world they'd like to learn more about, become an expert about it and teach the rest of us. They'd been so devoid of power over their own learning they couldn't believe that I could trust them to be an expert and teach others about Mexico, about Italy. I heard stuff like, "This is not what I'm used to. I'm used to reading the chapter and

answering the questions in the back. I've never done this before." They didn't know
anything about note taking; lots of them just copied whole sentences. (Goodman,Y.,
1991, pp. 86-87)

We learned and adapted from student responses. We focused more
attention on the learning process; for example, taking time and helping
students to ask questions so they weren't too general (What about slaves?) or
too specific. We met with students to go over their research folder with
rough notes and information before starting on their final project. And we
often shifted their final project to an oral report, or artistic presentation,
rather than a formal paper. The presentation is an important part of the
learning process, placing students in the role of expert and providing an
opportunity for them to organize their new understandings and share them
with others.

Toby initially organized her theme units chronologically, following the
American History textbook: i.e., precolonial, colonial, and Revolutionary
War. However, she encountered the age-old American History problem of
how to get past the Civil War. When I started teaching the fifth grade, I
wanted to try more global themes, such as War and Peace, that would allow
us to explore the United States across chronologies and geographies. The
global theme made it possible to address diverse issues and histories and to
ground human issues more contextually instead of in bits and pieces. We
used timelines, constructed with the students across the semesters, to give
kids a sense of chronology. When I started teaching in the fifth grade, I
thought I would do four global themes, but found I had time for two:
"Cultures in Contact in America" and "Childhood in America." Toby
eventually moved to one global theme: "The History of Civil Rights in
America."

I found that the individual I-search project did not work as well with fifth
graders as it did with Toby's middle-school students. A few
students—generally those with parents who were teachers—would bring in
high-quality projects, but other students did mediocre work and some
students never completed the I-search project. I decided to organize the
students into research groups, generally formed around similar topics or
interests. While each student had his own questions, the students worked
together to find resources, negotiate materials, record information, and plan
presentations. With the research groups, every student in the class
participated and enjoyed some success on a research project. Students
became learners/teachers and often worked very well with just a few group
conferences. This allowed me to more closely work with students who
needed extra help with reading, writing, and research. Group research
contributed to creating a learning community, and Toby also adopted
research groups, shifting her "I-search" to "We-search" studies.

Reading and Writing in Community Voices

A major influence on our work at Burton International was the opportunity to work closely with David Bloome, an ethnographic literacy scholar at the University of Michigan. Through ethnographic observation, David was able to gain insights that were difficult for Toby and me to see as we were teaching. Toby writes, "I have always believed that the ultimate responsibility of a teacher is to provide an environment where everyone is free to learn if they wish to. David's research has given me the power to constantly strive to make those words a reality. I know my classroom environment is crucial for all of my students, especially those that come from outside our majority American populations" (Curry, 1986, p. 4).

David observed a group of students in Toby's classroom brainstorming what they knew about the Civil War. After considerable discussion, they concluded that they knew nothing. One student was from El Salvador, at that time involved in a civil war, and one student from China later wrote about family at Tiananmen Square. While Toby had asked the students to share their own knowledge base, David observed the students sneaking a look at the history textbook in their desks.

I also observed that many of my fifth graders, given a research project, would come in the next day with a report that had often been copied from an encyclopedia. After years of answering the questions at the end of the chapter, students had a difficult time seeing book authors as fallible human beings with a subjective perspective. We wanted students to be aware that books were written by people. We wanted them to be critical as well as proficient readers and "read against the grain." As Toby says, "I told them, 'You can't trust one author or one book about anything. You need to read a variety of things, to piece together your information and learn that just because it's in a book doesn't make it true" (Goodman, Y., 1991, p. 87). We also wanted students to be aware of the learning experiences within their families and communities—the "funds of knowledge" that Moll and Gonzales (1994) describes in Latino communities.

We began to explore the idea of engaging in inquiry experiences that took students away from books as primary resources. David and Toby decided to try involving seventh-grade classes in ethnographic research of their own communities. For this project, Toby had the opportunity to be a participant observer while David, the teacher, involved students in observations and interviews within their communities. Students were asked to write a persuasive essay on an assigned topic (such as smoking or pollution) at the beginning and end of the project. David and Toby found that before the ethnographic study, students would generally cite published texts in order to support the argument. Few students cited people in their community, or their own personal examples. After the ethnographic project, students were much more likely to draw on their own expertise or that of people in their community as support for the argument that they were making.

I involved students in at least one community study project for each class theme. For "Childhood in America," students interviewed an adult about their childhood and wrote sketches based on their interview. During "Cultures and Contact in America," students did a family history project before developing inquiry questions. Each student did an oral presentation and made a display that was shared at a culminating celebration. The family histories introduced us to the histories of Michigan and America.

For example one student, Lisa Rousseau-Clark, had a grandfather who came from a sharecropping family in Virginia, and an Italian grandmother who came from Brooklyn. Both moved to Detroit when her grandfather was stationed at Fort Wayne. Another grandmother came from a German farming family in Western Michigan, while her grandfather's family were French-Canadians who followed the lumber to Michigan. Lisa wrote:

> When I started this project I felt kind of bad because we don't speak any other language, we don't have customs from another country, but now I have learned a lot about my relatives. I found out a lot of interesting things that I never knew before. It's interesting that people end up living where ever their jobs are. Like my Great-Grandfather Rousseau ended up in Saginaw because that's where the lumber industry was. My Great-Grandfather Krauss ended up in Freeland because that is where there was good farm land.
>
> I think my culture is an interesting one because I have four different ones… Italian, Appalachian, French-Canadian, and German. I want to find out more about each of the cultures and how my family has changed with each generation. I like learning about old cultures and traditions." (Goodman, D., 1991, p. 315)

Community study helped us to examine the difference between "hands-on" learning (counting plastic mice) and experiential learning (observing actual mice). It also helped us to consider the difference between firsthand experience (observing mice in the field) and simulated experiences (observing mice in a cage in the classroom). The richness of students' responses to firsthand oral history was striking:

> The fifth graders listen in rare silence as visitors talk of days gone by. They hear the street cars screeching through the busy neighborhoods where freeways now bypass the empty shells of burned-out houses. They see filled inkwells in rows of bolted desks where their desks and chairs are now scattered about. They taste the candy bought at the friendly corner store, which now greets them with steel bars and Plexiglas shields. (Goodman & Curry, 1991, p. 158)

In investigating "Childhood in America," I asked each of my students to interview an adult about what their life was like when they were ten years old. In the family histories, I used oral presentations and display projects to move students away from "reports." For this project, at the end of the year I helped the students to turn their interviews into a character sketch. Terrence interviewed his grandmother, "I was amazed when she told me how cheap things were back then. A loaf of bread cost five cents. Pepsi and Coca-Cola cost five cents too. Movies cost five cents. Now they cost five dollars." Matthew interviewed his Grandpa Al:

My grandpa was born in Italy. When he was about my age there was a war. The war was rough on them because sometimes there was no food. A lot of people had their houses blown up and it happened to my grandpa's house too. But luckily my grandpa's aunt pulled him out of the house when she saw the bomb coming towards the house. All the men in town were killed but my grandpa's dad because he was a baker and they needed him to bake bread so they could have something to eat. My grandpa only went to school for four years because when the war started school ended. After four years the war ended. While there was no school during the war my grandpa mostly played and looked for food. Once he was playing with a grenade but luckily he did not get hurt. Him and his family would eat leaves off trees and when the America soldiers were around my grandpa would beg for candy bars. My grandpa really didn't give a crap who won just as long as he got food.

Ethnographic studies demonstrate to students that their families and communities are important resources for learning and that the issues that are important to their families are relevant to the school curriculum as well. Wang Li (a pseudonym), a student in Toby's classroom, wrote about Tiananmen Square less than a year after he had emigrated from China:

On Sunday morning, June 4, 1989, I called China. My grandmother told me that all Saturday night soldiers killed students, maybe more than one thousand. The soldiers moved from the north of the square to the south of the square, killing students like they were sweeping a floor. When they saw someone who disobeyed them, they killed them. In just maybe two hours the very large square was quiet, not any noise.

On Sunday morning, my grandmother went to the square; she had permission because she is an officer of Chinese hospitals. She saw a student who wasn't dead. She tried to move his body, but he couldn't move, he just cried. Another student was caught in an explosion. His mother found all of his body except for his left leg.

I am very angry about things in China. When one student dies, he will fall down, but ten or more angry people will stand. The government can kill thousands of students, but they can't kill all the Chinese people. The students may die, but people will always remember them; they will be remembered in our minds and in our hearts. (Curry, 1992, p. 32)

Bringing the lives of children and families into the classroom curriculum, while sometimes raising painful issues, helps us to see a whole language classroom as not just a room full of books and learning centers, but rather as a cultural space with the possibility for all students to have access to literacy. Engaged in meaningful inquiry, students learn to read and write but also to construct oral and written texts that have personal meaning and extend their understanding of the human experience. They are becoming literate while engaged in posing and solving important problems in their lives. Toby writes:

> It was in Wang's culturally diverse school that I really began to understand language, learning, teaching, curriculum and what global studies are all about. I am a "whole language type," who loves learning, teaching and children. With the help of many teachers, especially my "peer mentor" Debra Goodman and ethnographic researcher David Bloome, I have learned what it means to create communities of learners and how to bring the community of our world into the classroom. (Curry, 1992, p. 32)

Community and family studies, inquiry learning, and other productive experiences (story writing, independent reading, etc.) reorganize the institutional relationship within classrooms and among classrooms, families, and children. During school-wide observations, David noted that the nature of learning experiences changed how the classroom was structured. When the classroom was organized around the mandated curriculum, typically "text reproduction" experiences, "students were confined to their desks and their own work" (Bloome, 1986, p.15). However, during "text production" experiences where students were engaged in creative work, inquiry, or group projects, "changes also occurred in the social organization of the classroom. The very nature of these activities required students to talk with each other and move around the room to get resources." Within these kinds of activities "differences surfaced in how students approached reading and writing activities based on their cultural and family backgrounds" (pp. 15-16). In other words, David found that "productive" or whole language learning experiences supported students from varied cultural backgrounds, "in terms of the classroom community, because the diverse approaches that students employed in reading and writing activities were legitimized by both the nature of the text production activities and by the teacher, cultural and family differences in how students approached reading and writing did not count as differences in class participation" (p. 16).

Our Learning Community

During the years that Toby and I worked at Burton International, TAWL groups and other whole language teacher support groups were growing across the U.S. and Canada. At national conferences, we met with other whole language teacher groups and shared what was going on in each area.

These meetings helped us to see beyond the bureaucracies and limitations of our own settings and eventually led to the founding of the Whole Language Umbrella.

Toby and I felt somewhat isolated in the Detroit Public Schools. Although we were sure there were progressive teachers in Detroit and in the Detroit area, it was initially difficult to find them. However, by 1987, through meetings, contacts, classes, and conferences, we had pulled together a group of people interested in whole language and formed the Metro-Detroit TAWL group. This group included teachers and administrators from districts spread around the Detroit area. Most of the initial members were teacher-leaders in their districts. We were active in the first years of the Whole Language Umbrella, and some group members helped me to publish the first WLU newsletter.

Within just a few years members of Metro-Detroit TAWL had formed several other groups, generally located within school districts: North Oakland TAWL, Troy TAWL, Monroe TELL (Teachers Exploring Language and Literacy), Birmingham TAWL, and Plymouth TAWL. Toby and I continued to meet with the Detroit teachers in the Detroit TAWL group. We met Jerry Oglan and other teachers from Windsor, Canada in the early 1990s. The leaders of these groups eventually became International TAWL, sponsoring the WLU conference in Windsor, Ontario in 1995 and continuing to meet through the '90s.

The TAWL group was a place where you could have "rough draft" conversations without repercussions. They generally started out as gripe sessions and how to deal with the constraints, stresses, and barriers to whole language teaching continues to be a topic for discussion. But topics and formats ranged based on the interests of group members. Through the artist-in-residence program at Burton International, Toby and I met a wonderful teaching poet named Larry Pike, and for a while the group met at the community college for discussions on writing and poetry. We found that posting topics for sessions often drew in people with special interests, and we also invited people, for example math educators, to help us think through a topic. We shared children's books and sometimes read novels or professional books together. TAWL meetings always involved lots of food as well as conversation. We kept track of children and partners and found close friends within the group.

Finding Our Voices

In 1989, NCTE sponsored the first "Day of Whole Language" and Bess Altwerger talked about whole language teachers as empowered professionals. She described "empowered professionals" as having both a personal and social meaning:

> When we apply this personal meaning of empowerment to whole language teachers, it means that we as individuals have taken control over our professional lives—that we are no longer personally willing to yield to external demands and expectations that we believe not to be in the best interest of our students. It means that we have found our voices, no longer willing to resort to covert teaching—to writing one plan and teaching quite another. (Altwerger, 1991, p. 26)

In one early study that David did at our school, he noticed a phenomenon he called "teaching in the cracks" (Bloome, 1986). As he observed teachers, he noticed that they began with a curriculum driven by textbooks and district mandates. However, teachers began to introduce more creative experiences between the mandated curriculum. For example, between the basal reading lesson and the grammar lesson, they would rehearse a play or introduce a creative-writing activity. These creative learning experiences took up more and more of the school day until they often were longer blocks of time than the text-based lesson. However, these holistic learning experiences were unofficial. They were never mentioned in the teacher's plan book or reflected in the students' report cards.

My own approach was somewhat similar, although perhaps more consciously subversive. I had the social studies textbooks and the basal readers under each student's desk where they were visible if I faced a surprise observation. (And students were expected to read them if they were not prepared for silent reading.) I had a block called "reading" in my plan book and did not go out of my way to point out that the basal reader was used less and less frequently until it became a once-a-year unit on basal readers. My fifth graders analyzed the readers for such issues as quality of texts and representation of gender, culture, and race.

While I tended to close my door and teach, Toby was more outspoken. She repeated Brea's story regularly and quipped that basal readers were just the right size for propping open the classroom windows. In addition to anecdotal stories, Toby and I collected plenty of evidence, both quantitative and qualitative, that whole language "worked." Through the Fifty Book Clubs, Toby could report the enormous number of pages read by her students. I kept track of the number of words my students wrote and the percentage of conventional spellings across the year. But the more critical evidence was the student's actual reading, writing, and thinking. End-of-the-school-year publications and student-authored pageants provided forums for students to present all they had written and learned. And we invited parents to tell us what they thought:

June 11, 1987

Dear Debi,

Rebecca told me you'd like an evaluation of the year at Burton International in your classroom. Here goes!

As a parent I look to my child. I was concerned initially with the new and different set-up. I was concerned with Rebecca's fear of no geography. "I don't know the 50 states." But here is what I found.

I found my bright child—a very good reader—become a great and copious reader. I found my child, sometimes reluctant to take pen in hand, not only writing but creating original works. I hear my highly emotional child tell of "circle time" where she talked about how she felt and heard how others felt and how they were all interrelated.

I found my child evaluating herself and others carefully and meaningfully. I found my child learning to respect and attempting to understand the different children in her classes and most of all looking for similarities.

I found my child looking into her past, talking with her grandmother, questioning where she came from. I found my child happy with what she found.

I found myself, also a reluctant writer, writing a log with my wonderful child. Telling her about me and learning about her.

I found myself, not fully understanding but trusting a teacher to love and teach my child.

With these public demonstrations and parent responses, Toby and I were suddenly left alone. We began to stop apologizing for what we were teaching. When asked "but are you preparing them for next year?" we responded, "Who's preparing them for me?" When Detroit adopted a new basal series, Toby frankly told the language arts curriculum specialist implementing the new program that we weren't using basal readers. The curriculum specialist went back and reported to her supervisors that we had developed an "enriched" program and had no need for the basal readers.

As we celebrated, I remembered asking one of my favorite professors why he suggested ways of incorporating literature into basal reading programs rather than suggesting literature as the reading program. He'd replied that basal readers were here to stay. Toby and I thought carefully about the compromises required for students in our district. We distinguished compromises made on behalf of students' immediate circumstances with our beliefs and public statements as professionals. In an interview published in 1991, Toby said:

I don't want to hurt kids because of my beliefs. There used to be a test in Detroit, the ABC writing test, and the kids had to write a horrible little paragraph on this standard paragraph form. It was the notorious five sentence paragraph: topic sentence, three supporting sentences, and a concluding sentence. It's not real writing, but it would get them a passing grade. So I compromised. I taught my kids how to take the test. I told them, "This isn't real writing, but this is how you can write for this test." But I also warned them that they would come up against other teachers who would ask them to write like this. (Goodman, Y., 1990, p. 90)

This story illustrates how Toby's whole language classroom empowered students, as well as teachers, as agents of their own learning. As David wrote: "What characterizes Toby's class is her demand that you care about what you do…. If you read a good book you are expected to have an opinion and share it because what you think matters. If you write an essay or a story, what you write should matter to you." In Toby's classroom, opinions and dissent also mattered. He continued, "If you want to resist, that's okay, but you have to be serious about it and provide alternatives. You have to seriously engage Toby in your resistance." David also described Toby's classrooms as "a conspiracy between her and her students":

I remember one incident when the district monitor was coming to check whether students had been using the seventh-grade basal reader and mastering the designated competencies. Neither Toby nor her students had any time for such nonsense. They were busy reading myths and making up myths of their own. So Toby passed out the reading skills competency checklists to her students and told them to check off the ones they were able to do, including those that had been checked off in previous years. For Toby, schooling was not going to get in the way of learning, and it was not going to get in the way of the important work they were doing. (Bloome, 1991, p. 229).

Re-reading these stories today, I am reminded again of how passionately we cared about our students and the opportunities for them to do important work. I think of how hard we worked to provide space for students to "care about what you do" in face of the constraints of "schooling" and in a world where the voices of teenagers and children are not valued. I remember the impatience and disappointment we felt at conferences or workshops with educators and researchers who disregarded the significance of decisions taken out of the hands of teachers and families.

Teachers that I worked with in Detroit often wondered what our teaching lives, and our students' lives, would be like if we had the opportunity to teach without the constraints of tests or state and district mandates. We wondered what our lives would have been like with 25 instead of 33 students and with a budget for buying paperback books. Perhaps our ideas would have been less defined, less sharply honed then they were in the face of adversity. But we suspected we would be able to accomplish more. I said in an interview:

Toby and I are totally against tests; we're against them because they label children, they dictate curriculum. They're used to evaluate teachers, to track children, to terrify and control parents. And here we are, telling kids you're all capable, you're all wonderful, and then these tests place them on a bell-shaped curve and tell them they're incompetent. We decided that our kids are going to do more than those in an economically deprived area are supposed to do. On the other hand, we decided when we make presentations to teachers that we're not going to answer the question "How do your kids do on standardized tests?" We're not going to give credence to testing. (Goodman, D., 1991, p. 91)

We responded proactively by sticking to our agenda for ourselves as well as for our children, by spending our time on things we cared about, and by insisting on important work and refusing to be sidetracked. When Toby heard that there might be an opportunity to open new "schools of choice" in Detroit, we gathered a group of teachers and wrote a proposal for a whole language school, which I describe in the next chapter.

We were also part of a movement of educators in CELT, NCTE, TAWL, and WLU who took us seriously and provided us with forums for speaking out. Vera Milz, one of my mentors, first asked me to present with her when I was a student teacher. David Bloome suggested a panel about "reading and writing in community voices" and asked me to describe how I teach reading and writing through family histories and community studies. My first reaction, which surprises me now, was that I didn't teach reading and writing. And then I thought of all the texts that the children used and created: picture albums, newspaper articles, obituaries, family bibles, stories, notes, questions, and family trees. Bess Altwerger said, "Never before have so many articles written by classroom teachers appeared in professional journals" (1991, p. 26). Writing and speaking at conferences helped us to keep learning more about how to be whole language teachers.

We were inspired by Bess Altwerger, who reminded us that we must be socially as well as personally empowered:

We as whole language teachers must develop a sense of social empowerment that reaches beyond our own individuality, our own classrooms and our own schools. We as a group must adopt as our ultimate goal the eradication of social inequality and injustice, and work to create an educational system that transforms, rather than reproduces and perpetuates, these societal conditions. We must recognize our moral obligation to our students to do more than just make them literate. We must resist efforts to reduce critical thinking to politically and socially vacuous thinking skills but engage our students in critique of real-life issues so that they will be able to tackle societal problems that will face them in the future as they transform and improve our society. Whole language can be more than a pedagogy of language and literacy—it can be, in Giroux's (Giroux, 1988,) words, the "pedagogy of possibility and hope." (1991, p. 27)

Whole Language as a Transformative Pedagogy

Ira Shor (1987) describes the "real potential of teaching" as the possibility of "confirming or challenging socialization into inequality" (p. 14). Carole Edelsky (1996) expresses these opposing forces as "conserving" or "transforming" movements within education. Transformative forces seek to "challenge socialization into inequality" by challenging the discriminatory assumptions and practices imbedded in our society and reflected in our schools and classrooms. During the late 1980s and early 1990s, as I describe in another chapter in this book, there was an increase in the possibilities for teachers and children to negotiate the curriculum in their own classroom. Today, as teachers once again face controlling district and government mandates, the January 2005 issue of *Language Arts* had "Teaching in the Cracks" as the issue theme.

In a climate of political attack, many whole language educators have gone underground. For me, however, the moral of the story I've told here is that you can't promote change by closing your door and teaching quietly. You have to speak up for what you believe. As a teacher educator today, I outline for graduate students two forums for discussion. The first is a theoretical one: What is the nature of literacy and literacy learning? And what is the best way to help children become literate? It is critical that we continue to explore and debate these questions. The second forum is more overtly political and greatly impacts on scholarly research and debate: Who gets to make decisions for teachers and children? I never want to minimize the political struggle that all teachers face. A resource teacher told me recently that her use of the words "whole language" in a proposal going to the district board of education were stricken by the language arts coordinator, while the names of commercial "reading" programs that focus entirely on phonics and skills were acceptable for the presentation. I'm not advocating for young, untenured teachers to buck the system. Toby's frank admissions were accepted because she was experienced and well liked. The children of the DPS language arts leaders were in her classes. Toby continued to serve on district committees, in spite of setbacks and frustrations, and worked closely with the head of alternative schools for Detroit.

What I am suggesting is that teachers advocate on behalf of children as learners, for curricula and structures that support children as learners, and against curricula and structures that are conserving rather than transforming educational practices (Edelsky, 1996). I'm suggesting that teachers find ways to address issues and controversies that are important in the lives of children, particularly avoiding self-censorship. I'm especially suggesting that teacher educators, working in more protected communities where academic freedom and faculty governance is at least the professed ideology, advocate for teachers as decision makers. At the same time, we must continue to create whole language classrooms and curriculum at the university level where issues of equity and social justice, and even terms like *whole language* can be explored and debated.

But I'm not suggesting we do it alone. At the most recent meeting of the Whole Language Umbrella, there was a call for reestablishing the local TAWL groups. While several groups are still active, many, such as Detroit TAWL, no longer meet. I am suggesting we speak out and proudly identify ourselves as whole language teachers but also as part of a transformative teacher's movement.

References

Allen, R. V. (1965). *Attitudes and the art of teaching reading.* Washington, DC: National Education Association.

Allen, R. V. & C. Allen. (1982*). Language experience activities.* Boston: Houghton Mifflin Co.

Altwerger, B. (1991). Whole language teachers: Empowered professionals. In J. Hydrick (Ed.), *Whole language: Empowerment at the chalk face.* New York: Scholastic.

Atwell, N. (1987). *In the middle.* Portsmouth, NH: Heinemann.

Bloome, D. (1986). *Cultural diversity and writing instruction.* Paper presented at the National Council of Teachers of English, San Antonio, TX.

— (1991). Great teachers: Toby Kahn Curry. In K. Goodman, L. Bridges-Bird, & Y. Goodman (Eds.), *The Whole Language Catalog,* (p. 229). Santa Rosa, CA: American School Publishers.

Bridges-Bird, L. (Ed.). (1989). *Becoming a whole language school: The Fair Oaks story.* Katonah, NY: Richard C. Owen.

Cambourne, B. (1988). *The whole story: Natural learning and the acquisition of literacy in the classroom.* New York, NY: Scholastic.

Church, S. (1996). *The future of whole language: Reconstruction or self-destruction.* Portsmouth, NH: Heinemann.

Cleary, B. (1983). *Dear Mr. Henshaw.* New York: Morrow.

Curry, T. K. (1986). *Teaching/ Learning in the cracks.* Session: Cultural Diversity and Writing Instruction. Paper presented at the National Council of Teachers of English, San Antonio, TX.

Curry, T. K. (1992). Freeing student voices: Building a "living" multicultural curriculum. *Focus, Michigan ASCD* (Spring), 32-35.

Delpit, L. (1995). *Other people's children: Cultural conflict in the classroom.* New York: The New Press.

Edelsky, C. (1996). *With literacy and justice for all: Rethinking the social in language and education* (2nd ed.). London: Taylor & Francis, Ltd.

Edelsky, C., Altwerger, B. & Flores, B. (1991). *Whole language: What's the difference.* Portsmouth, NH: Heineman.

— (1996). Whole Language: What's New? In C. Edelsky (Ed.), *With literacy and justice for all: Rethinking the social in language and education* (2nd ed.), (pp. 108-126). London: Taylor & Francis, Ltd.

Fisher, B. (1998). *Joyful learning in kindergarten* (Rev. ed.). Portsmouth, NH: Heinemann.

Freire, P. (1994). *Pedagogy of the oppressed.* New York: Continuum.

Giroux, H. (1988). *Teachers as intellectuals: Toward a crtiical pedagogy of learning.* Westport, CT: Bergin and Garvey.

Goodman, D. (1991). Community study: A focus for social studies and language learning. In K. S. Goodman, Lois B. Bird, Yetta M. Goodman (Eds.), *The Whole Language Catalog, (p. 315).* Santa Rosa, CA: American School Publishers.

— (1999). Growing up whole language. In C. Edelsky & A. Marek (Eds.), *Reflections and connections: Essays on the influence of Kenneth Goodman,* pp. 187-210. Cresskill, NJ: Hampton Press.

Goodman, K. (1986). *What's whole in whole language?* Portsmouth, NH: Heinemann.

—. (1996). *On reading.* Portsmouth, NH: Heinemann.

Goodman, Y. (1990). *Teaching as a political activity: A conversation between Toby Curry, Debra Goodman, & Yetta Goodman*: Unpublished transcript for 1991 teacher interview.

— (1991). The teacher interview: Toby Kahn Curry and Debra Goodman. In N. Atwell (Ed.), *Workshop by and for teachers 3: The politics of process* (pp. 81-93). Portsmouth, NH: Heinemann.

Goodman, D. & Curry, T.K. (1991). Teaching in the real world. In Y. Goodman, W., Hood, & K. Goodman (Eds.), *Organizing for whole language.* Portsmouth, NH: Heinemann.

Goodman, Y., D. Watson, & Burke, C. (1987). *Reading miscue inventory: Alternative procedures.* Katonah, NY: Richard C. Owen.

Goodman, K. S., Smith, E. B., Meredith, R., & Goodman, Y.. (1987). *Language and thinking in school: A whole language curriculum* (3rd ed.). Katonah, NY: Richard C. Owen.

Goodman, Y, Hood, W., & Goodman, Y. (1991) (Eds.), *Organizing for whole language.* Portsmouth, NH: Heinemann

Graves, D. H. (1983). *Writing: Teachers and children at work.* Portsmouth, NH: Heinemann.

Harste, J., Woodward, V.A., & Burke, C. (1984). *Language stories and literacy lessons.* Portsmouth, NH: Heinemann.

Ladson-Billings, G. (1994). *The dreamkeepers: Successful teachers of African American children.* San Francisco, CA: Jossey-Bass.

Macrorie, K. (1984). *Twenty teachers.* New York: Oxford University Press.

—. (1988). *The I-Search paper.* Portsmouth, NH: Heinemann.

Merriam, E. (1991). *The wise woman and her secret.* New York: Simon and Schuster.

Moll, L. C., & Gonzalez, N. (1994). Lessons from research with language-minority children. *Journal of Reading Behavior, 26*(4), 439-455.

Norton, G. (1989). What does it take to ride a bike? In L. Bridges-Bird (Ed.), *Becoming a Whole Language School: The Fair Oaks Story,* pp. 105-114 .Portsmouth: NH: Heinemann.

Paley, V. (1995). *Kwanzaa and me: A teacher's story.* Cambridge, MA: Harvard University Press.

Rosenblatt, L. (1978). *The reader, the text, the poem: The transactional theory of the literary work.* Carbondale: Southern Illinois University Press.

Shannon, P. (1990). *The struggle to continue: Progressive reading instruction in the United States.* Portsmouth, NH: Heinemann.

— (Ed.). (1992). *Becoming political: Readings and writings in the politics of literacy education.* Portsmouth, NH: Heinemann.

Shor, I. (1987). Educating the educators: A Freirean approach to the crisis in teacher education. In I. Shor (Ed.), *Freire for the classroom: A sourcebook for liberatory teaching* (pp. 7-32). Portsmouth, NH: Boynton Cook.

Short, K. G., Harste, J. C. & Burke, C.. (1988). *Creating classrooms for authors and inquirers* (2nd ed.). Portsmouth, NH: Heinemann.

Short, K., & Burke, C. (1991). *Creating curriculum: Teachers and students as a community of learners.* Portsmouth, NH: Heinemann.

Taylor, D. (1983). *Family literacy: Young children learning to read and write.* Portsmouth, NH: Heinemann.

Weaver, C. (1990). *Understanding whole language: From principles to practice.* Portsmouth, NH: Heinemann.

— .(1991). Whole language as good education. *The Whole Language Umbrella, 2*(2), 1-10.

Whitmore, K., & Crowell, C. (1994). *Inventing a classroom: Life in a bilingual, whole language learning community.* York, ME: Stenhouse Publishers.

Note

1. It was difficult to decide how to name the authors I cite in this chapter since many of these published researchers are colleagues and friends. I decided to call those colleagues that I worked with by first names and to use last names for writings published by colleagues a and researchers outside of Detroit.

The Whole Language Movement in Detroit: A Teacher's Story: Part Two

DEBRA GOODMAN

Changing the Story of a Whole Language School in Detroit's Center City

Whole language, for us, is not just a vision of education, but a vision of the world and the way people connect with each other. For it is in the sharing—in the telling, the listening, the recording, the reading, and the retelling—of our stories that we become visible to each other, that we become part of human history, and that we begin to change that history together. (Bloome & Solsken, 1991, p. 82)

Introduction

This is the story of how a group of teachers, students, parents, community activists, administrators, university colleagues, poets, and storytellers were involved in *changing the story* of an inner-city public school. The Dewey Center for Urban Education started with a proposal written by six Detroit teachers. Along the way, the proposal was adopted by a school community and shaped by the school's history and the actions and interactions of all participants. Toby Kahn Curry [now Loftus], a major author of the proposal, describes the school community in a book proposal:

*Changing the St*ory is a new refreshing tale from Detroit. It is the story of the conception, implementation, and "becoming" of a whole language school in the Cass Corridor, a notorious neighborhood in Detroit's center city, a neighborhood known for its unemployment and economic depression where children and adults must wage a daily battle against drugs, prostitution, and crime. But like our new school, The Dewey Center for Urban Education, the Corridor is a place of hope and determination, peopled by many unsung heroes who choose to live and work in the area, people who aren't afraid to take a risk or search for a new solution to the many social problems that face all urban Americans. The daily lives of these community members have been an enormous source of strength for us as we move forward with our program. (Curry, 1990, p. ii)

The Dewey Center opened in the fall 1989 at a moment when interest in whole language peaked and many whole language projects came to fruition. The first Whole Language Umbrella conference was held in St. Louis in July 1990. I was active on the WLU board, and the Detroit TAWL group edited the first WLU newsletters. At the same time, Toby and I began collaborating with a University of Michigan group exploring curriculum that respected the "authority and expertise of learners" (Stock, 1995). The Dewey Community Writing Projects in the summers of 1989 and 1990 grew out of these discussions.

David Schaafsma (1993) describes how pedagogy evolved through storytelling during the community writing projects: "Through the daily stories we told, we were revealing our learning theories, and, upon hearing others' accounts, we reshaped those theories. We seemed to be building a curriculum through storytelling" (p. xvi). Our teaching stories became a "larger story" like the "Samarkan histories: with each teacher's story we begin the tale again from another perspective, another point of view, and we see how much richer and more complex the tale becomes, and how much more valuable multiple perspectives can be for capturing the complexity of the classroom" (p. xvii).

Changing the story became a metaphor for our process of becoming a whole language school. Toby writes:

The creation of The Dewey Center has meant a myriad of new experiences for many different people: children, teachers, parents, administrators, community members, and university researchers. We all have our own perspectives, insights, and observations about these experiences, but we also have a shared belief that our story is worth documenting and discussing with others. Schooling in America is being redefined, innovative educators across our country are rethinking and restructuring traditional schools to meet the needs of an ever changing world. The narratives that evolve on these pages trace the change and restructuring of one school and one community, but this is certainly a story that can happen elsewhere. (Curry, 1990, p. iii)

Unfortunately, we were so busy living this school change that the multi-vocal book Toby proposed was never completed. In the following pages I share my own story of the Dewey Center and the process of "creating a curriculum through storytelling." In this retelling, I draw on my own memories, source documents (i.e., the school proposal, conference notes and papers, student writings), interviews during my doctoral study, and recent surveys and conversations with Dewey Center teachers. Additional resources include Schaafsma's published study (1993), papers written by Dewey teachers (Goodman, 1992; Curry, 1992; Curry, 1998), and the transcript of a conversation between Yetta Goodman, Toby, and me (Goodman, 1990) for the "teacher interview" in Atwell's " *Workshop by and for Teachers 3: The Politics of Process* " (Goodman, 1991).

Writing the Dewey Center story is difficult. There are so many stories, and so many ways to tell them. There is the story of a school where doors were locked at 3:30 every day becoming a bustling site of after-school events, morning and afternoon latchkey programs, teacher/parent meetings, workshops and writing groups, and evening poetry readings. There is the shift from what one teacher describes as "monotonous teaching as well as learning" (Gatt, 2003) to a school where "we are all writing—from 8th grade to first, " as Yetta Goodman said during a 1992 WLU conference. There are stories of learning and teaching in a community with high incidences of asthma and AIDS, where needles and condoms are found on the playground, where family members may be in prison or killed by gunfire, and young children learn to be tough. There are stories that Rose Bell[1] and other community activists share of filling "the projects" with irises and gathering clothing and supplies for young mothers.

This is the story of a group of Detroit teachers, African American and White, committed to building a learning community for Detroit's children. It is the story of middle-income, professional, mostly African American families driving their children into the inner city to learn alongside children from lower income families, also mostly African American. It is a story of collaboration and conflict, moments of liberatory teaching and moments of compromise. The painful and hopeful stories that compose this history, told in the classroom and among parents and teachers, involve complex issues of poverty, race, gender, culture, community, identity, language, learning, pedagogy, and schooling. Toby writes:

> This is a story of one school and many lives. When we changed the story of the Couzens Community School we altered the lives of many students, teachers, and community members and began to redefine the community where they work and live. Change is tough. One person's dream is another person's nightmare. Giving up the comfort of what is known for the uncertainty of the new can be terrifying. We have faced many obstacles and staunch resistance. We have only just begun the journey and our destination is still uncertain. In an urban school district, like Detroit, plagued with numerous financial and social problems there are never any guarantees. While our success has been monumental, the struggles have been never ending. (Curry, 1990, p. ii)

This chapter provides a glimpse of the monumental successes and never-ending struggles of the Dewey Center story. I start with a chronology. I describe how a group of teachers, working with children and parents, began to rethink language learning and teaching practices. I discuss critical aspects of becoming whole language teachers including inquiry, dialogue, collaboration, and negotiation. I describe the complexities in bringing teachers, students, and families together to construct a whole language school community. I conclude with some things we learned from living the Dewey story and some things I learned from this retelling.

A History of the Dewey Center

Proposing a Whole Language School

By the late 1980s, the political climate in education was more open to innovation, providing a window for whole language educators. The Michigan Board of Education adopted a holistic definition of reading as an interaction between reader, text, and social context. Toby and I participated in conversations exploring whole language pedagogy with educators across the country and in Canada. We joined a growing number of classroom teachers presenting at conferences, teaching university courses, and writing articles and books (see, for example: Atwell, 1987; Goodman, Goodman, & Hood, 1989; Fisher, 1991). Toby and I taught a graduate course in whole language at Wayne State University from 1989 to 1992. During that time, we observed a shift from teachers saying, "All very interesting, but I could never do that in my school" to teachers making profound pedagogical shifts during just one semester.

Burton International School, where Toby and I taught, was part of Detroit's small "Alternative Schools" (schools of choice) Department. At district-wide conferences, Toby and I began to meet teachers and parents who shared our interest in transformative (Edelsky, 1991) classrooms and schools. In 1987, the superintendent of schools organized a task force on alternative schools and Toby was asked to participate. Toby describes the "findings" of the task force:

> What came out of this year-long task force was that schools of choice and the magnet schools had happy kids and teachers who wanted to be there. The children had high attendance, they liked coming to school. The parents were satisfied. Debi and I were both working at a school with a multicultural population, The Burton International School. The Task Force said programs like Burton could be replicated. At Burton we had five hundred kids on the waiting list. Community members of the Task Force became politically active. The current president of the Detroit School

board and three of the other board members came out of this group. (Goodman, 1990, p. 1)

The election of community activists to the school board, with strong support from the Detroit Federation of Teachers, reflected a movement towards "empowered" neighborhood schools. Toby describes how the idea for The Dewey Center came out of a conversation with Linda Coleman, a kindergarten teacher at another alternative school: "That was right about the time Ken's book *What's Whole in Whole Language?* (Goodman, 1986) came out. Another teacher was at my home one day and she picked up a copy of the book and said, 'This should be another alternative school. We should start our own whole language school.' And I said, 'Alright, Linda, we'll just go ahead and do that' " (Goodman, 1990, p. 1)

Toby brought together a small group of teachers at her house. We represented teachers from kindergarten to middle school. Toby, Linda Coleman, and I were White teachers in a predominantly African American district, and we asked African American colleagues Sandy Martin and Joanne Wilson to join us. We started by brainstorming our ideal school without consideration for mandates or constraints.

The proposal that grew out of these conversations describes a school where: instruction is organized in theme cycles; multi-age classrooms and cross-age learning experiences encourage a family-like community; all staff members are teachers; everyone writes and publishes; evaluation is an ongoing process; and discipline is a growth experience and not punishment. As quoted in the mission statement for our proposal:

> The Dewey Center will be a learning environment for everyone—children, parents and staff. Our approach to learning and teaching will be holistic and developmental. Our focus of study will be the Sciences and Humanities. The tools we will use for our studies will be writing, reading, speaking, listening, and thinking. Program development and daily planning for the special needs of each child will take place in collaborative teams of teaching staff, informed by the latest knowledge of how children learn. Students and parents will be actively involved in every aspect of our school lives.

It was Toby's idea to name our proposal after John Dewey because of powerful connections between whole language curriculum and Dewey's experience-based and student-centered learning. Dewey wrote:

> If one attempts to formulate the philosophy of education implicit in the practices of the new education, we may, I think, discover certain common principles amid the variety of progressive schools now existing. To imposition from above is opposed expression and cultivation of individuality; to external discipline is opposed free activity; to learning from texts and teachers, learning through experience; to acquisition of isolated skills and techniques by drill is opposed acquisition of them as a means of attaining ends which make direct vital appeal; to preparation for a

more or less remote future is opposed making the most of the opportunities of present life; to static aims and materials is opposed acquaintance with a changing world. (Dewey, 1963, p. 19)

We were also inspired by the importance Dewey placed on democratic classrooms and educating for democracy. Dewey wrote, "The limitation that was put upon outward action by the fixed arrangements of the typical traditional schoolroom, with its fixed rows of desks and its military regimen of pupils who were permitted to move only at certain fixed signals put a great restriction upon intellectual and moral freedom" (1963, p. 61). Whole language involves freedom to choose learning experiences and negotiate the curriculum with the teacher.

For Detroit teachers and families, whole language was more than a learner-centered, literature-based program. It was a curriculum with the potential for addressing inequities in students by creating a multicultural, antiracist curriculum. Dewey wrote, "But the fact still remains that an increased measure of freedom of outer movement is a means, not an end. The educational problem is not solved when this aspect of freedom is obtained. Everything then depends, so far as education is concerned, upon what is done with this added liberty. What end does it serve? What consequences flow from it?" (1963, p. 61). Finally, we also shared the concerns of Detroit parents, particularly African American parents, that our children not be involved in "experimental" and untried programs. Naming the school proposal after John Dewey also illustrated that whole language builds upon a long tradition of progressive pedagogy and research (Shannon, 1990).

While imagining our ideal school was exhilarating, I never imagined the proposal would be accepted. I describe Toby as "the real optimist of the group....I'd been burned so many times, I was more paranoid looking over my shoulder and Toby was always more open...with her views. She never thought you had to teach behind closed doors" (Goodman, 1990, p. 2). Toby said, "I had gotten in trouble but I had done it really openly." When we began writing the proposal, Toby remembers me saying, "I'll go along for the ride, help write the proposal, but really Toby, it'll never fly. Can you imagine what we're facing?" (Goodman, 1990, p. 1).

The Proposal "Flies"

What the best and wisest parent wants for his own child, that must the community want for all of its children. Any other ideal for our schools is narrow and unlovely; acted upon it destroys our democracy. (Dewey, 1980, p. 5)

What we were facing was an off-again, on-again minefield of public opinion, city schools' politics, and the ever-present probability that months of hard work could be discarded or co-opted in a moment. In the fall of 1987, responding to the task force's recommendation, the press attacked the superintendent for considering new schools when Detroit had ongoing financial concerns. The superintendent announced there would be "no growth and development" that school year. However, in February 1988 a quiet internal memo invited proposals for new alternative schools. Six weeks were provided to draft proposals, but our proposal was ready. When proposals were reviewed, "ours got the very highest mark of any proposal because it was the only one that was philosophically-based, comprehensive and well thought out" (Goodman, 1990, p. 2).

However, Aretha Marshall, Director of Alternative Schools, suggested we needed an actual site to make the proposal a reality. At the same time we were contacted by Hattie Montague, a longtime community activist. The Couzens School, six blocks from Burton International, was slated to be closed and she had heard of our proposal. The Couzens School was built during the 1960s baby boom to house 1,000 children. By 1987, however, enrollment was less than 200 children in preschool through eighth grade. The neighborhood, once a thriving center-city community, included city blocks of empty lots dotted with boarded buildings, homeless shelters, and a few remaining businesses. Most children lived in the Jeffries Homes, subsidized townhouses which families called "The Projects." With a beautiful library and many large classrooms, the building was perfect for innovative programs, collaborative teaching, and school-wide centers. After several meetings and conversations, Montague, the Concerned Citizens of Cass Corridor, and the Cass Community United Methodist Church endorsed the Dewey Center. The proposal was revised to reflect the school community.

Montague organized a parent meeting to discuss the proposal. For the first time in years the school was open in the evening and about 40 parents attended, along with a few administrators and teachers. After the meeting was scheduled, an assistant principal at a nearby school asked to present her own proposal for an alternative school designed for African American children's "learning needs." The proposal author was African American, as were Couzens' principal, Hattie Montague, and Aretha Marshall. At the meeting, parents questioned why their children needed a special program rather than a whole language curriculum for all children. The Dewey Center for Urban Education proposal was overwhelmingly approved.

Gaining the support of teachers was more difficult. When Toby presented the proposal at a staff meeting:

The staff wanted an explanation of whole language and so I started telling them what whole language wasn't because that was really easy for me after reading Ken's discussion about what whole language isn't (Goodman, K., 1986). I talked about my own classroom and the kinds of things I was learning. I discussed the research that I had been reading. People were just shaking their heads. I didn't get attacked but they were just waiting for it to be over. (Goodman, 1990, p. 3)

Hard Choices: Schools of Choice, School Communities, and Educational Policy

While some Couzens teachers were immediately excited about the whole language curriculum, most teachers were skeptical. National discussions of whole language had not reached Detroit Public Schools, and many teachers viewed whole language as something Toby and I had invented. Couzens teachers were accustomed to strict discipline and teacher-directed classrooms. They expressed doubts that our experiences at Burton International, where White and Black families and middle-income and working-income families were well integrated, would translate to Couzens where students lived in a neighborhood considered the toughest in the city.

We considered allowing the school to be closed and reopening the building with new teachers and a reorganized student body. We were aware of whole language schools around the country, including community schools like Fair Oaks (Bridges-Bird, 1989) and schools of choice such as La Escuela Fratney (Peterson, 1994). The Manhattan New School (Harwayne, 1999) started with handpicked teachers and primary grades, expanding each year. However, neighborhood Tucson schools (Wortman & Matlin, 1995) with supportive administrators and teacher study-groups were making gradual shifts to a whole language framework.

Toby and I believed that whole language curriculum did not require "super teachers" or special children. We had concerns about schools of choice ultimately contributing to existing inequities in urban districts. At their best, Detroit's alternative schools were places where parents, teachers, students, and community members worked to create a shared vision of a school community. Schools such as Detroit Open School provided stellar examples of the possibilities for education in Detroit. At their worst, Detroit's alternative programs were showcase schools skimming "the cream" across the city, allowing a few—generally privileged—families to avoid standard-fare education without addressing pedagogy district-wide. While preference was given to neighborhood children, application deadlines and other policies created obstacles in communities where families had less school savvy.

On the other hand, The Dewey Center for Urban Education was possible because of the schools-of-choice movement and the support of the

Alternative Schools Department. Aretha Marshall's goal was to expand exemplary programs to include many more schools, teachers, and families. Later, as Marshall saw what we were accomplishing at Dewey, she realized that whole language is a pedagogical framework that crosses programs, content areas, and developmental levels. At that time, she organized whole language speakers and sessions for the citywide alternative schools.

Still, the Dewey Center proposal authors believed strongly that curriculum reform needs to reach neighborhood schools for public education to thrive. We wanted to create a theoretically grounded, community-based school, without any gatekeeping for neighborhood children. While we never imagined the struggles involved in asking an existing faculty and student body to make a shift to a whole language philosophy, I believe we were right in working to build a school with the Couzens community. By positioning ourselves as insiders, we were eventually accepted as part of the community, working with families to make the school a safe haven in a troubled and sometimes frightening neighborhood.

In the end, the faculty did endorse the proposal. We asked them to support the proposal on its own merits. However, many teachers reasoned that the proposal would keep the school open and if the community wanted the Dewey Center, they wouldn't stand in the way. We went to the school board with endorsements from teachers, parents, and community. Board members voted to let the Couzens school stay open, allowing our proposal to sink or swim without official approval.

We spent the next school year preparing for the new school program. A committee of teachers, parents, and building and district administrators began meeting to orchestrate the transition. Ken Goodman came to the school for a public meeting attended by teachers and parents across the city. We asked citywide families to enroll students for the fall semester in support of a transitional program. We would use the additional enrollment (about 70 students) to open three multi-age classrooms at the primary, upper-elementary, and middle-school levels. Linda Coleman, Toby, and I would teach in these classrooms.

The transition process was not ideal. While Toby had administrative credentials, district seniority prevented us from bringing her in as principal. Toby and I continued teaching full-time at Burton International during the Dewey Center planning process. We were never able to use the reading budget (earmarked for expensive basal readers and workbooks) for trade books or other literature. Nor were "start-up" funds provided for new classrooms. As is a common practice in city schools, teachers spent a lot of their own money on books and materials.

However, with the help of an alternative schools grant writer, we were awarded a three-year "restructuring grant" from the state of Michigan.

Strategic use of district funding, along with the restructuring grant, provided professional development, curriculum development, a full-time librarian, parent workshops, a part-time parent coordinator, artists in residence, some books and materials, a school publishing center, and a professional library for teachers. The restructuring grant also established a structure for shared school leadership, supporting an atmosphere of collaboration and dialogue.

Becoming Whole Language Learners and Teachers

Mary Jo Regnier describes how she begins the school year with her first and second graders, "I start by saying, 'We're all a family. We're here all year. We're here to learn. All of us are teachers, helping one another learn.' Then I ask the children. 'What would you like to learn?'" (1994). For all of us—teachers, administrators, parents, and students—becoming a whole language community involved becoming learners as well as teachers.

We began the planning process with a detailed proposal outlining broad changes in curriculum, learning experiences, evaluation, grouping, and scheduling. However, the proposal was based on the proposal authors' experiences and *our stories* of becoming whole language teachers. Whole language at the Dewey Center had to evolve within that community. Whole language is not a set of practices but a theoretical framework that teachers bring to the classroom. Becoming a whole language teacher cannot be mandated, forced, or hurried. For meaningful conversations to occur, teachers had to be stakeholders in school leadership and have the freedom to make professional decisions in their classrooms.

Extra planning time (one period each week) was provided for grade-level cluster meetings (primary, upper elementary, and middle school). Administrators, cluster leaders, parents, and staff formed a leadership team. Weekly faculty meetings were reorganized to include committees, small group discussion, professional development, and sharing. Restructuring grant funds supported a week of professional development before school started each fall, including time for setting up classrooms and collaborating with other teachers.

I can't overemphasize the value of professional development, particularly time for teachers to talk and plan together. Teachers exchanged ideas, shared concerns, discussed learning experiences, planned collaborative inquiry projects or theme studies, and so on. Dewey Center teachers needed time and support to be learners as well as teachers. Becoming whole language teachers involves similar processes to those Mary Jo describes above: inquiry, collaboration, and dialogue.

Professional Development: Learning through Inquiry

In fall of 1988, Toby and I met with a small group of teachers and administrators in the Couzens' library. I remember a lot of tension, and one teacher "was sitting there downcast looking very sullen and distant and he was not the only one." Toby responded in her direct and disarming way, "We were going around introducing ourselves and I was making a chart of who everybody was for myself so I could connect up names and faces. And he was sitting there with a sour expression and I think I said, 'Do you want to be here? I sense from your body language that you don't want to be here.'" The teacher, Emmanuel Gatt, explained that he needed to know more about whole language before he could help with planning. He promised to be our biggest advocate once he understood whole language. Although whole language defies simple definitions, I launched into a short presentation "that was geared towards what the teachers wanted to know right at that time" (Goodman, 1990, p. 4).

Emmanuel is a White teacher who had taught at Couzens for 24 years, starting as an intern in a program for student teachers working with "inner-city, high-risk students" (Gatt, 2003). Hattie Montague was impressed with him and "made sure" he was offered a teaching position. He was dedicated to the children in the community and was respected by families and the administration. He involved his fourth graders in school plays, science fairs, and other extracurricular experiences. In a survey, Emmanuel describes the "method of teaching and learning" during his first 24 years: "Everything was structured. Each subject was allotted time to be taught and learned. Most often the subjects were unrelated—handwriting, spelling, English. It was monotonous teaching as well as learning the content matter from the student's point of view" (Gatt, 2003).

Emmanuel describes his initial struggle with understanding whole language:

> Even after several workshops I had a difficulty understanding its meaning and purpose since I was structured to teach each subject matter separately. I needed a definition of Whole Language that was simple and direct. It took a couple of years of constant observations, questioning, and reading published books on Whole Language before my brain comprehended what Whole Language was inviting teachers to accomplish. (Gatt, 2003)

For Toby and me, Emmanuel's story was symbolic of the change process at Dewey. Whole language teachers are also whole language learners. They bring amazing experiences, resources, and expertise to professional conversations. They need authority over their own learning, choosing where to focus their inquiry. While other teachers immediately tried the teaching practices we suggested, Emmanuel requested readings and asked questions, seeking a theoretical understanding before exploring teaching practices himself. Later, he published child-authored books with his class and was instrumental in finding ways to apply whole language pedagogy to math and science curricula.

During the transitional year, the Alternative Schools Department provided funding for eleven staff development sessions on Saturdays and after school. Participation was voluntary, but teachers received a stipend for attending. With a growing interest in whole language, teachers at other schools asked to attend professional development sessions. City-wide participants were very enthusiastic and shared their excitement with Couzens staff. Aretha Marshall and her staff worked closely with Toby and me during the initial staff development, but came to trust us after observing the first sessions. We resisted suggestions to focus on practice and give teachers weekly assignments to try out specific learning experiences. I remembered that, "We said to the staff, 'Look, our goal is for you to think about this; don't even worry about what you are going to do. We just want you to think about it this year. We are not implementing this year.' We wanted them to understand it's a three to five year process. And people started to relax and be able to say, 'I don't have to learn this all at once'" (Goodman, 1990)

Toby and I shared our own inquiries into Goodman's (1986) pillars of whole language, David Bloome's notion of productive (i.e., creative writing) and reproductive (i.e., copying) texts, and our interest on community study. I had recently heard Brian Cambourne describe the "conditions of language learning," a pedagogical model based on observations of children learning oral language in families (see Cambourne, 1988). Both Toby and I found this model enlightening, bringing together beliefs about language learning and teaching, and providing for theoretically grounded classroom practice. Cambourne's conditions became a framework for constructing curriculum and evaluating learning experiences at the Dewey Center.

We wanted teachers to explore and refine their own beliefs rather than adopting ours. We raised contrasting theoretical perspectives, creating an atmosphere friendly to questioning and professional disagreements. Toby and I explored whole language theory with stories of learners and experiences in our classrooms. We asked teachers to talk about their best experiences as students. These experiences are typically functional, meaningful experiences such as listening to a book read out loud, participating in a school play, or going on a field trip. These stories provided examples of teaching strategies. We felt teachers could best decide how to adapt these ideas to their classroom teaching.

Most teachers were skeptical but open to discussion. Interest in whole language grew as teachers began to share experiences and possibilities. A few teachers opposed the whole language program and eventually left the school. Several teachers were very excited about the new direction the school was taking. Clara Jane Thompson, an African American teacher, was active in the local reading council and the International Reading Association. The whole language orientation was all she needed to take off, and she started a reading and writing workshop that year, holding daily individual conferences with all her students.

Paulette LeDuc and Ilse Hamers, both European Americans, worked with students with language impairments who often started talking at six or seven. They had discovered that functional language experiences (i.e., taking messages to other teachers, singing songs, reading predictable books, and publishing their own stories) were most supportive for their children's oral and written language development. Paulette says, "When the whole language idea was first proposed I was very excited. Finally, I had an official name for what I had been trying to do with my students. It was like my work with the students was finally validated" (LeDuc, 2003).

Conversations and inquiry continued throughout the next five years as the Dewey Center program expanded. We created a professional library and held children's literature lunches. Teacher and parent inquiry groups explored literature discussion, miscue analysis, classroom research, and so on. Paulette remembers these meetings as a highlight of the Dewey program:

> I enjoyed the series of Saturday parent/teacher workshops. It was good to share ideas with colleagues. Our teacher writing club was most refreshing for me. It was a vehicle for me to express my thoughts, aspirations, joys, frustrations as a teacher in a large, urban, floundering school system. The workshops gave me hope for the rational. So much irrationality in expectations had been set forth as mandates in my teaching. (LeDuc, 2003)

Whole language starts with the theoretical orientation and beliefs of the teacher, but at the same time whole language is a "theory in practice" (Edelsky, Altwerger, & Flores, 1991). At the Dewey Center, professional development was grounded in collaborative teaching and in dialogue focused on direct observations of children engaged in meaningful learning experiences.

Collaboration, Dialogue, and Meaningful Work

The school opened in the summer of 1989 with the Dewey Community Writing Project. For two summers middle-school students explored their community through oral history and writing workshops, in a collaborative project with the Center for Educational Improvement at the University of Michigan. The small summer program, involving eight teachers and forty students, provided a space for teacher inquiry and reflection. We learned about possibilities for professional development through collaborative teaching, observations, and dialogue, and we learned about the importance of meaningful work in the lives of young writers.

We published an anthology of community writing each summer. Toby writes, "The writing of *Corridors* has served in many ways as the connecting pathway or link between the separated lives of students, teachers, community residents, and the life force of inner-city Detroit" (Curry, 1989, p. 1). Students visited neighborhood businesses and interviewed community activists, learning about the history and resources of the community. James Cook, an eighth grader living in the community, writes:

> If I could write about any community in Detroit, it would be the Cass Corridor. Because of drugs and unemployment, many people moved away. But at one time, there were more people on Brainard between Second and Third than in most small towns in Michigan. Today the Cass Corridor is mostly a bunch of burned down buildings. There are lots of drugs and prostitution, but I don't think it's as bad as its reputation. In the late forties and fifties, a lot of people came to Detroit because of jobs in factories. Many of them went to the Cass Corridor, which was one of the only places where you could get an apartment quickly. (Cook, 1989, p. 1).

Students met community activists such as Rose Bell who described helping teen mothers, planting flowers, and fighting against drugs. One student asked, "Isn't it dangerous to be a community organizer?" Mrs. Bell responded, "It's dangerous walking out of your door in this neighborhood." Still, she encouraged kids to get organized, get involved, and help change their community (see Goodman, 1991, p. 85).

Our metaphor "Changing the Story of an Inner-City School" developed in staff conversations during the summer project. While engaging students in "changing their community," we were changing how we viewed students. Teachers shared observations and stories about the same learners, and our insights—and the stories we told—became new stories. As the stories we told about learners changed, the students themselves appeared to change. Students that teachers initially described as "non-readers" blossomed, but also teachers shifted in describing and interpreting observations of learners.

Collaborative faculty meetings also provided a space for frank discussions that rarely occur at administration-led faculty meetings. Following a walking trip, Jeanetta Cotman, a fifth grade teacher at Couzens, said she was not comfortable with students eating food in public and was upset that other teachers allowed it. Although the group of students was racially mixed, Jeanetta was primarily concerned about the African American children. Susan,[2] an African American teacher, supported Jeanetta, arguing that African American students are singled out for negative treatment and teachers need to help them be aware of their appearance in public.

What struck me about this incident is that it never occurred to the four White teachers that "eating on the street" might be offensive, although Jeanetta felt that the incident was an example of White teachers not caring about African American children. I grew up in Detroit, attending predominantly African American schools, and had heard teachers express similar concerns. However I did not anticipate objections to eating in public. Dana, a young African American teacher, was familiar with Jeanetta's reaction but associated it with an older generation, illustrating the complexities of teaching identities. Jeanetta and Susan grew up in the South and both were parents.

In a district where around 90% of students and about half the teachers are African American, I had never experienced such open discussion about race at a faculty meeting. Delpit (1995) describes "alienation and miscommunication" that occur when concerns of African American parents and educators are not part of professional conversation. Discussions of issues like race may be emotionally charged and divisive. African American colleagues have told me they sometimes find it easier to just let things go. However, in a collaborative project, where each teacher participates in decision making, there is more reason to raise and discuss critical issues. Shared leadership and open dialogue provide the possibility for teachers to understand each other's experiences, beliefs, and concerns.

Becoming a Whole Language School

Chaos and Never-ending Struggles

The Dewey Center opened officially in August 1989, and all eyes were on Toby, Linda, and me to set up "model" whole language classrooms. We each experienced the most difficult teaching year of our careers. Most of the new, citywide students were placed in our classrooms because the families were interested in whole language. This meant I had sixteen students adjusting to a new school, including one troubled 10-year-old who constantly heckled me during class discussions. I also received two of the most challenging neighborhood fourth graders.

Most neighborhood children were well cared for, though their families often struggled to pay bills, and the community suffered from poor health, violence, and substance abuse. In some cases utilities were cut off, and keeping clothes washed was difficult. While the neighborhood was primarily African American, it was an historic immigrant center, and some of the poorest residents were white Appalachian families looking for work in Detroit. There were several homeless shelters and we frequently had children join us for a few days or weeks until their family was relocated. Toby wrote,

"My new school, the Dewey Center, is geographically five blocks from my former school. Five city blocks, but economically and culturally a million miles" (Goodman & Curry, 1991, p. 163).

We anticipated a long pedagogical transition, but we never anticipated the chaos and confusion of the first few years at Dewey. Teachers trying holistic practices felt like unsure beginners. Emmanuel says, "I realized I had to unlearn my discipline which I felt comfortable doing for many years and rethink how students would benefit from this new philosophy. This involved forfeiting my comfort zone as decision maker and structure enforcer" (Gatt, 2003). Experienced whole language teachers struggled to construct a classroom community in this unfamiliar setting. In earlier years, I would observe students closely and construct small groups, placing students who needed support under the wing of nurturing peers. That year, three students were more challenging than any student I had worked with before. While most students were capable and eager to learn, it was difficult to get the class listening to each other for a group discussion. Arguments and fights were commonplace.

In the past, class discussions of conflicts provided students with alternate ways of responding. In this group, many students argued that if someone "gets in my face, knock them down." I grew up in middle-income Detroit communities and had never had to survive in the Cass Corridor. During the summer project I drove a fifth grader to her family's basement apartment. As I drove away, bricks and bottles were thrown down at the street. My first thought was to get out of there quickly, and I left thinking about the children growing up in that community. I could not argue with children about how to live in their world.

I respected the students' choices of how to survive outside of school. However, inside the school walls we needed to work together to create a safe place to learn. The school of choice brought together children from a wide range of economic backgrounds, opening up conversations that benefited all students. Citywide students, generally growing up in African American professional families, provided alternative perspectives. "My daddy says you don't have to fight to be a man," one student told his classmates. At the same time, neighborhood children shared maturity and resilience in response to a sometimes difficult childhood world.

Students' experiences *inside* school also influenced responses to whole language invitations. Toby describes her sixth and seventh grade class that year: "Several of my students have been retained once, some, twice. Many think they can't read and have never tried to read a book without 'lots of pictures.' Most of them have never done any real writing, and many think they can't write because they can't spell. My kids have come into our whole language classroom from what I consider to be the horrors of fragmented learning" (Goodman & Curry, 1991, p. 163). Although students were not reading and writing like previous groups, our experiences during the summer project illustrated they were not less capable. Toby wrote, "Each context is a new one. The same kinds of things that worked for me and the students at Burton International are not working in the same way at the Dewey Center. I must take the time to know my students, to learn who they are and what they know" (Goodman & Curry, 1991, p. 166).

Most of the children had never read a novel, so Toby read aloud Mildred Taylor's *Roll of Thunder, Hear My Cry* (1991). She said:

> For most, it's their first experience with powerful historical fiction—a story that focuses on a black family's survival in the racist, rural Mississippi of the 1930s. Together we analyze the plot, discuss the characters' thoughts and actions, make comparisons of the historical setting with 1989 city life, and make predictions about the story based on what the author has already revealed to us, the readers. I love to see literature and history come alive for my students. Their comments show how serious they are, how much they care about the book, and how eager they are to learn. (Goodman & Curry, 1991, pp. 163-164).

In my fourth and fifth grade classroom, many students were excited by choices and invitations and became quickly engaged in learning experiences. Others missed the familiar routines of teacher-led instruction. They requested assigned desks and questions at the end of the chapter. When we brainstormed what we wanted to learn, children suggested school-like topics (trees, rocks). When we negotiated a focus for thematic inquiry, they chose the traditional fifth grade topic: States. Without experiences with learner-centered workshops, students misunderstood or mistrusted the classroom structure. Some students viewed learning centers as "free time" and declined the learning "invitations" I extended.

Delpit (1995) argues that the indirect style of progressive White teachers may be confusing to African American students familiar with more direct adult/child interactions: "If such explicitness is not provided to students, what it feels like to people who are old enough to judge is that there are secrets being kept, that time is being wasted, that the teacher is abdicating his or her duty to teach" (p. 31). Years later, when I observed one Dewey classroom for my doctoral study, second grade African American children understood indirect instructions such as "Would you like to close the door?" I think cultural patterns of communication influenced classroom communication during those first years because the situation was new to all of us. The students and families responded with an understandably growing mistrust of unfamiliar White teachers proposing learning experiences that challenged common views of "schooling." We had to earn the trust of children and families before we could become a community of learners.

In response to "the students in front of me," I moved center time to the afternoon and provided assigned seats for students requesting them. I continued to offer functional, meaningful language experiences but fewer choices. We focused on one learning experience at a time, although students still shared their expertise in small groups. I was frustrated, however, because I felt I was "losing the child by working with the whole group" (Goodman & Curry, 1991, p. 148). During workshops, conferences, and small-group teaching, children have more opportunities to interact and ask questions, and I am able to observe and scaffold students' responses.

Delpit reminds us that when whole language teachers involve students in negotiating the curriculum and organizing the classroom, they have an important role in *making learning experiences and teaching practices explicit* to students. I had conversations with students about my expectations and my rationale for classroom structures and experiences. I explained that I sometimes ignored students who were fooling around because I was busy teaching and not because I didn't care. I placed students in the role of co-teachers, asking them to identify problems with student behaviors and suggest solutions. Initially, all suggestions involved what the teacher should do to the offending student. But how could I control everyone's behavior and teach at the same time? We began to see that we all had to work through our problems together.

When students come up with ideas—such as having extra math lab time or moving quiet reading to the morning—these suggestions tend to work. We tried workshops and learning centers again. Over the next three years, my room was organized into four areas: classroom library, math & science, research/theme center, and a general writing/work/art space. I adopted Toby's idea of a daily "plan of study" which explicitly lists all assignments and invitations available. They could choose what to work on, but they could not choose to do nothing. Once students set a daily plan, they were expected to follow through. Students who had completed all of their work each week received a sticker on a class chart. During my first week at Dewey, four students had stickers. By December about half the class "completed their work" within the week. (By the beginning of my third year every student completed all the learning experiences offered during the first week.)

Parents shared their concerns, and I listened and acknowledged their expertise. I explained that my goal was for students to take responsibility for learning. Engaging students in "meaningful work" provides opportunities to practice language, math, and thinking strategies. Just as learning to read always involves "miscues," learning how to be responsible for your own learning involves some "fooling around." Students who were not working independently were reeled in on Fridays and provided with more direction during the following week. Parents could see this happening and it made sense.

"There is something missing"

Toby had an easier time getting her class running smoothly that year, but she worried that learning experiences were not connected with students' lives. She wrote, "Everyone has a writing folder, and we're almost ready to publish our first book, 'The Real Me.' There is something missing, and I think it relates to a basic mistrust that students have of schools and teachers. I haven't been able to convince my kids that I'm genuine and in return their participation in the program has lacked authenticity" (Goodman & Curry, 1991, p. 167). Toby describes how students' "Real Me" stories describing double Dutch, stickers, and posters did not "reveal some bigger truths about their lives and their goals for the future." She wrote, "There is only our classroom door that separates many of my kids from drug addicts, alcoholism, prostitution, community violence, and poverty. It seems that both my students and I are driven to ignore these harsh realities during our five hours together each day" (p. 167).

We believed that connections between school and community were the place to start, but these complex layers of poverty and mistrust created barriers to involving students in a safe classroom community in the school. Toby wrote:

> In the past, I've been a great one for talking to others about student ownership, but this school year it has been extremely difficult to translate the words of ownership into real student-controlled learning. I've watched and waited for my kids to take ownership over their reading selections, organization of their time, topics for their writing, and decisions about where our studies should take us. (Goodman & Curry, 1991, pp. 165–166)

It wasn't that the children had no sense of community. We knew from talking with students and community residents that "the projects" included extended families and a strong community grapevine. Toby describes learning as much about her middle school students "by watching them during their thirty-minute outdoor recess as I do in our four or five hours together in the classroom (not an easy admission for a fifteen-year teaching veteran)." She explains: "I know they understand ownership because of the successful social events they coordinate. Their first party of the year ran so smoothly that I turned the time over to them the second time a holiday came up. The group organized a class basketball game without consulting or including me. Unfortunately I am left out of these events—not yet a member of this group" (Goodman & Curry, 1991, p. 166).

One day, when I was working in the publishing center, a passing sixth grader tossed a candy wrapper into the room. For me, this act—using the publishing center as a trash can—was symbolic of the disregard and disenfranchisement many older students still felt for the school. We had not come close to our dreams of a school where everyone had an important role in the learning and teaching community. Toby wondered, "In a community where many kids never make it through high school, is there hope that my kids can become productive members in our democratic society? We are struggling together to define our place in the world and to make meaning out of our school life" (Goodman & Curry, 1991, pp. 162-163).

Making Meaning Out of School Life

> The only freedom that is of enduring importance is freedom of intelligence, that is to say, freedom of observation and of judgement exercised in behalf of purposes that are intrinsically worthwhile. (Dewey, 1963, p. 61)

Over the following years, we worked to create a community where we "define our place in the world and make meaning out of our school lives." Reva was in my first fourth and fifth grade class. On a survey at the end of fourth grade, she described why she liked our class, "I have freedom. It's not boring. It's not stupid. It has better classroom activities." After two years at Dewey, Reva's mother, a high school teacher, selected a specialized middle school closer to home. A few weeks into the semester, Reva returned to Dewey. She writes, "Every day when I came home from school I begged my mother to transfer me back to Dewey Center. She was very reluctant. But I kept up the hustle. I knew my mother was very enthusiastic about cooperative learning and the whole language program." Reva's new school "has a very traditional concept" which "did not make a good impression on me." At Dewey, "the classes are more inspirational" and "we do not have to sit around and listen to the teacher talk all day."

What is important to Reva about the Dewey Center is the "freedom" and "inspirational" classes. When students focus on meaningful and interesting work, their proficiencies as readers, writers, and thinkers develop. These learning experiences build connections between students' lives outside of school, their lives inside of school, and their role in the larger communities that surround home and school.

Many Dewey Center programs and learning experiences built connections between family, community, and school. Mary Jo Regnier invited local senior citizens to read to her children once a week. Seniors would each read a book to small groups of children, who rotated until they had heard all of the stories. Nina Moore, the eighth grade homeroom teacher, had taught in the Couzens community for many years. One year, she asked her eighth graders to brainstorm "what was good about gangs." The students, at first incredulous about gangs as a "school topic," began to consider and share how gangs create a social community. Nina and the students created different kinds of "gangs" in the classroom that year. At the same time, she opened a door for frank discussion of the students' lives outside of school.

Other Dewey learning experiences helped build connections between children's lives and the wider communities outside of school. The *New York Times Magazine* published an extensive feature on "The Tragedy of Detroit" (Chafets, 1990), and Toby was outraged by the negative tone. She posted the article on the class bulletin board and the students explored the misperceptions and realities of Detroit and other cities. She read Jonathan Kozol's (1995) *Amazing Grace* to her sixth and seventh grade class, which describes a community in New York City. When Toby read the section on AIDS, several students started crying. We discovered that many problems in the South Bronx, such as a high incidence of AIDS and asthma, have parallels in the community around the Dewey Center.

Emmanuel Gatt's gardening club began as a large garden on school property. Several classes were involved in gardening projects. Emmanuel helped Mindy LePere's first and second graders to plant a butterfly garden where they released the butterflies they had observed from the larval stage. The gardening club became an official 4H chapter. Toby organized a series of poetry readings at the school where local poets and our middle school poets shared their poetry. The audience included followers of the local poets, community members, and parents who came to hear their children.

In addition to finding resources in the school, Dewey students were involved in projects that contributed to the community. During the second year, our new principal supported service learning. She suggested shifting the eighth grade graduation from the typical ceremony honoring a few high achievers to a "rite of passage" celebrating all participants. Each eighth grader presented proposals to the principal for self-improvement, service to family, and community service. The kids stopped fighting with siblings and helped out more around the house. They cleaned up their block or ran errands for an older neighbor. One girl, living at a nearby homeless shelter, started an after-school program at the shelter. When her family relocated across town, she took several buses in order to graduate. It was the only full year in one school that she'd had as a middle schooler.

When the *Michigan Chronicle* (Detroit's African American newspaper) did an article on the summer writing program, Toby met the managing editor, Danton Wilson. Toby says, "As a professional writer, he was telling how schools so often kill writing for children. He said the reason he became a writer is because he had a fifth grade teacher who was so special." Wilson came to Toby's classroom and let the kids interview him. He said that if they submit articles to the *Chronicle,* he would consider publishing them. "All of a sudden, the kids figured they had a voice—they could talk and write about their experiences and investigations" (Goodman, 1991, p. 84). Students interviewed teachers and community activists for their published column.

We began to see students making connection between school experiences and their own lives. During a theme study of "The Struggle for Human Rights," Toby's class watched "Eyes on the Prize," a video documentary. Allen came in one day saying, "Mrs. Curry, you'll never guess what happened to me yesterday. I felt like one of the kids in Little Rock Central High back in 1954." Allen and his cousin had gone to a White suburb with a church youth organization. They were the only Black kids among four hundred students, and some kids harassed them. Toby says, "He saw the relationship of his experience to the integration of Little Rock Central High School." Toby talked with the family and Allen wrote about the incident for the *Michigan Chronicle.* Through inquiry and writing, Allen was able to share a painful incident with his teacher and community and put it into an historic perspective.

After three years, our first group of eighth graders had completed middle school at the Dewey Center. Destiny, the president of that eighth grade class, was the sixth grade girl who had tossed a candy wrapper into the publishing center as if it was a trash can. When I asked about her shift from the outsider to school leader, she told me that her brother had talked to her about choices, and she had made a decision to turn herself around. As the story of the candy wrapper represented the disenfranchised middle school students, Destiny's shift from angry rebel to school leader inspired us with the possibilities for transformative, community-based education.

Monumental Successes

The read'n Girl's	The Readin' Girls
We are read'n to gether.	We are reading together.
We are friends.	We are friends.
We work to gether. We	We work together. We
share. We love eaiher. We	share. We love each other. We
help earh er. we are girl.	help each other. We are girls.
We don't tzs. We play.	We don't tease. We play.
The ead.	The end
by Charlene and Donnikka	by Charlene and Donnikka

This poem, written in Mary Jo Regnier's classroom, hung in the principal's office as a representation of the literate community that evolved at the Dewey Center. Mary Jo said, "Every child is a reader. In order to become a better reader, you study authors. Children learn to read through literature. When I first heard Frank Smith talk in person, he said, 'Teachers don't teach children to read. Authors do.' I didn't understand that at first, but now that I've moved to whole language, I've discovered that's exactly what happens. You let the book engage the child" (Regnier, 1994).

Mary Jo attended the staff development sessions at Dewey during the planning year, and joined the Dewey Center later as a teacher. She describes a dramatic change in her life as a teacher exploring whole language theory:

> I've been teaching since 1959 and these are the memorable years. Because the program is child-centered, each experience is new. It isn't staged. It comes from them. There's more enthusiasm, and I think the kids learn more too. Before I was structured, everything was out of a manual. Social Studies textbooks, basal readers. Everything was narrow. Now I have freedom. So much is incidental. There's so much conversation and exchange of ideas. In the old tradition the teacher was always right and everything's from the teacher. In the last five years my role and my image diminish. I become less and less a teacher. I feel like I'm one of the teachers and I'm one of them now. Oh—I make the adult decisions, but we're all teachers and learners together. You're always addressing the kid in you. (Regnier, 1994)

The Dewey Center became an oasis of pedagogical possibilities within whole language conversations. Teachers' understandings of the significance of whole language—and our school—shifted with a Dewey Center conference in spring, 1991. Colleagues organizing a whole language conference in Windsor, Ontario, across the river from Detroit, welcomed a preconference day at our school. Every Dewey teacher was involved in some way, from parking to decorations to tour guides, and so on. A hundred guests from across the two countries visited the Dewey Center. They spent the morning visiting classrooms in session on student-led guided tours. In the afternoon, Dewey teachers and others provided break-out sessions. Although the participants raved, the most important impact was on the Dewey teachers and students. They could see that whole language was broader than the school, and that we were inventing something of great interest to the educational community.

The school developed and attracted a highly talented and dedicated staff who were becoming whole language teachers together. Reading together, researching our classrooms, and sharing our stories—we were pushing the boundaries of teaching and learning. We explored theoretical understandings, abandoning some practices and revising others. It was a community where we could argue about whether learning experiences and teaching practices were consistent with our understandings of how children learn language. It was inspiring how ideas built off each other. In kindergarten, Linda Coleman started "exploration time" first thing in the morning, setting up tables with blocks, art materials, or water trays for kids to explore. Many teachers adopted this alternative to morning "bell work" or "journal writing"—a discovery learning time that sometimes led to more formal learning experiences. Our children came to know themselves as readers, writers, and learners.

I observed an Author's Day Celebration in Susan Austin's second grade classroom in June 1996. The children circulated, reading their "autobiographies" to the family members present. Mrs. Griffin, Kristine's mom, listened to as many as she could, and responded enthusiastically to every child. At the end of the celebration, she spoke to me about whole language at the Dewey Center:

> My daughter has been in whole language from the beginning. And it's a joy to be around a child who has a whole language experience. Because learning for them is a joy. It's an adventure, and they're always coming up with something new. It's never the drudgery of "I have to do this, we have to do this." It's the excitement of what I can learn—how this applies to my life.

Mrs. Griffin had three children at Dewey and compared talking to children in whole language classrooms to talking to college students:

> I think the most exciting thing is the fellowship that I have with my children. It's a difference in that it's not like I'm mother and I'm just helping them with their homework, but it's like we're friends and we're exploring things together and they're giving me feedback and I'm talking to them and they're sharing how they feel and how they attack problems. And that's just exciting. (1996)

Mrs. Griffin illustrates the school at the Dewey Center. Families were included in every aspect of the planning process. They were welcome classroom visitors, and teachers offered many invitations for parent participation. The enthusiasm most families had towards the school philosophy was driven home when we realized the school name change was not official. Some neighborhood families wanted to keep "James Couzens," because of the community history it represented. When we named our proposal after John Dewey, it was really a working title, and we didn't really imagine changing the school name. However, active members of the parent community researched Dewey's work. At the meeting, parents talked about John Dewey, about experience-based learning, and about democracy and education. In respect for local parents, Brian Conaway, head of the school community organization, suggested that we maintain "Couzens" for the auditorium. By an overwhelming majority, The Dewey Center for Urban Education was approved as the official school name.

The Decline of Whole Language at Dewey

During our first years at Dewey, a progressive school board brought in a new superintendent known for her support of schools of choice, including whole language schools. She was an elementary teacher herself and brought great hope to Detroit teachers by speaking at a union meeting. Instead of "training" every teacher with the flavor-of-the-month curriculum, the new superintendent initiated a *menu* of professional development options. I attended the Language Arts planning meetings. Committee members were excited about whole language and said I was just the person they needed. I wrote several options for whole language staff development with the Dewey Center as a professional development site. However, when a professional development clearinghouse was held, we were not invited and whole language was not included in the professional development menu.

Working with the Alternative Schools office, we designed the Communication Arts High School. Toby met with enthusiastic print and broadcast journalists who agreed to offer field internships. She publicized the program, interviewed students, recruited staff, worked out schedules, and ordered supplies. Toby was to be the assistant principal in charge of the school, housed in the Dewey Center. However, the Language Arts department convinced the superintendent to hire a principal for the tiny high school, and district policies prevented Toby from interviewing for the job. At one board meeting, a Language Arts administrator hissed, "You'll never get that school."

We were bewildered by the actions from the Language Arts department. However, our principal pointed out that we had designed two language arts schools without consulting their department. Although department staff were never supportive or encouraging, we committed a political faux pas by not seeking their approval. Just before we opened the high school, the new superintendent disbanded the Alternative Schools office. As a proponent of schools of choice, the superintendent wanted all areas and programs to include alternatives. This well-meaning but misguided decision removed the innovative leadership that protected the Dewey Center from conservative forces within the district.

The superintendent was a strong supporter of "school empowerment," and we were excited about the concept of local leadership and reallocating school resources. We wanted to use textbook funds for literature and provide materials to support new teachers. However, many teachers were wary of "empowerment," with concerns that local schools were responsible for ALL decisions such as fixing roofs and buying toilet paper. The incentives offered to empowered schools provided encouragement for a gradual transition. However, in a bizarre and ironic move, the superintendent attempted to mandate empowerment by making it a contract bargaining issue. There was a six-week strike with teachers fighting against being empowered. The superintendent isolated herself from teachers and was not reined in by the board.

The Dewey Center may have survived this crisis except that the new principal was an authoritarian who had difficulty sharing leadership. Without the Alternative Schools office, our collaborative leadership structure broke down. The principal had some good ideas and voiced support of whole language, but nothing could happen without her approval. A wonderful fifth grade teacher organized a school Kwanzaa celebration. The administrative oversight made it such an ordeal that she vowed never to do it again and left Dewey after one year. The principal alienated teachers and staff. A teacher who was robbed in her classroom was chided for giving the man money. The faculty filed union grievances, but the principal became more entrenched. Experienced whole language teachers began leaving and the principal encouraged them to go.

Becoming Whole Language Teacher Activists

The invitation to "become" lives on in the teachers, students, and families that participated in the Dewey Center, in the stories we tell and the work that we continue to do. The Dewey Center was not a curriculum or a program but a process of becoming whole language teachers and learners. When Toby and I first envisioned the school, we pictured a place where we would enjoy teaching. We envisioned a place that we could call home, where we could practice becoming whole language teachers in a supportive community.

The Dewey Center was that place. We were surrounded by thoughtful colleagues who were working together to change teaching and schooling. My colleagues were a powerful thought collective and a wonderful group of friends. However, we didn't anticipate what it was like to be a vanguard, bringing whole language to ambivalent teachers, questioning parents, and administrators with little vision of whole language curriculum and leadership. We had a talented teaching staff, initial district and community support, and the state restructuring grants. We worked with families that loved and cared for their children. We tried to provide a caring place where everyone could learn.

We learned that it's not possible to establish a whole language school without theoretically grounded, knowledgeable curriculum leaders who know how to work with teachers and families. Dewey's school leadership team including parents, teachers, and administrators created a forum for collaboration and dialogue. However, one authoritarian principal was able to destroy shared governance and any possibility of a curriculum based on dialogue. We learned about the critical importance of funding. Detroit Public Schools have always been terribly underfunded. Teachers scramble for mismatched furniture, especially tables and book shelves, and often buy materials themselves. However, the textbook allotment would have purchased incredible classroom libraries. We could order "supplemental literature" within the text program, but monies for textbooks and consumables went unused.

The State of Michigan restructuring grant provided a framework for change. This small grant—$300,000 over three years—supported artists in residence, created a school publishing center, and provided teachers with a small budget for literature and other materials. State restructuring grants are a powerful model of how governments can support innovative schools. A small amount of money for an existing public school goes a long way. However, this grant program was discontinued in favor of funding largely unsuccessful charter schools.

With the families in the Dewey community, we faced the "savage inequalities" of school districts funded by property taxes. Most Dewey teachers are Detroiters, active in community politics and fighting injustice through letters to the editor, union meetings, community organizations, and so on. We knew there were limitations to what we could do from within our classrooms to change the conditions in which children lived. Nor did we see ourselves as missionaries, bringing salvation to inner-city children. Contrary to suggestions in the 2004 presidential debates, no amount of reading, writing, and calculating will overcome poverty and discrimination. As Toby and I wrote, "Why are all of society's problems shunted into this small corner of the world so that these preadolescents are confronted with them every day?" (Goodman & Curry, 1991, p. 169).

However, we came to see whole language as a pedagogy of possibility. "By designating this new school as a magnet school and inviting students from all over the city, we hope to open the world of possibilities beyond the narrow communities where that each group lives" (p. 169). We could study the civil rights movement, talk to community organizers, and engage children in the political process—attending city council meetings or going to hear Nelson Mandela when he first came to town. Whole language pedagogy also provides students with agency over their own learning in many small ways: making choices, forming a committee to run a center, talking about family and community experiences, posing their own questions for learning. With a focus on learning processes, whole language provides what Delpit (1995) calls the "codes of power."

Working in a community where children's lives and futures are at stake made it critical (and unavoidable) to constantly ask ourselves if we were doing our best for them. I described earlier how children seemed to change as our stories about them changed. Our stories illustrate that the stories we told changed teachers as well. Those of us who came to Dewey as "weak, liberal, ineffectual teachers" were forced to think through what it means to have what Freire (1994) calls a "liberatory pedagogy." While we didn't let go of this ideal, we were pushed to consider what it means to truly create a democratic classroom.

During the time we worked at Dewey, children's lives changed for the worse. Homeless shelters were closed as the governor ended funding for the homeless—and homeless adults lived in the fields near the school. Welfare funds for families were cut, recreation budgets slashed, and funding for education eroded. Children in the community grew up in families where the possibilities were narrow. They witnessed police brutality and the toxic literacies (Taylor, 1996) of courts and public services. These are not problems a teacher can fix within the classroom.

If we are concerned about our students and about these larger social issues, we have to fight them outside of the school setting. However, we can also work to create democratic classrooms where children and parents' voices are heard. Where experiences make sense, and where children take control over their own learning. Toby writes:

> When students feel empowered as learners, they begin to think about the choices that lie ahead of them. Our children have taught us that students who are valued and given the opportunity to closely examine and explore the critical issues of their lived lives are able to make healthier choices for their own futures and the futures of their individual communities. (Curry, 1998, p. 20)

Mrs. Griffin also relates whole language pedagogy with children's lived lives:

> You know the learning just doesn't stop with the assignment. It carries over into life itself. And I think if we just have faith in our children, the learning process, if we have faith in their ability – that in the long run we'll get more problem solvers. We'll get happier people able to deal with their problems. And that investment in that whole learning. They care more. Because it's built in - in whole learning - that you got to care for one another, you've got to listen. (1996)

Toby says, "Creating a literate, safe haven is probably the most critical goal that I have for myself as a teacher." She describes "building this safety net on the first day of school" and continuing through the summer:

> Everyone has a classroom job and everyone is expected to participate....At Thanksgiving and Christmas we collect food for needy families and deliver it to the rescue mission behind our school. In every way I can imagine, I blanket my students

in love and acceptance. Above everything academic, I have learned that I must strive to nurture the humanity of my children. For without our humanity, what are we? (Curry, 1998)

Postscript

I last visited the Dewey Center in June, 2003. As I approached the school I noticed another apartment building has burned down and there are more empty fields of grass and weeds. The school looks good. All the windows have been replaced, and the roof is trimmed with blue siding. There is a preschool playground with attractive equipment. It is the last day of school for teachers, and several Dewey teachers, including Emmanuel Gatt, are retiring. Emmanuel talks about his 34 years teaching in one community. He talks about the important work with children. He uses gardening metaphors like cultivate and harvest, and I remembered the community garden he created with the gardening club.

Susan Austin is now teaching kindergarten. Open Court has been adopted by Detroit because of the new national "No Child Left Behind" legislation. Susan tells me they have a workbook for everything. She shows me a stack of unused Open Court workbooks designed to prepare kindergartners for the fourth grade state test. She pronounced the workbooks "a huge waste of money." However, she had spent the year cooperating with the Open Court program, at least for phonics. I talked later with a group of Dewey whole language teachers about coping with Open Court. None of them are using the writing workbook. One teacher rebelled completely, saying, "What are they going to do, fire me?"

I talk with the Headstart teacher who started as a paraprofessional at Couzens. She expresses concern over the changes in Headstart, focusing less on child development. I visit Nina Moore in the eighth grade classroom. Her room is meticulous and she shows off her well-organized closets. She tells me she had no plans to retire. I asked her about Marco, who was in my dissertation study, and she tells me he has won a science fair award and will be on the high school basketball team. She says he had become quite a good reader. As she talks of him and other students, her perceptive observations and interests came through. I remember the no-nonsense, caring, hard-working, and dedicated middle school teacher I'd always admired. Calm in the face of the storm.

I left the building with a similar mixture of feelings to those I had in 1979 when I first started substitute teaching in Detroit Public Schools. The reality of urban schools is totally different—both much worse and much saner—than the impressions we read in the news. In the most depressed communities, and working under incredible constraints, there are groups of teachers who care deeply about children. I'm not talking about special teachers. I'm talking about most teachers. Whatever their beliefs, they work ceaselessly, often thanklessly, to help children. Although they whisper about difficult times, and some are moving on, they are not burnt out. They are not going through the motions. Even when I disagree with their pedagogy, I am always impressed with their professionalism and the way they try to create safe spaces for children to learn. Teachers have tremendous potential, like all learners, and respond to the invitations provided by administrators, communities, school districts, and now state and national governments. We can invite them to build on their strengths, to always become thoughtful and professional (whole language) teachers. Or we can invite them to follow scripted programs. How is this even a choice?

Writing the two chapters for this book has been both amazing and depressing. I'm amazed at the work we were doing and the level of thinking and reflection in the 1980s and '90s. And I wonder if anything I'm doing now is as important as the work that many small groups of teachers were doing in communities across the U.S. and Canada at that time. I am writing the story of a powerful teacher's movement in Detroit at a time when the phrase "whole language" has become taboo, and even whole language proponents are debating whether the term has served its purpose.

Writing has renewed my understanding that whether or not we use the term "whole language" is not the point. It's whether we allow people to narrow our definitions and our understandings of the possibilities to move beyond narrow perspectives of teaching and schooling. I believe that dropping the term whole language because it is under attack only contributes to the de-skilling of teachers as professionals. But the point is that we need to do important work with our students. We need to push our thinking forward and avoid nodding to perspectives that reduce our possibilities as teachers. We need to continue to grow in teaching literacy for social justice and constructing schools for all children.

References

Atwell, N. (1987). *In the middle*. Portsmouth, NH: Heinemann.

Bridges-Bird, L. B. (Ed.). (1989). *Becoming a whole language school: The Fair Oaks story.* Katonah, NY: Richard C. Owen.

Bloome, D., & Solsken, J. (1991). Naftali's Profession. In K. Goodman, L. B. Bridges, & Y. Goodman (Ed.), *The Whole Language Catalog,* p. 229. Santa Rosa, CA: American School Publishers.

Cambourne, B. (1988). *The whole story: Natural learning and the acquisition of literacy in the classroom.* New York: Scholastic.

Chafets, Z. E. (1990, July 29). The tragedy of Detroit. *The New York Times Magazine.* New York: 21-51.

Cook, J. (1989). The Cass Corridor. *Corridors: Stories from inner city Detroit.* Dewey Center Community Writing Project. Ann Arbor, The Center for Educational Improvement through Collaboration.

Curry, T. K. (1989). Corridor. *Corridors: Stories from inner city Detroit.* The Dewey Center Community Writing Project. Ann Arbor, The Center for Educational Improvement through Collaboration.

— (1992). Freeing student voices: Building a 'living" multicultural curriculum. *Focus, Michigan ASCD* (Spring): 32-35.

— (1998). The best we can. *Language Arts Journal of Michigan 14(2)*: 19-22.

Delpit, L. (1995). *Other people's children: Cultural conflict in the classroom.* New York: The New Press.

Dewey, J. (1963). *Experience and education.* New York: Collier Books.

— (1980). *The school and society.* Carbondale, IL: Southern Illinois University Press.

Edelsky, C. (1991). *With literacy and justice for all: Rethinking the social in language and education.* London, New York: The Falmer Press.

Edelsky, C., Altwerger, B. & Flores, B. (1991). *Whole language: What's the difference.* Portsmouth, NH: Heinemann.

Fisher, B. (1991, revised 1998). *Joyful learning in kindergarten.* Portsmouth, NH: Heinemann.

Freire, P. (1994). *Pedagogy of the oppressed.* New York: Continuum.

Goodman, D. & Curry, T. K. (1991). Teaching in the real world. In Y. Goodman, W. Hood, K. Goodman (Eds.), *Organizing for whole language,* pp. 137-169. Portsmouth, NH: Heinemann.

Goodman, K. (1986). *What's whole in whole language?* Portsmouth, NH, Heinemann.

Goodman, K., Goodman, Y. & Hood, W. J., Eds. (1989). *The whole language evaluation book.* Portsmouth, NH: Heinemann.

Goodman, Y. (1991). The teacher interview: Toby Kahn Curry and Debra Goodman. In N. Atwell (Ed.), *Workshop by and for Teachers 3: The Politics of Process,* 81-93. Portsmouth, NH: Heinemann.

Harwayne, S. (1999). *Going public: Priorities and practice at the Manhattan New School.* Portsmouth, NH: Heinemann.

Kozol, J. (1995). *Amazing Grace.* New York: HarperCollins.

Peterson, B. (1994). Building social justice classrooms in an unjust society. *Talking Points*: 2-6.

Pointer, J. (1989). Pride. *Corridors: Stories from inner city Detroit.* The Dewey Center Community Writing Project. Ann Arbor, The Center for Educational Improvement through Collaboration.

Schaafsma, D. (1993). *Eating on the street: Teaching literacy in a multicultural society.* Pittsburgh, PA: University of Pittsburgh Press.

Shannon, P. (1990). *The struggle to continue: Progressive reading instruction in the United States.* Portsmouth, NH: Heinemann.

Stock, P. (1995). *The dialogic curriculum: Teaching and learning in a multicultural society.* Portsmouth, NH: Heinemann.

Taylor, D. (1996). *Toxic literacies: Exposing the injustice of bureaucratic texts.* Portsmouth, NH: Heinemann.

Taylor, M. (1991). *Roll of thunder, hear my cry.* New York: Puffin Books.

Wortman, B. & Matlin, M. (1995). *Leadership in whole language: The principal's role.* York, Maine: Stenhouse.

Unpublished Sources:

Curry, T. K. (1990). Changing the story: The evolution of a whole language school in Detroit's Center City (Introduction for Book Proposal), unpublished.

Gatt, E. (2003). Written Survey

Goodman, Y. (1990). Complete unpublished transcript for "The teacher interview: Toby Kahn Curry and Debra Goodman". Goodman Y. 1991 above.

Goodman, D. (1992). *Changing the story in Detroit's inner city.* Whole Language Umbrella, Niagra Falls, unpublished notes.

Goodman, D. (1996). Whole Language Umbrella Conference Notes. Niagra Falls, NY.

Mrs. Griffin. (1996). Transcribed from videotaped interview with D. Goodman.

LeDuc, P. (2003). Survey.

Regnier, M. (1994). Audiotaped interview with D. Goodman.

Notes

1. In most cases I have used participants' actual names with their direct permission, or because names are published in other documents. In some cases I have omitted names or used pseudonyms.

2. A detailed account and discussion of this incident is a major discussion in Schaafma's book *Eating on the Street*. I'm using the first name pseudonym requested by Susan for the book.

CHAPTER FOUR

A Brief History of Whole Language and the Winter Workshops: From Miscue Analysis to Liberatory Pedagogy

CAROLE F. STICE, NANCY P. BERTRAND, AND MARYANN MANNING

W hen we were asked to write about our experiences at the "Whole Language Winter Workshops," we knew why. Among the three of us, we have attended all eleven. As we began sharing our memories of those days, we realized they were always embedded in the context of what was happening in reading instruction at the time. It was out of the political arena that whole language and the Winter Workshops emerged. This chapter, then, recounts the early days of the whole language movement as it attempts to chronicle the Winter Workshops. We are honored to have the opportunity to tell this story.

The Winter Workshops were held for ten days every other December beginning in 1976 and continuing through 1994, with one last workshop in 2000. They were created in response to requests from teachers for help in understanding the latest research on language, language learning, and the reading process. We found them to be powerful resources in our teaching lives, influencing our classroom practices, informing our research, guiding our professional reading, and ultimately changing our views of the world. Through these wonderful workshops, we came to better understand research on literacy and its implications for teaching. Our efforts to apply that information to our own classroom instruction were supported and enhanced. It is a pleasure to share with you our perspectives on and memories of those events.

Whole Language

Whole language is the application to classroom instruction of research findings from a wide array of fields collectively referred to as socio-psycholinguistics. As an educational movement, whole language has its roots not only in the areas of linguistics, cognitive psychology, and child language learning but in the powerful child-centered, hands-on philosophy and democratic ideals of John Dewey and 20th-century progressivism.

By the early 1970s, just when so much was coming to be understood about language development and how human brains work, progressivism was being edged out of U.S. schools. Mastery learning, with its criterion-based hierarchy of so-called reading "skills," was being ushered in—mostly for purposes of measuring teacher accountability.

While some teachers have always been naturally holistic, the whole language movement, per se, first materialized in the late 1970s in response to the ways in which the then "back-to-basics" effort was being applied, specifically to the teaching of reading. Rather than putting children through programs that drilled them on isolated aspects of words, many teachers believed in keeping language whole and helping children learn to read and write as they used the language, engaging in authentic literacy events and natural language contexts.

In the early 1970s, research findings about both oral and written language learning, were making their way into classes in colleges of teacher education in most developed and developing countries around the world. Combined with the tenants of progressivism, the term "whole language" appeared in the U.S. It gained popularity in direct proportion to attempts by bureaucrats to control curriculum.

Back-to-Basics

Both whole language and the Winter Workshops began during the previous "back-to-basics" movement of the 1970s. In the mid-1960s, when Maryann and Carole began teaching, behavioral objectives (i.e., "the learner will" bla, bla, bla) were still a thing of the future. No lists of so-called reading skills were used to drill children on arbitrary, isolated aspects of the tenuous relationship between oral and written language. When grade-level objectives relating to reading (typically only a dozen or so per grade) began to be provided by state departments of education, textbook publishers, and school systems, classroom teachers latched on to them for guidance. In addition to wanting to know what various "experts" said should be covered at each grade level, the main dilemmas for elementary classroom and "remedial" reading teachers in the 1960s were:

1. at what age should formal reading instruction begin, and
2. should teachers teach whole words, i.e., the "look-say" approach, or phonics, or both? (See Chall, 1967)

In the 1960s, most K-6 classroom teachers taught developmental reading as part of a self-contained classroom curriculum. They used the basal reader series adopted by their school systems. Basal readers back then were almost completely written by college teachers following a formula that controlled vocabulary, sentence lengths and types, spelling patterns, and so forth. Teachers typically arranged the children into three or more reading groups based on their reading abilities and employed the directed reading lessons and activities found in teachers' manuals (Betts, 1946; Stauffer, 1969). They introduced the story with a brief discussion, introduced the "new words" before the children read the story, set a purpose for the reading, had children read silently at their seats, read aloud in "round robin" fashion, asked preset comprehension questions from the teachers' manuals, and employed various workbooks, usually for phonics, word study, and comprehension. These activities kept two groups busy while the teacher "worked" with the third. Children were drilled on synthetic or analytic phonics and phonics rules. They worked on structural analysis including compound words, syllables, roots, affixes, while stacks of flash cards were used to teach so-called "sight" vocabulary. Teachers believed that word recognition led to comprehension — not the other way round.

Some taught their students to preview before reading, a technique, which typically involved skimming and scanning when applied to nonfiction. Outlining and other study techniques such as the SQ3R were taught to older students. Some teachers read aloud to their students and a few even had their students reading trade books. The more avant-garde gave their students magazines and newspapers to read in class.

Writing, however, was separate and seen mostly as mechanical, like handwriting. Creative writing gained momentum in the 1950s and '60s, but it was typically approached with "cute" or "catchy" sentence stems and other forms of story starters. The writing process itself was just beginning to be studied. Most educators believed young children couldn't write creatively. Besides, even if they could, it didn't matter. Their writing wouldn't be any good, and writing didn't help them learn to read anyway. Like today, most teachers were hard working and well intentioned. They worried when the programs they employed did not produce the results they sought, when despite their best efforts some children still struggled. They wondered why, if learning to read was indeed a matter of learning phonics and/or memorizing sight words, some children who received solid instruction consistently failed to thrive. Many turned to instructional kits and programmed materials such as SRA or DISTAR. Educational publishing companies flourished by promising the next panacea.

Following Johnson's Great Society of the 1960s and the infusion of millions of dollars into public education, politicians began to clamor for greater teacher accountability. If politicians were going to give public schools so much money, they wanted to be certain it was well spent. They wanted to see results. Schools began to think in terms of minimum standards. To that end, lists of objectives for reading began to appear along criteria for meeting each objective. Amid cautions that these so-called "minimum standards" would inevitably become *maximum* standards, materials and test developers changed "objectives" to "skills."

It seemed a subtle and unimportant difference, but in retrospect it was a major shift. The focus had changed from what *teachers* were supposed to know and do, to what *children* were supposed to know and do. Skills lists grew exponentially until each publisher's list contained hundreds of "skills," all to be "mastered" by American school children in pursuit of minimal competency in literacy. These so-called "skills" provided even more fodder for materials from textbook publishers, curriculum developers, and above all, standardized test makers.

Many teachers questioned where all these "skills" were coming from and why each state or publisher's list differed somewhat in sequence as well as content. How was that possible, they wondered, if learning to read was truly a matter of mastering a set of known "skills" in hierarchical sequence?

To the best of our knowledge, none of the hundreds of reading skills that made their way into these minimum competency lists were ever empirically derived. No reliable, replicable studies were ever conducted to determine if readers really learn to read by acquiring a series of isolated skills, much less just what those "skills" might be. Nor were any reliable, replicable studies ever conducted to determine the order in which such skills, if they existed, were supposed to be sequenced. Thus, the "skills" view was initially predicated solely on what a few educators *assumed* readers did and what they needed.

Beginning in the late 1960s, and running well into the '80s, school systems across the country increasingly attempted to mandate mastery-learning curricula. These test-teach-test programs were an assembly-line approach to child learning. It was as if we thought educated adults could be "manufactured" from uneducated children by employing a nuts-and-bolts approach to learning. Skills mastery models increasingly bogged teachers down in paper work and minutia. Furthermore, they bored children out of their wits while obfuscating the real reading process for both groups.

Gaps in teacher knowledge back then were fairly substantial. For one thing, we did not understand the importance of *what* our students read. For another, we didn't yet know enough about *how* proficient readers read—that what each child brought to the text was as important as what was in the text. We did not grasp the universals of the reading process that all readers, regardless of language, must employ. We certainly weren't aware of how each text in a sense teaches the reader how to read it (Meek, 1988). Nor did we fully appreciate that it is the aggregate effect of engaging with a large number and wide variety of texts, read for real reasons, that ultimately produces proficient readers.

It was generally assumed at that time that children should read without making mistakes—another serious blunder. That is, teachers believed the best readers read with complete accuracy. The role of error in reading and in learning to read was misunderstood. The role of oral versus silent reading was also misunderstood. Before the recursive and *transactive* nature of the reading process was fully described, teachers taught children to attack words with their arsenal of "skills." When children encountered an unknown word during reading they were told to "sound it out." Since studies revealed that good readers knew a great deal about sound-letter patterns, including subdividing words into syllables, it was assumed that teaching children about sound-letter patterns would make them good readers (See Adams, 1990). More faulty logic.

Reflective teachers, teachers who were themselves avid readers, knew there had to be more to reading and to teaching reading than just telling children how to sound out unrecognized words. They knew the heavily scripted lessons in their kits, programs, and textbooks didn't cover the less obvious aspects of proficient reading.

By the mid-to-late 1970s, it was clear to many teachers that the mechanistic nonsense students were being asked to perform often failed to help them internalize reading. Many teachers who understood children's learning and language development and who had worked with young children for a while saw that much of what they and their students were being asked to do was not only unhelpful and irrelevant but often harmful.

Out of dissatisfaction with this "bits and pieces" approach to teaching reading, a grassroots movement among classroom teachers began to take shape. Teachers rebelled against what they were being told to do, not because it was too much work or because they didn't understand it, but because they didn't believe in it. The term "whole language" was coined toward the end of the 1970s to identify differences between teaching for meaning and application and instruction based on drilling for acquisition of a hierarchy of isolated skills. By the end of the next decade, the term whole language was widespread.

Reading Process Research

From the 1940s through the 1980s, research in linguistics, psycholinguistics, socio-linguistics, neurophysiology, child language development, cybernetics, and the reading process, among other areas, provided new insights into language, learning, and literacy. The processes proficient readers and writers employ began to be described. How young children developed control over their oral language was documented, and the relationship between oral language development and control over written language was explored (See Goodman, 1984, 1990; Halliday, 1975; Wells, 1986).

Among other things, they realized that children actively engage in thinking and problem solving as they learn language; that they understand more language than they are able to produce; that mimicry is only a small part of language learning; and that children use what they already know to anticipate and perceive in both oral and written language forms. These insights had enormous implications for instruction.

In 1967, Ken Goodman published "Reading: A psycholinguistic guessing game." This article caused quite an uproar. Here was someone looking at reading in new ways. Ken said children recognized more and different words when the words were embedded in a story than when they were "read" from a list. Therefore, he asserted, there must be more going on during real reading than just the application of memorized words (sight vocabulary) and/or decoding from letters to sound. Otherwise there would be no difference in children's word recognition levels between the two encounters with print. He spent the next three decades discovering and describing what reading is and how children learn to do it (See Gollasch, 1982; Goodman, 1986, 1993, 1996).

Like so many other teachers and teacher educators around the world, we wanted to know more about this new view and the reading process research from which it derived. By the mid-1970s, articles and books about miscue analysis and the psycholinguistic view of reading were appearing. We went to IRA and NCTE sessions trying to find, sometimes in vain, a vacant seat or floor space in any room where either Ken or Yetta Goodman was speaking. We read most everything the Goodmans wrote, as well as anything from Dorothy Watson, Carolyn Burke, Dorothy Menosky, Roger Shuy, Frank Smith, Don Holdaway, Brian Cambourne, Jerry Harste, James Britton, and Margaret Meek, to name but a few.

We wanted to incorporate Reading Miscue Analysis into our teacher education courses, but learning to do a miscue analysis without instruction and social interaction was difficult. Few professors, ourselves included, felt able to adequately teach miscue analysis. We needed an opportunity to study with the experts and time to really learn, not just hear presentations at conferences. So, as Carole Stice was driving Ken to the airport following his keynote address at the Metropolitan Nashville Annual June Reading Conference in 1975, she asked him how people like herself might study with him.

The Winter Workshops

Both Ken and Yetta Goodman had accepted faculty positions at the University of Arizona in Tucson. Oddly enough, they were not in the Reading Department; they were employed in Elementary Education. Tucson in December was sunny and usually warm with excellent and plentiful southwestern culture, cuisine, and reasonable hotel accommodations before the influx of January tourists. Since most college professors were between semesters, December seemed a perfect time and Tucson, the perfect place.

In the fall of 1976, the first invitations were sent announcing a ten-day workshop with the Goodmans on *Miscue Analysis Applications for Teacher Educators*. This initial Winter Workshop was co-sponsored by the College of Education, the Department of Elementary Education and the Bureau of Educational Services at the University of Arizona, along with the Goodmans themselves. Approximately thirty persons attended, among them such notable educators and authors as Bill Martin, Jr. All the sessions were led by either Ken or Yetta Goodman.

Participants experienced "A Mardsan Giberter for Farfie," "The Down-hole Heave Compensator: A Tool Designed by Hindsight," "The Boys' Arrows," the first sentence of "Poison" by Roald Dahl, and "The Boat in the Basement," (Goodman, 1996; Whitmore & Goodman, 1996) We listened to taped recordings of children reading from real texts. We grappled with how to answer the 32-item taxonomy for each miscue being examined. We saw how reader expectation, grammar, cultural background, and prediction interacted to affect oral reading. As we examined our own reading, we saw that the process really *was* highly complex, involving the recursive interaction among our linguistic, cognitive, and experiential background knowledge.

Even if we didn't yet fully understand the reading process, we were gratified to know we had been right. Reading was more than sounding out words, recognizing high frequency or sight words, and/or applying structural analysis and context clues. All the traditional content and views of reading we had previously been taught took on the aura of folklore. Before us were scientific studies of reading—empirical, objective, and exploratory.

The success of the first workshop was evident when, in 1978, a second invitation was extended. It read: "Dear Friends and Colleagues, Because of many requests a repeat conference focusing on the use of Miscue Analysis in teacher education will be held in Tucson, Arizona from December 13 to December 22, 1978. The primary focus of this conference is to provide teacher educators with insights emerging from Miscue Analysis which can be applied to college courses and in-service workshops." The staff was once again Ken and Yetta Goodman. This time sessions focused on the following areas:

- The Reading Process
- Comprehending and Reading
- A Comprehension-Centered Language Curriculum
- Using Miscue Analysis in Teacher Education
- Using Miscue Analysis in Educational Research
- Developing Miscue Analysis in Educational Research
- Readability and Miscue Analysis

Also, participants were taken to a nearby Navajo Reservation to see classrooms where children, in the hands of informed teachers, were engaged and learning under difficult conditions, with limited resources.

By 1982, whole language as an educational philosophy and movement was becoming known, and the focus of the Winter Workshop changed accordingly. That year the title was *Whole Language and Miscue Analysis Workshop for Teacher Educators*. The staff had increased as well. In addition to Ken and Yetta, Dorothy Watson and Myna Haussler were listed as presenters. The invitation was extended not only to professors of reading, language arts, and other related fields but also to in-service and curriculum directors and to those preparing themselves for such positions. The workshop was now also sponsored by the Center for the Expansion of Language and Thinking at the University of Arizona. For the first time, course credit was made available.

The invitation cited opportunities "to develop course outlines and materials focusing on miscue analysis as a means of making future teachers aware of the reading process and language development." Two miscue strands were offered: one for beginners and one for those who had attended the workshop before. A special strand for those interested in using miscue analysis as part of their own research was also offered.

Participants visited a whole language first-grade classroom in an inner-city primary school in Tucson. The teacher, one of the Goodmans' students, was Bob Wortman. During that visit, we watched the *children* explain what they were doing and why they were doing it. Some were making Christmas cards; a few were making piñatas; some were making gingerbread men; still others were working with Bob exploring the number 100 using nuts, lima beans, barrettes, and blocks. Captioned artwork from shared literature hung from the ceiling; a mural of desert flora and fauna with labels graced the back wall. The children could read everything in the room, and they did. They told us about their class and asked us questions about who we were and why we had come to visit them. It was the most exciting and dynamic first-grade classroom we had ever visited.

For the 1984 workshop, the title was *The Whole Language and Miscue Analysis Workshop*. As advertised in NCTE publications, it promised to be similar in structure to the 1982 workshop, but this time all levels of teacher educators, from early elementary through adult literacy, were invited.

By 1986, the workshops had become international. Of the 80 participants attending the *Whole Language in Teacher Education Workshop*, as it was called that year, 20 were Canadian and one was Australian. Orin Cochrane, principal of the David Livingstone School in Winnipeg, brought several of the school's faculty members with him. In addition, Peter Krause, then Superintendent of the Lakeshore District in Quebec, also attended. Administrators from the U.S. were present as well. As word of whole language spread, more than 20 of the 80 participants that year were elementary classroom teachers. Another interesting addition was the number of people involved in the publishing industry. Richard C. Owen Publishers, Heinemann Educational Books, Firefly Books, Silver Burdett Ginn, and The Wright Group were represented.

Again sessions for beginning and advanced miscue analysis were offered. For the first time, an alumni strand was provided at the request of repeat participants. Advanced psycholinguistic research in reading and writing and its application to instruction were a focus. The four pillars of whole language—whole language, whole learning, whole teaching, and whole curriculum (Goodman, 1986)—were introduced. Special attention was given to the reading-writing connection, whole language evaluation, "kidwatching," authenticity in learning engagements, and the transactional model of the reading process.

Some evenings, Ken returned to the hotel to meet with small groups and answer questions. He must have felt that some of us required more guidance and support than others as we struggled to comprehend new terms, ideas, and theories. He must have assessed our miscues and misperceptions and was very patient with us as well as generous with his time. Other evenings we engaged in professional readings and discussions, attempting to make new connections and extend our understandings.

The 1988 workshop was perhaps the largest. This workshop offered the addition of a research strand for participants to present their own research relative to miscue analysis and/or whole language. Whole language as a grassroots movement was growing in the U.S. and other countries, but most participants did not have access to whole language schools or even good whole language classrooms for that matter. Consequently, school visits were planned to kick off the workshop. Many participants were from areas where whole language had not made an impact. They were anxious to see real whole language teachers in schools that prided themselves on their whole language philosophy.

Bob Wortman, whose first-grade classroom we had once visited, had become principal of Borton Primary School. He was one of several area principals and teachers who welcomed us into his school. For some of us, these were among the first whole language classrooms we'd ever seen. We can still recall with perfect clarity the children proudly showing us their classrooms, their writing, artwork, and other products from their current unit of study. One bilingual second grade was studying oceans. The children talked at length about what they had read and what they had learned about oceans. They were also quite proud of the butterfly garden behind the school that all the children were helping create. Tucson, they explained, is along the migratory path of many species of butterflies that winter in Central America. They told us they wanted the butterflies to stop and rest for a while at their school.

The children's affection for their school, their level of ownership and sense of accomplishment, their celebrations of learning, and the level of parental support were a joy to see. We left wondering how the essence of such a place might be recreated elsewhere.

December 1990 brought over 100 participants and yet another new name, *The Whole Language and Literacy Processes Winter Workshop*. New major topic strands included: "Teacher Educators and Staff Developers" led by Dorothy Watson, "Bilingual Education and Whole Language" led by Barbara Flores, "Whole Language for Beginners" led by Lois Bridges, "Middle School and Secondary" led by Bruce Appleby, and "Administration and Whole Language" led by Bob Wortman. Participants were asked to preregister for one strand. Several minicourses were also offered to explore topics such as Vygotsky and whole language, early literacy, literature sets, invented spelling, thematic units, and of course miscue analysis.

The 1992 workshop was set up much as the 1990 one, with the addition of a topic strand on the role of ethnography in classroom research. However, the most noticeable difference was that of the 57 participants, 12 were from

Puerto Rico and six were from Argentina. Participants also came from Venezuela, England, and Canada as well as from ten states across the U.S.

The *Tenth Biennial Whole Language and Literacy Processes Winter Workshop* of 1994 was bittersweet. Most of the 100 participants realized this would likely be the last time such a gathering would take place. They came from all around the world: Mexico, Venezuela, Argentina, Uruguay, Canada, Egypt, Puerto Rico, Taiwan and well over a dozen U.S. states. We learned songs in several languages, told child-learning stories, and shared many of the joys and some of the hardships of teaching.

The topic strands were continued as well as a variety of minicourses. We learned about the latest updates on the reading process as well as research on whole language. New that year was a book signing for participants who had published. Participants enjoyed more presentations, sharing experiences from various countries, and being read aloud to from children's books from a variety of cultures and in a variety of languages and dialects.

Also new to this workshop was the sharing of articles blaming whole language for everything from declining test scores to global warming, it seemed. The political attacks on the whole language movement were vehement and startling. It seemed, however, that as whole language was being vilified in the United States, it was growing and producing powerful results elsewhere, especially in Hispanic countries.

The eleventh workshop was held in the winter of 2000. By that time, the term whole language was no longer being used in most publications because publishers believed it hurt sales. Publishers who had made their companies' reputations through publishing whole language materials began asking their authors to use other terms. Teachers were under attack and the entire movement was in jeopardy.

Therefore, it was only fitting that the Eleventh Winter Workshop be titled *Foundations of Whole Language: A Liberatory Pedagogy.* As one would expect, this workshop was highly multicultural, with new participants from Egypt, Colombia, and Paraguay. Two participants were from the Moscow School in Russia. Coincidentally, one participant was from Moscow, Idaho!

While the format continued to be the same, the most notable difference was the offering of concurrent sessions designed to enable participants to share both their research and the practical applications of whole language beliefs and values. Seventeen presenters discussed everything from music literacy, to studies of literacy and gang membership, to journal writing in a Puerto Rican kindergarten, to studies employing miscue analysis to assess learner growth in reading over time. The topic strands continued, as did the minicourses. That year, a wonderful addition was a literature-sharing tea hosted by Kathy Short where she and others shared hundreds of beautiful books for children and adolescents.

Despite the attacks on whole language and the personal attacks on the Goodmans, the 2000 Winter Workshop continued to focus on building understanding and valuing diversity. Although the title was *Foundations of Whole Language: Toward a Liberatory Pedagogy*, the reading process was still the major strand, as was whole language in teacher education; this time, however, there was no miscue analysis strand. Instead, Barbara Flores and Ruth Saez-Vega, both former students of the Goodmans and teacher educators themselves, led the "Pedagogia del Lenguaje Integral" strand.

Although there had been slight changes in the workshops over the years, the schedule remained fairly constant. Rituals and celebrations are mainstays of whole language classrooms and, consequently, of the Winter Workshops. Each day began in song, followed by a language story or a read-aloud. Community building, an integral part of whole language theory, was an integral component of the Winter Workshops. Participants were invited to share stories depicting their cultures. *Possum Come a Knockin'* by Nancy Van Laan is one of Yetta's favorites and "Miss Daisy" from *Listening for the Crack of Dawn* by Donald Davis, one of Ken's.

Mornings always included a large group presentation by Ken or Yetta, with one frequently interrupting the other. Ken shared his current thinking about the pillars of language learning or the reading process and how his research continued to inform his thinking and his research. Yetta presented her research about child language development or what she had learned most recently as an avid kidwatcher (Goodman, 1978, 1984, 1990).

Breakout sessions directed toward literacy development, teacher education, elementary or secondary teaching, administrating quality, learner-centered schools, and/or literacy research followed the large group morning sessions. Over the years, guest speakers provided participants with invaluable information and insights from their own work: Roach Van Allen talking about language experience; Rob Tierney and Dorothy Watson sharing kid-tested, instructional strategy ideas; Carole Edelsky talking about her own childhood literacy and her research in Karen Smith's classroom; Luis Moll sharing his marvelous research into family funds of knowledge; and Denny Taylor providing examples from her research into the often devastating power of the written word as paper trailing affects persons in systems such as social services and criminal justice. One year Tom Birdseye shared a draft of the children's novel he was working on and invited participants to be part of an author's circle.

As in all good whole language classrooms where children learn and play together, the participants in the Winter Workshops also felt a sense of community. Each year, the Goodmans invited everyone to be part of their extended family. They opened their home to participants—all 100 of us sometimes—at least one evening during the ten days. They let us meet and get to know their family, including their three daughters and several grandchildren. They lead us in singing, with Yetta playing the guitar or dancing, inviting everyone to join in. Each of the ten-day workshops was alive with the joy of learning and the fun of being together.

No Winter Workshop was complete without several outings; browsing at the children's bookstore and shipping our purchases home; shopping trips to Nogales, Mexico; attending services at the San Xavier Mission; buying Indian flat bread; and walking through the Sonoran Desert Museum to see roadrunners, prairie dogs, and western diamondback rattlesnakes. On more than one occasion, we toured and feasted at Old Tucson, where western TV shows and movies were filmed. Usually, there were trips to the top of nearby Mt. Lemmon, cold winter's night rides through Sabino Canyon lighted only by a full moon, and before Christmas and Hanukkah, driving tours through Winterhaven, the area in Tucson where neighbors vie to see who can mount the best holiday lights display. Enormous saguaro cacti decorated for Christmas are an unforgettable sight to the non-desert dweller.

A favorite ritual was the closing ceremony at the end of the ten days. Forming a circle and joining hands, we bid each other farewell. One year we sang three versions of "This Land Is Your Land"—one for Canadian participants, one for U.S. participants, and one for those from Latin America. Another year we each said "thank you" in a different language or language variation, e.g., "Much obliged."

After each Winter Workshop, we returned to our own corners of the world, fortified with new knowledge and ideas for how to pass the information we had learned on to our students. Our understandings of reading, writing, and learning had developed and deepened. Having learned more about miscue analysis, especially how it informs us about the reading process, we left empowered, knowing how better to help our own students learn to assess the strategies used by readers in their classrooms. Energized with new insights and in possession of greater courage because we knew we were not alone as we returned home, we were always able to improve our own instructional practices and promote higher levels of literacy in our various locales.

We had seen classrooms where children from economically distressed backgrounds, long considered the most at-risk for school failure, were in charge of their own learning, asking their own questions, immersed in literate practices, and collaborating with their teachers to plan classroom engagements. We saw that they were learning and growing in amazing ways. We had been in classrooms where teachers talked about learning theory, explored critical pedagogy, and understood what was meant by authentic engagements as well as what it means to be a co-creator of curriculum with their students. We saw the classroom results of these types of engagements. We knew whole language worked, because we'd seen it.

The Winter Workshops enabled us to increase our understanding of socio-psycholinguistic processes as we widened our professional networks. Insights and findings from reading process research and related fields shared with us from the first Winter Workshop taught us that common sense views of language and literacy were mostly myth; that they were overly simplistic and largely inaccurate. As we learned what proficient readers do when they read, how learner background mediates comprehending, and how perception during reading works, we began to identify the strategies proficient readers use to navigate text. We learned how to help struggling readers, to show them how to monitor their own reading as they focus on making sense of text. In short, we came to better understand the interrelated components of the transaction between reader and writer and what the implications of these insights are for both evaluation and instruction.

Looking back today, the whole language movement was very much like the "open education" movement of the 1950s in that it never was understood or implemented to any great extent. That is, there was more talk about whole language than there ever were classrooms or teachers who actually understood and applied it. Like open education, there were teachers and schools claiming the term but going about business as usual.

In the early 1990s, a survey throughout Tennessee revealed that a mere 2% of elementary teachers in the state actually held a whole language philosophy that was sufficiently well developed to produce whole language classrooms (Bertrand, 1994; Stice, 1995). The vast majority of Tennessean teachers have always believed in and employed systematic phonics together with a heavy emphasis on the basal-reader-directed reading-thinking approach. Until the introduction of incentive programs to encourage independent reading, most didn't even really use many trade books in their reading programs to supplement their basal reader lessons.

Like open education before it, teachers and administrators around the country have grossly misunderstood whole language. Some thought, and probably still do, that it meant not teaching phonics. Some thought it meant teaching reading the way they always had but with trade books instead of basal readers. Some thought it meant letting children read whatever they wanted, spell words any way they wanted, and then do whatever they wanted with no instruction, direction, or support. Some thought it meant more of an emphasis on writing. Many believed it to be a creative alternative for use near the end of the school year after the children had taken the state achievement tests. Some saw it as fun and something different to do on Friday afternoons. Perhaps worst of all, large numbers of educators thought it meant going back to a focus on whole-word learning and/or whole-group instruction.

As the Winter Workshops always pointed out, teaching reading was never a question of teaching phonics or not teaching phonics. Phonics is one of the cue systems that readers use. Knowledgeable teachers understand that. Phonics supports reading and writing, but it is not a method of teaching reading (Goodman, 1993).

Today the "back-to-basics" initiative across the U.S. claims to favor achieving balance, balancing the reading trade books with direct instruction in guided or leveled readers along with writing. In some instances, the balanced approach is thought of as striking a compromise between phonics instruction and actual reading. Few think of the need to balance reading, writing, speaking, and listening in classrooms. Few consider balancing the four pillars of education: whole language, whole learning, whole teaching, and whole curriculum.

Summary

Whole language in its early iterations focused on explicating the reading process and creating child-centered classrooms. That was the fundamental gift of the movement. We thought it would end the notion that reading was merely a matter of saying words correctly.

Now it's a new era—the 21st century—and what teachers are being told to do is remarkably like what everyone was doing back in the 1960s and '70s. This current round of "back-to-basics" will not produce "every child a reader by third grade," especially if we are interested in readers making sense of what they've read. Human beings do not grow as the result of being measured. We grow as the result of being nourished. We grow from the wealth of our experiences—the richer and more authentic the better.

A liberatory pedagogy suggests that education's purpose is to help children become information getters and critical thinkers, and that to do their jobs teachers must be more politically savvy and active. When this latest attempt to turn children into proficient readers by putting them through phonics and phonemic awareness training fails, we hope teachers will not allow themselves to be blamed. They were, after all, only doing what they were told. Teaching, taken out of the hands of teachers and put into programs, means that the *programs* are responsible for the results—doesn't it?

As we learned in the Winter Workshops, "back-to-basics" fails to recognize the most fundamental principle of all: reading is a process and processes are acquired as learners engage in them, not as learners study about them. Over the 25-year span of the Whole Language Winter Workshops, this one fact was pointed out perhaps more than any other. Learning to read is as natural as learning to talk. Just as children learn their mother tongue by *really* talking and listening in real contexts, so children learn literacy by *really* reading and writing! As Ken and Yetta have always said, there is nothing more basic, or more liberating, than that.

References

Adams, M. (1990). *Beginning to read: Thinking and learning about print.* Cambridge, MA: MIT Press.

Betts, E. (1946). *Foundation of reading instruction.* New York: American Book Company.

Bertrand, N. (1994). Welcome to our rainforest: Whole language orientation and implementation. In C. Kinzer, D. Lue, J. Peter, L. Ayer, & D. Frooman (Eds.) *Multidimensional aspects of literacy research, theory & practice. Forty-third Yearbook of the National Reading Conference,* pp. 249-256. Oak Creek, WI: National Reading Conference.

Chall, J. (1967). *Learning to read: The great debate.* NY: McGraw-Hill.

Gollasch, F. (Ed.) (1982). *Language and literacy: The selected writings of Kenneth S. Goodman Vol. I: Process, theory, research.* London: Routledge & Kegan Paul.

— (Ed.) (1982). *Language and literacy: The selected writings of Kenneth S. Goodman Vol. II: Reading, language, and the classroom teacher.* London: Routledge & Kegan Paul.

Goodman, K. (1996). *On reading.* Portsmouth, NH: Heinemann.

— (1993). *Phonics phacts.* Portsmouth, NH: Heinemann.

— (1967). Reading: A psycholinguistic guessing game. *Journal of the Reading Specialist, 6,* (4): 126-135.

— (1986). *What's whole in whole language?* Portsmouth, NH: Heinemann.

Goodman, Y. (1978). Kidwatching: An alternative to testing. *National Elementary School Principal, 57,* 4: 41-45.

— (1984). The development of initial literacy. In. H. Goelman, A. Oberg, and F. Smith (Eds.), *Awakening to literacy.* pp. 102-109 Portsmouth, NH: Heinemann.

— (1990). *How children construct literacy: Piagetian perspectives.* Newark, DL: IRA.

Halliday, M.A.K., (1975). *Learning how to mean.* London: Edward Arnold.

Meek, M. (1988). *How texts teach what readers learn.* Exeter, England: Thimble Press.

Stauffer, R. (1969). *A directed reading-thinking approach.* NY: Harper & Row.

Stice, C. (1995). Low numbers-high hopes: A survey of whole language in Tennessee. *The Tennessee Reading Teacher. 23: 2,* 10-15.

Wells, G. (1986). *The meaning makers: Children learning language and using language to learn.* Portsmouth, NH: Heinemann.

Whitmore, K. & Goodman, Y. (1996). *Whole language voices in teacher education.* York, ME: Stenhouse.

CHAPTER FIVE

Whole Language Nurtures Social Justice Inquiry

MONICA TAYLOR AND GENNIFER OTINSKY

Background

We, Monica Taylor and Gennifer Otinsky, have been working collaboratively now for two years on a whole language social justice project in which Montclair State University (MSU) preservice teachers from various content areas and Grover Cleveland Middle School (GCMS) sixth graders explore issues of racism and social justice together through inquiry. Our collaboration developed as a result of joint efforts to establish a MSU professional development school partnership with the middle school. As we will discuss in detail below, together we opted to partake in a Summer Leadership Associates program which was offered by MSU's Agenda for Democracy. It was during this program in the summer of 2002 that our collaborative project was born.

Through coordinating two preservice field courses that are taught on-site with a sixth-grade social studies curriculum, we were able to devise two units that provide all students involved an opportunity to explore social justice/whole language teaching tangibly in a safe community. The MSU students, who often understand social justice and whole language concepts theoretically, have an opportunity to experience these teaching paradigms in practice. The sixth graders have the opportunity to explore difficult issues alongside adults who may have more experience with research. We have the opportunity to team-teach, collect data, and reflect on our beliefs about social justice and whole language together. All members of our community have the experience of both providing scaffolding for others as well as receiving support through scaffolding, so that we all partake in our multidimensional zones of proximal development (Vygotsky, 1978).

Below is a dialogue between us, Monica and Gennifer, about how we are becoming whole language teachers/social justice agents, what our current views are about these paradigms, and how we have used these principles together with our preservice teachers and sixth graders. We believe that by providing these multidimensional components of our identities through discussing our past, present, and future beliefs and practices, we can help others to realize or reaffirm their own identities as whole language teachers/social justice agents. In our eyes, you cannot become a whole language teacher without also becoming a social justice agent.

From Where Do We Come?

Monica: To begin our dialogue, I think that it would be really useful to try to describe some of our childhood/adolescent literacy/learning experiences to shed light on how we began the process of becoming whole language teachers. Unearthing our similarities and differences may also help us to understand the ways in which we have developed our partnership which is an integral part of our social justice project. So Gen, what are some of your memories about literacy?

Gennifer: My mom always read to my sisters and me when we were kids. I don't know if it was because she was an educator and realized the importance of reading readiness (did educators know back then what we do now?), or if it was just instinctual for her. Her parents had both been well educated, her mother a teacher and her father a veterinarian and the head of the Veterinary Science Department from the time of its inception at Louisiana State University. Education and reading were important in their family. My father was also an avid reader when I was growing up and still is now. Again, education played an important role in his life as his father set an example and went back to college as an adult to get the education he had never had the opportunity to have as a young man out of high school. My grandfather graduated from college (while working full time and supporting his family) the same year that my father graduated from high school. The formal portrait that my grandmother had taken of them together in their caps and gowns has always been a favorite of mine. Even with his college degree in history, my grandfather continued to work in the same factory job at a chemical company where he had always worked. He had not gotten his degree to advance in his career or make more money; rather he had gone to college for the simple love of learning. I guess with all of these examples and inspirations as I was growing up, it was inevitable that I would find significance in education. (Is it any wonder that my sisters are also both educators?)

Monica: From where do you think that this thirst came? I have a similar story—I wonder why our grandparents felt so strongly about education? Was it a cultural issue? Did they believe that education equated to success? Do you have any insights?

Here is my story. I grew up very close to my maternal grandmother, Nanny, who was a kindergarten teacher for 25 years. When I think about my own influences in terms of literacy and learning I always think of her. She was first-generation American growing up in New York City in the 1920s. Education and reading were extremely important in her family and she and her two sisters all attended Hunter College at a time when most women were not educated. They all became teachers. Nanny, thirty years later, returned to Hunter to receive her Masters in Early Childhood Education. She strongly viewed one's education as a mark of success. Like your grandfather it wasn't so much about advancing in one's career, rather it was about learning for learning's sake. When I finished my Ph.D., she proudly told everyone that she met that she had two Ph.D.'s in the family—her son and her granddaughter.

Growing up with my parents, who are also well educated, I began to understand that learning was something that is done all the time and not just in the context of school. Through travel, culture, the arts, languages, reading, and exposure to others who were different from us, my parents helped me to realize that learning is hands-on and experiential. They did this both through inviting us to have different experiences and also through modeling this attitude to life as well. They encouraged me to be successful both in and out of school. I think that these learning experiences helped me to value hands-on, authentic, holistic learning for my own students when I became a teacher. I know what it feels like to explore ideas in an authentic way for my own understanding and gain. No wonder my students respond when they have ownership of their learning. I was enormously lucky—privileged, really—to have these opportunities and assume that I would go to college.

The other aspect of my upbringing that I remember clearly is that my parents always invited us to participate in the dinner-table conversation but they never purposely discussed topics that were "child" appropriate. They discussed politics, or current events, or their critiques of literature, art, music, or theater and they expected us to discuss these issues with them. They listened to our views and appreciated our process. They encouraged us to be critical thinkers, even if it meant arguing with our teachers or people of authority in school. This was not always pleasurable—in fact dinner could be quite tense—but we learned to speak up for ourselves.

Gennifer: It's funny how different we were in this respect. Although dinner conversations were an integral part of our family life, I don't recall engaging in such deep intellectual dialogue with my parents. We were encouraged to do our best in school, and we always succeeded but were not encouraged to question authority. In fact, until a situation forced me to question authority in my first teaching job, I blindly accepted authority for the most part. I was a "pleaser" in school and work. My own learning about social justice, largely through our collaboration, has taught me to honor my own convictions more firmly.

Monica: I am curious to hear about our literacy experiences growing up. As I often ask my own students to recall their pasts in the hopes of informing their present. What were your experiences growing up with language and literacy?

Gennifer: As I grew up, books became a wonderful escape for me. Not that I had any sort of traumatic childhood that required escaping, but I was so used to seeing my parents and my older sister reading, that I figured I had better join in or be left behind! I distinctly remember that it was the summer before fourth grade when I really became passionate about reading. Until then, I had always found it to be somewhat boring, and don't remember really choosing to do it if I didn't have to, unless none of my friends were available to play that day. Sure, I still loved to hear the teacher at school read aloud to us or have my mom read aloud to me in the back of our station wagon as we were on some long road trip and my dad had declared a temporary moratorium on the singing of camp songs, but it just wasn't something I thought of doing for myself.

During the summer before fourth grade, however, I suddenly felt like I must be missing out on something. My older sister would sit for hours at a time devouring book after book. When the Bookmobile came to our neighborhood (our town had a very small library which my mom would take us to but which never seemed all that inspiring) it was the event of the week to which we all looked forward. I remember rushing to the bottom of our street to jump aboard and see what new delights the Bookmobile would have to offer that week. My sister always seemed to be reading the Nancy Drew mysteries or the Trixie Belden mysteries, so I thought I would give them a try as well. Little did I know then that Trixie Belden and her pals would usher me into the world of independent reading that still consumes much of my free time today! This absolute love of reading and the escape that it provides from the worries and responsibilities of the "real world" is what I try to communicate to my students every single day that I go to school. My love of reading came from the experience of doing it for my own pleasure and interest and not necessarily in response to the request of my teachers. I valued reading for authentic reasons, much like what I know and embrace of whole language teaching.

Monica: I had the same sort of feeling about reading; it was a wonderful way to enter other worlds and see what it was like to be in another's skin. Having lived in many different places where it was often challenging to make new friends, books provided me with a safe haven where I could always escape. I would read voraciously—actually, when I have time I still do. I loved Nancy Drew, the gothic mysteries, the Little Women series. I still have those books tucked away. I still feel excitement when I enter a library or go to a bookstore.

I've always tried to remember how I learned to read, especially once I started learning about early literacy and whole language. But the only memories I have are of either Nanny reading to me or of us reading together. I was already a good reader when I started school. In fact, I helped my grandmother begin her kindergarten classes before I started my own experience as a kindergarten student. I remember reading a story to the children while my grandmother spoke with their parents. It was only once I entered school, during first and second grades, that I remember being told that we needed to drill letters and sounds. I couldn't understand the purpose of this, since I already had many successful reading strategies.

During the fifth grade, my dad was horrified by the history curriculum in my international school in Greece, so he decided to begin our own private tutoring sessions. Boy, did I dread those sessions. He had a love and background in the classics, so he required me to read a chapter of *Plutarch's Lives* and then meet with him to be orally examined. The text was way above my reading level—I knew that there was no way I could look up all of those vocabulary words—so I read for meaning as best as I could. I knew that I just had to have a little bit of information to answer his questions. And I got away with it. Years later he was shocked that I had only been in the fifth grade for those sessions. Looking back, I realized how much I learned about being a reader. I tell this story to my students as a way to illustrate the reading process.

I wonder if my passion for reading and discovering the world rubs off on my students. I am always so surprised when preservice teachers tell me that they are not readers.

Gennifer: Although I've always thought of myself as a reader, I did not always identify myself as a teacher. In fact, I did not plan to be a teacher. As the middle child of three girls, I was always trying to do the unexpected to ensure that I would get plenty of attention (typical middle-child-syndrome behavior!) Although a favorite pastime of my sisters and my friends was to play school down in our basement (my mom would bring extra dittos and workbooks home from school for us to play with), and although I almost always insisted on being the teacher (more from a desire to be in charge than a real desire to teach, I'm afraid!), I actually fought the call to become a teacher when I went away to college. Instead, I chose to follow my passion for performing and became a musical theatre major. Eventually I figured out that if I decided to make a career out of performing, rather than just enjoy it as a hobby as I still do today, I would have to suffer through too many anxious and frustrating auditions. I started contemplating other majors. I already had enough French credits to be well on my way to earning a degree in that, so I continued my French studies. And then I finally accepted what I had been trying to avoid for years: that pursuing a degree in education would be a good fit for me. After all, isn't there a huge element of performance in our daily teaching? And besides, the students are a captive audience!

Somehow I guess I always knew that I would end up in the classroom, and I have found it to be exciting and invigorating ever since I decided to accept my "birthright" and become an educator! Furthermore, since I had loved so many of my teachers from my middle-school years, I decided that middle school would be the perfect venue for me. Luckily, James Madison University had a degree to offer specifically in middle-school education. Armed with that and my French degree, I set out to find a teaching job.

Monica: I also tried to avoid my calling as a teacher. I was always involved in teaching while I was in school and then college. I would volunteer to tutor kids or assist in a classroom. I am the oldest of four children so I was used to nurturing and mothering everyone. In fact, I think that I was the person who taught my younger brother to read. I knew that I had teaching instincts but I thought that I wanted to pursue something that was more "glamorous." I decided to study French and Italian at the University of Pennsylvania with the hope of entering into international business. After interning in a large corporate accounting firm during the summer of my junior year in college, I realized that the business world was not for me. I began to think about pursuing a career in teaching although I had few teaching credentials. I was able to get a teaching job in New York City with a conditional substitute license. I began my career as a Spanish/French middle-school teacher in an urban alternative public school in New York City. I think it was my first experiences of urban teaching that led me to think about my beliefs about social justice.

Although I grew up in a relatively conservative family, I had a variety of experiences growing up that began to lay a foundation for my social justice frame. As a young child growing up in New York City, I was exposed to people of many cultures and backgrounds through my daily interactions. My parents were great advocates of learning about other cultures so we would often explore foods, music, art, and cultural events together. My mom would take me to Chinatown or Spanish Harlem to buy seafood, fruits, and vegetables at the open air markets. We traveled on the subway frequently. I attended bilingual preschool and elementary school and in the summer participated in an integrated camp for gifted children where I interacted with urban children from diverse backgrounds.

At the age of eight I moved abroad, living in France, England, Greece, and Bahrain for a total of four years. It was at this time that I developed an openness to all people. I really had no choice since I had to adapt to new environments, languages, and cultures frequently. In Bahrain, when I was eleven, I participated in a volunteer program where we would work with lower income children to provide toys, books, and food. We traveled into these communities on a bus and invited the children to come aboard. This was my first memory of witnessing such a drastic discrepancy between people. I had never seen such poverty and I remember feeling very confused and disheartened.

Throughout high school and college, I volunteered to tutor students in lower income communities. As I mentioned previously, I knew I could teach and I found working with urban children rewarding. When I began teaching at the alternative public middle school in New York City, I realized how naïve I was about urban life. I had thought that I knew New York but I really did not know New York at all. It was really my middle school African American, Caribbean American, and Latino students who opened their worlds to me. Most of my students traveled from Harlem and often invited me to visit their neighborhoods and communities. I was able to see the complexities of their lives and cultures and learned to understand and value their identities.

I also want to mention that I was raised in a home with strong women who advocated for women's rights. During the seventies, when my mother got divorced and was struggling to care for her children on her own, we often listened to Helen Reddy's "I Am Woman." I was encouraged to be ambitious and successful and to be aware of the ways in which women are treated unfairly. When my mother bathed me, she had pictures of Mother Teresa and Gloria Steinem on the ceiling so that we could discuss significant women. I think Nanny also modeled the characteristics of a strong advocate of women's equality and the values of education. The influences of my family coupled with my own experiences helped me to understand the importance of teaching for social justice, of helping my students to hear multiple perspectives and listen for the voices that are so often unheard. I want my students to find their voices as social activists and change agents.

And whole language? Well, those roots have been with me always. I began my journey of becoming a whole language teacher initially because I had whole language instincts, not because I was formally educated in whole language. As I mentioned earlier, I began my career as a teacher through the back door. I had grown up among teachers, tutored urban kids in high school and college, but was resistant to studying to become a teacher. And yet as I was about to graduate from college, I thought that teaching was something that I could do and enjoy. So with only one education course under my belt, I was hired as a Spanish and French urban middle school teacher. Most of what I knew about teaching was either from my own experiences in school or from instincts. I had spent much time in my grandmother's kindergarten classroom and I understood that children had to be engaged to learn. I can't say that that first year was easy—actually the first five years were a struggle—but the kinds of learning that I created with my students were whole language based. I understood and later studied sociolinguistic theories to support my beliefs that my students would learn language, learn about language, and learn through language if the topics we studied were relevant and meaningful to them. I tried to create learning experiences that helped them understand the value of language. I did not teach vocabulary in isolation; rather I tried to connect it to life experiences. I wanted them to have ownership of their learning and value it not because they were receiving a grade but because it enriched their lives. The grammar, vocabulary, and spelling were important because they helped them to make meaning and communicate; but those parts of language were merely tools, not the purpose of their lessons.

Whole language also made sense to me because it created spaces for students and me to explore issues of social justice in informal and formal ways. Although I had grown up in New York City, teaching in a public alternative middle school was quite an eye-opening experience. I had thought that I had a good understanding of urban life, but through interactions with my students I was introduced to their families, cultures, and communities. I had always loved hip-hop, but they expanded my horizons; in turn, I shared my culture with them. A whole language philosophy invited us to explore and connect our lives through the use of inquiry. We were able to begin to have difficult conversations that emerged through learning about topics that were relevant and interesting to us.

Of course, as I started taking graduate courses in language and literacy during my second year of teaching, I began to realize that my instincts were correct—that there were actual theories that could back up my beliefs about language learning. And I have to say that I didn't really trust my instincts until I was studying with Ken and Yetta Goodman several years later in Arizona. It's not that I didn't continue to teach in a holistic way, but I didn't value the way that I was teaching. I would close my door so that other teachers did not have a chance to comment on my teaching. I was not secure because I did not see or hear that others were teaching the way that I was. In graduate school, I began to realize that whole language was more than a teaching perspective: it was a way of life.

Gennifer: The irony of my contributing to a chapter in this book is that, until recently, I never considered myself to be a whole language teacher. In fact, I sometimes lamented the fact that students who reached my sixth-grade language arts and social studies classes had been taught by "whole language hacks" in the elementary schools of my district. I mean, how else could I explain some of these students' apparent lack of phonemic awareness as evidenced by their atrocious spelling or their inability to use apostrophes to form possessives correctly? This was a direct result of the whole language movement, I thought. I had heard other "grammar purists" who had taught for many more years in my district blaming whole language, and I just thought that they must know what they were talking about since they had so much more teaching experience than I did. I figured that I would just have to start from square one with my students to try to undo the damage that had been inflicted upon these poor victims of the whole language movement.

Looking back on my own teacher training, however, I realize that I never truly understood what the whole language movement was about and had in fact always been one of those "whole language hacks" I had previously impugned. My gross misunderstanding can be summed up as this: Whole language means kids don't learn how to read by learning the rules of phonics; they only learn through memorizing site words. Kids should never be taught grammar out of context; if they are given plenty of good models, they will somehow magically learn the correct usage of semicolons and apostrophes.

Monica: This does not surprise me, though, because whole language is misrepresented, misconceived, and misunderstood. I have never heard about whole language being memorizing site words. I wonder how many other misrepresentations are out there. This is one of our major impediments in the whole language movement.

Gennifer: Until recently, this is what I thought was meant by the term "whole language." I have learned, however, that even though I choose to sometimes teach grammar out of context (gasp!) and occasionally even assign "skill and drill" homework to reinforce these grammatical concepts, I can still have a whole language classroom. I probably would have never come to this realization on my own, however. I recently had to be told that I am a whole language teacher by you, a university professor of education with whom I have been collaborating and who has spent the better part of three years in my classroom working with my students and me. You were shocked to hear me say that I didn't consider myself to be a whole language teacher. After you explained to me what your beliefs were about whole language, a light bulb went off. Of course I am a whole language teacher. I couldn't imagine teaching any other way. I had been teaching this way strictly by instinct, though, not according to some explicit rules or methodology that I had learned in an education course. I had discovered this way of teaching through doing, through trial and error, through my own inquiry in the classroom—through the same techniques I encourage my students to use in the classroom on a daily basis.

Monica: And of course in my eyes you are absolutely a whole language teacher—you combine a variety of teaching strategies with the focus of teaching language arts and social studies. You encourage students to take ownership of their learning and you construct learning opportunities that are authentic. You provide students with a variety of learning options so that they can be creative, use a variety of mediums, and build on their strengths. You help them to build their knowledge about grammar and spelling because these tools are essential for communication. You are becoming a whole language teacher using whole language practices, through doing, trial and error, and inquiry. And you have naturally connected whole language to the exploration of issues of social justice.

Gennifer: Okay, I'm glad you brought up the idea of whole language being a great way to explore issues of teaching for social justice. Although I've been teaching language arts and social studies for eleven years, I never really took a deliberate stance toward including issues of social justice until my partnership with you began a few years ago. At that point, I never imagined that my working with you and becoming involved in the summer Leadership Associates program at Montclair State University would end up having such an impact on my future teaching practices and ideas. Until we deliberately co-taught this unit on social justice, I had always addressed tough issues as they occurred but more in an out-of-context way. For example, when studying certain historical happenings in social studies class, such as the slave trade in the United States, we of course included discussions of injustice along with the historical facts. Or in language arts, when reading a novel or short story with some theme relating to social justice, I always tried to highlight the issue and have a meaningful discussion or debate regarding the topic as a topic alone, rather than just in relation to the plot. Until you and I started collaborating as a result of our shared experience in Leadership Associates, however, I never considered just exploring with my students the idea of social justice purely for the sake of social justice.

Monica: I feel so lucky to work collaboratively with you in your classroom. Staying in touch with sixth graders helps me to expand my understanding of the ways that they use language and explore issues of social justice. I think we should begin to talk about our collaboration and the Leadership Associates program.

Gennifer: In association with the New Jersey Network for Educational Renewal, a division of the National Network for Educational Renewal, the Montclair State University Agenda for Education in a Democracy organizes a Summer Leadership Associates program. One of the primary goals of the Agenda is to guide educators to understand their roles and responsibilities as professionals in a democracy and as promoters of social justice. The Leadership Associates Program is designed to fulfill that goal, encouraging educators to develop a deeper understanding of the moral dimensions of teaching in a democracy and to examine their own roles in their respective institutions so that they can become more effective agents for change. Together, as we grappled with issues of democracy, race, ethnicity, stereotypes, hate, and agencies of change, you and I realized how powerful our collaborative exploration was and we wondered how we could replicate this inquiry for our students.

We decided that we would co-teach a unit on writing personal memoirs in my sixth grade language arts classroom, and use it to model constructivist teaching techniques for your preservice teachers who would be a part of the class every day for three weeks. It was such a successful and enriching experience for both of us, my students, and your students, that we then decided we would have to attempt to provide a similar experience for all of our students the next semester as well. This time we decided that we would have your new group of preservice teachers join my students in a social studies class instead, and that we would co-teach a unit specifically on social justice. Even though it did not necessarily fit into a category of my curriculum, U.S. history from pre-Civil War to the present, we knew that the overarching concepts of social justice would apply to every historical concept that I typically cover with my students. The three-week departure from my typical history curriculum seemed like it would be time well spent. We used an inquiry model as our guiding force, partnered my sixth graders with your preservice teachers who had been learning throughout their teacher training about teaching for social justice, whole language ideology, and using inquiry in the classroom, and we once again had an unbelievably successful experience.

Monica: I would like to talk about this portion of the project in more detail because I feel that the experience of teaching social justice collaboratively has strengthened our views of whole language teaching. We knew that the sixth graders would gain a tremendous amount from the scaffolding provided by the preservice teachers, but we had no idea how my preservice teachers would gain from the experience. My students made such comments as "We are doing what with the sixth graders? A social justice project? Why would we ever do that? What do they know about stereotypes and social justice? Why should they know anything about social justice yet?

They are so young and innocent." My preservice teachers were at the end of their teacher education program at a university that values and endorses culturally responsive teaching and critical pedagogy. They were enrolled in my course on teaching and learning that is taken at the beginning of their student teaching semester. How could they be so surprised that we would dare to teach issues of social justice to sixth-grade students? Didn't they see the connection between "reading the word and reading the world" (Freire & Macedo, 1987)? Where did their disconnect begin? Why were their assumptions about middle-school students so limited and naïve when it came to issues of race, ethnicity, class, and gender? How would they ever be able to teach for social justice in their own classrooms? At what age or grade level would they deem their students ready to discuss injustice?

Several of the readings during the course addressed issues of race and ethnicity and teaching for social justice. As the preservice teachers discussed the readings with me in the hours prior to attending your sixth-grade class, they questioned the appropriateness of addressing the topic with the middle schoolers. They then had the opportunity to try out these practices when they entered the classroom and worked side by side with the sixth graders. They were able to grapple with issues of race and social justice teaching in a small group setting with me, and then they actually had to discuss and put into practice similar issues with the sixth graders. We believed that being co-learners with the adolescents would allow them to experience what they were reading and discussing in theory. We hoped that these experiences would facilitate their development of beliefs and understandings about teaching for social justice through a whole language framework. We encouraged the preservice teachers to be reflective and asked them to culminate the experience by writing a philosophical statement about teaching for social justice.

As we discuss our beliefs about whole language and social justice teaching, we realize both frameworks share the same tenets. Our lens on whole language/social justice teaching includes several important principles that guide our practice. We believe that teaching begins with the individual student; hence the topics of inquiry should be relevant to her life, and the ways that she explores her topic should be shaped by her interests and learning styles. The types of curricular activities are designed to encourage students to question and think critically about topics that are presented, whether from the teacher, text, media, family, or community. Students are encouraged to engage in authentic reading, writing, and thinking. In our work, we strive to be multicultural, antibiased, and pro-justice. This means that we hope to have students both celebrate their differences as well as ask the difficult questions of whose voices are missing or unheard and why. We strive to uncover the ways in which some people are privileged and have access to wealth and power while others live as objects of discrimination and injustice. We believe that our students can only develop these concepts if they have hands-on experiences and if they explore burning questions that are generated from their own lives. Ultimately we hope that our social justice inquiry will raise the consciousness of all of our students and would encourage them to become active members of society and potential change agents. We also look forward to a new generation of teachers who have adopted a pedagogy of change.

We are particularly committed to the importance of social justice teaching within our classrooms because the majority of our students are White and from middle- to upper-income suburban communities. We believe that many of our students take their positions of privilege for granted, both from material and social perspectives. They have had little to no interaction with people who are different from them. They view racism and other acts of discrimination as isolated incidents between individuals rather than institutionalized and societal norms. We hope to open our students' eyes to the social inequities and help them to gain an understanding of the ways in which privilege and inequity are interconnected from a historical point of view. We believe that our students deserve to understand the roots of injustice and the ways in which inequalities are perpetuated so that they can grow to make informed and ethical decisions as citizens in our society. We firmly agree with Edelsky (1999) when she writes, "If whole language is to promote democracy, justice, and equity, whole language educators must recognize the undemocratic nature of the existing political system in the United States. Despite secret ballots, rhetoric, and governmental structures, the United States is a long way from being a democracy" (p. 9).

We are aware that prior to our collaboration our sixth graders have had the opportunity to explore reading and writing authentically. Many of their former learning experiences have been with whole language teachers and therefore they are familiar and open to invitations to have ownership of their learning experiences. In a sense, because of their positions of privilege, they have been invited to think critically (Anyon, 1981) although not necessarily about issues of social justice. Our preservice teachers have, on the other hand, had mixed literacy schooling experiences. For many whole language/social justice is a significant leap of faith.

We are aware that there has been much critique about whether or not whole language is indeed critical and a vehicle for social justice. We embrace the ways in which Edelsky (1999) and others "re-theorize" whole language. In our eyes, whole language and social justice cannot be separated. We view a whole language framework as an essential vehicle to promote democracy and social change. We are presenting one example of our collaboration—a unit that we do in the spring—but this is only a small glimpse of the kinds of work that we are doing daily with our students, both sixth graders and preservice teachers.

Gennifer: We largely considered how much the sixth graders would learn through the scaffolding of their adult counterparts, but we did not even imagine the implicit learning that our preservice teachers would experience. We recognized that the multiple layers of scaffolding that could potentially develop within the collaborative learning community would clearly illustrate our whole language beliefs about teaching and learning. We all provide scaffolding for one another depending on the learning task. We never questioned whether or not the topic of social justice was appropriate for either set of students; we both believed that the kind of critical exploration that we had undergone during our summer Leadership Associates program was vital for all students.

Monica: Before we share an example of our collaboration, I think that it is important to acknowledge that we by no means feel that we are experts. Our work together has provided us with the opportunity to continue to explore what whole language/social justice teaching and learning means. We feel that working together helps us to critically examine our theories and practices. We have unresolved issues that we would like to discuss briefly in the conclusion.

Gennifer: Let's talk about the ways in which we set this up. We have now been doing a collaborative inquiry for three years. We actually received a two-year Inquiry grant from the New Jersey Network for Educational Renewal last year, which has been supporting our research and practice. For this discussion we will focus on the spring semester when we explore more general issues of social justice. During the fall semester, we explore racism.

During the professional semester at the university, preservice teachers take an intensive teaching and learning course for the first three weeks of their student teaching. During this semester, they review concepts and teaching strategies and prepare for their student teaching experience. You teach your section of the course on-site at the middle school during the time that I am teaching a sixth-grade social studies class so that the two groups of students can work together.

We have constructed a social justice unit that coincides with the sixth graders' theme of civil rights in hopes that the various activities of the unit would act, as Greene (1978) writes, as "a series of occasions for individuals to articulate the themes of their existence and reflect on those themes until they know themselves to be in the world and can name what has been up to then obscure" (pp. 18-19). We believe that this principle of naming the obscure will resonate on many levels with both the sixth graders and their adult co-inquirers. We have selected the context of social studies because we agree with Stock's contention that "the students' spoken and written language is their most readily available, most powerful means of learning" (1995, p. 17). The three-week unit therefore incorporates a variety of literacy teaching strategies including written reflections, brainstorming, poetry, reader response to texts, film, and visual images, writing workshop, inquiry research, role-playing, and multimedia presentations.

We have developed a three-week unit that includes community building; identity sharing; explorations of race, class, and gender; introduction to the term social justice; models of social justice activists; and culminates with time in small groups to develop and explore a self-selected inquiry question that will be presented to the group.

Monica: Gen, why don't you explain some of the actual inquiry invitations in more detail?

Gennifer: Students are randomly placed into groups of approximately four sixth graders along with two preservice teachers. After some whole-class discussion regarding the concept of a cycle of inquiry (Short et al., 1996) and some large-group brainstorming of possible social justice questions that might warrant some exploration, individual groups take a day or two to decide upon a topic in which all group members are interested. The following several class periods are spent in the media center where groups are able to work on planning their methodology and carrying out their research. The final goal towards which they are working is creating a poster board that allows them to present their findings visually. The requirements are that the board shows the original open-ended question they are investigating, their methodology and bibliographic information, their results and findings, and finally their plan for how they will take some action regarding the question and their findings. In other words, now that they have discovered possible reasons and causes for the social justice problem they investigated, what will they do to attempt to improve the situation?

The inquiry topics have been very diverse. One sixth grader's uncle recently ran for a seat in the U.S. Senate and lost to a millionaire, which prompted her group to ask the question: If a person can't run for office because they don't have money, then is it a democratic society? Another group, coincidentally comprised of five females and only one male, asked the question: Why hasn't a woman ever been elected president in the U.S.A.? Other groups wondered about the following: How does Title IX affect sports? Why was the Jewish community so discriminated against during WWII, and what are the ramifications of it today? Are athletes more important than teachers? Why are there more African Americans than Whites in jail? Do celebrities give back to their communities? Why is there world hunger? Why don't women have positions of power in the U.S. today? Why do some school districts have more money to spend on education than others? Why doesn't America recycle more?

Results are often impressive. We spend two class periods for groups to share the results of their inquiries, along with their proposed action plans. Action plans range from student-run after-school classes designed to educate fellow students about their issues, to bake sales to raise money for established charities that donate in some way to the cause in question, to letter writing campaigns to politicians. In the past, students have discussed ways to help support politicians for office who endorse Title IX, created a free garage sale in Black communities so people can get what they need without having to steal, and advertised to friends about Paul Newman's products since the proceeds from these sales help fund his charities.

Monica: We were very impressed with one group that decided to write a letter to the editor of the local paper, hoping to share their concern with the community:

> Editor:
>
> We are doing a school project. We have a question for you. Why hasn't there been a woman President in the United States? Doesn't this country need change? There are many woman rulers in other countries. Some of them are: Susanne Camelia-Romer from the Netherlands, Jennifer Smith from Bermuda, Queen Elizabeth II of England, and many more.
>
> We surveyed about 50 people, and asked them, "If there was a woman running for President, would you vote for her?" Three people said, "No," but they were all men. Thirty-three people said, "Yes," and the rest said "Maybe." Some reasons that people said that there hasn't been one before, is because of tradition, fear of change, and some people said that women are not capable of such a task.
>
> But, as you can see, women are capable, from all the other rulers in other countries. So, we are concluding that our country is ready for a change. Someone should step up to the plate. Women are ready to become presidents in our country.

The collaborative inquiry projects provide students with the opportunity to investigate an issue that truly meant something to them. Through the intense collaboration with the preservice teachers, the assignment allows the sixth graders to learn about the ways in which we all struggle with research, attempting to develop a report that encompasses multiple perspectives. Students begin to realize the power of language and the ways that they can potentially take action. As a culmination to the social justice unit, we ask students to write a reflection responding to various prompts. By doing this, we hope to gain an understanding of what the participants learned about social justice throughout our unit and through their inquiry projects. We also want to find out what the preservice teachers learned about teaching about social justice.

Gennifer: We have been thrilled with some of the responses we have received from your students and mine in the reflections we have asked them to do. Overall, the students have developed a more articulate way to explain social justice. For my students, social justice involves fairness and equality. The following is a list of some of the definitions written by the sixth graders when asked, "What does social justice mean to you?" I think including their actual words is important because their definitions are powerful and clearly illustrate their perspectives. Some of the students have written that social justice means:

- Everyone is treated fairly and no one is misjudged.
- Justice for all people no matter the size, race, sex, or class.
- Being able to be "you" and not being discriminated against.
- Learning about people's cultures and their ways of life.
- Socially treating everyone equally.
- People being treated equally throughout the justice system.
- Not judging people.
- Being able to have the same rights and service as all other citizens.
- All people are created equal but are not always treated equally.
- The justice to speak or think what you want to.

We then asked my students to explain to us what they have learned through their inquiry projects. Again, rather than paraphrasing or explaining their responses, we feel that their words speak for themselves. Some of the sixth graders have learned that:

- More money is spent on the military and less is spent on education.
- Most people with a better education are White.
- Even in the richest country, there is poverty.
- Some people who are really wealthy can get away with bad things.
- The media shows stereotypes, even if you don't notice them.
- How many people of different ethnicities drop out of school.
- Men hold higher positions in the workplace.
- It is hard for someone without money to have a position in the government.
- People are always discriminated against.

I think that these reflections clearly reveal the power of collaborative inquiry when exploring issues of social justice. The students have been able to draw significantly from their research and rethink some of the assumptions that they hold about others and about people who are in positions of power.

They have also been pushed to rethink their own positions in society and to brainstorm ways through which they can be social activists. Our inquiries have invited some sixth graders to think about power and their own positions in society. They are beginning to think about how they can question adults in authority like their parents or even the president. Some are thinking about what their roles are in a democracy—and whether "democracy" is the right term for our government system.

Monica: What is even more exciting to me is that many sixth graders continued to use this whole language/social justice lens throughout the rest of the school year. They seemed to begin to look at the world from a different perspective. I can recall that one sixth-grade male student was furious with a car commercial during the Super Bowl. He was troubled that the car that won the race was White. He began to think of the many ways that stereotypes are reinforced through the media. These new questions came directly from his group inquiry on the ways that the media portray stereotypes. He spent the rest of the spring bringing in examples of injustice that he had witnessed on television. He began to question language that in the past he would have ignored or not noticed. Unfortunately, not all students were able to internalize the social justice framework. Do you remember the incident with the student teacher?

Gennifer: How can I forget? I was furious and frustrated. After three weeks of social justice inquiry, one of my students used the term "lesbian" in a derogatory way to address a student teacher. These inquiries affect students in different ways. One of our new questions is how to infuse social justice beliefs into the daily lives of our students?

Monica: Yes, and this is a perfect segue to share some of what the preservice teachers learned through the experience because they address this exact point. Many of the preservice teachers realized that whole language/social justice teaching is a lifestyle. One woman wrote in her teaching philosophy:

> Social justice is so multifaceted that as a classroom teacher I must begin at its core. First, in my personal and professional life, I must want to live in a socially just manner and want to see others around me being treated with justice. I must be willing to reflect honestly on my own hidden biases. Without this advocacy and passion, social justice will not have a pure and genuine chance to thrive within my classroom.

I am impressed that some of my preservice teachers were able to realize the need for personal reflection and interrogation of these paradigms before they are implemented in the classroom. It seems that many preservice teachers recognized the ways in which they must have ownership over their teaching and curriculum. A whole language/social justice lens involves critique, reflection, and thoughtfulness. This reflective statement by another woman illustrates these principles. She writes:

> I think that it is very important that a teacher doesn't teach against her conscience. I believe that it is best not to align oneself with texts, people, or rules that hurt children. As educators, we need to root our struggles for social justice in the work we do every day, in a particular community, with a particular group of students.

Gennifer: Every time I read this I am struck by this pre-service teacher's depth of understanding. I think she clearly discusses the need to not only encourage our students to be critical but also to be critical teachers ourselves, advocating for our students and placing them at the center of our teaching and learning.

Monica: Another preservice teacher talks about the ways in which her beliefs about whole language/social justice will inform her practice in the classroom. She states:

> It is crucial for me to teach my students to think critically about social justice and what it actually means to live in a democratic society. Teaching for social justice needs to be integrated into every aspect of the classroom. It includes helping my students learn how to recognize injustices within society, not just those on the surface; how to think critically about how those injustices affect the subordinate groups, themselves, and society as a whole, and finally how to find their voice as part of society to help them become "truth tellers and change makers."

Although many preservice teachers embraced and took ownership of their beliefs about whole language/social justice, some students struggled to incorporate these principles within their content area or the context of their student teaching experience. One preservice teacher who worked with us in the fall and spring was quite reluctant. Although he had discussed these concepts in other coursework, he wasn't sure what it meant to him as a future teacher. By the end of the spring social justice inquiry, he began to embrace whole language/social justice beliefs and practices. He was frustrated, though, when he began to student teach and realized the changes that would have to be made in his cooperating teacher's classroom. He began to realize the political implications of his new paradigm and the potential struggles that he would have to face in the future. He wrote:

> Now that I have started student teaching, I am not sure how to teach for social justice. The sixth graders [at GCMS] were challenged to think at a higher level than I'm allowed to encourage in the eighth-grade class where I am working. The sixth graders were given projects that stimulated research, critical thinking, and fostered a sense of inquiry. The students that I am working with are asked to sit quietly, take notes, do well on assignments and not cause disruptions.

I really feel for this preservice teacher and realize that part of preparing teachers for their careers is helping them to find their political voices. As a teacher educator, I have to spend more time helping my preservice teachers to find strategies to negotiate the system. I think that this is an area that needs to be further developed in the field of education in general and more specifically when it comes to whole language/social justice teaching.

Gennifer: We cannot forget to mention that many of our students still don't acknowledge social justice issues. This is probably true for your preservice teachers more so than the sixth graders.

Monica: That is another important point. We have a few preservice teachers that have resisted us all the way. They have embraced transmission or direct instruction as their model of teaching, and they see themselves as the authorities in the classroom. They are uninterested in encouraging critical thinking or dialogue, and they envision only one way of looking at their content area. What is our role with these preservice teachers?

Gennifer: We are also, as I mentioned before, exploring ways to help the sixth graders infuse social justice into their daily lives. This is something that we are working on currently. We are working with some teachers in an elementary school in an urban district to develop an authentic collaborative inquiry with their third graders and our sixth graders. We would like to foster a partnership with children who are different from us so that our students have the opportunity to work beyond their assumptions about people who are different from them. We do not want it to be a show and tell experience or a look at what we have and you don't. Rather we hope that our students will have an opportunity to get to know, work collaboratively with, and provide scaffolding for children, as your preservice teachers have done with us.

Monica: I am really looking forward to this new dimension of our project. So what have we learned in terms of social justice and whole language?

Gennifer: Since our partnership has taken off, I feel like I have learned so much and have been able to offer my students so much more in terms of exploring issues of social justice in a more meaningful and authentic way. At first I thought this was strictly because of your mentoring (I mean after all, I lovingly refer to you as the Queen of Social Justice) but have come to realize that it goes much deeper than that. It's not just that you are this font of information and experience about issues of social justice, because I have been a very real part of the idea formulation as well; it's more that we have become our own support network for each other. Because we are in this together and because we often feel like together we are making it up as we go along (no matter how many hours we have already spent preparing and planning for every possible contingency), we have learned to support one another and encourage one another to take the risks that we might not have taken if we had been in the situation alone.

Monica: I think that you bring up a very important point: social justice, or whole language for that matter, can't be done in isolation. It is risky, time-consuming, challenging, and ever-changing. These types of inquiries that we do with students are open-ended and unpredictable. We never know where they are going to take us, and we need each other as a sounding board. I had always wanted to do this kind of work in my own classroom as a middle-school teacher, but it was difficult to do it alone. I really feel like that kind of community-of-learners approach where teachers support one another as learners as well as facilitators of learning is really what whole language is all about.

Gennifer: As the feeling of support allows us to take some risks we might not have taken otherwise, the program begins to take on a life of its own. When we first started collaborating, we did it in a very safe way. Since we weren't exactly sure what to expect from our attempt to co-teach in a situation where students would range from my eleven- and twelve-year-old sixth graders to your twenty-something through fifty-something preservice teachers, we decided on a relatively conservative approach. We taught a unit in my language arts class on writing personal memoirs. Using a constructivist model, we allowed the multiage class to formulate their own definition of personal memoir and then compose their own memoirs in a supportive and collaborative environment. We were so encouraged by the amazing response the two populations had to learning in this sort of multiage environment that we decided to try again, except this time we would co-teach a unit on social justice in my social studies class. Again, we were thrilled at how well the two groups collaborated and found that even the sixth graders really seemed to grasp and understand many of the very abstract concepts of social justice that had been explored. Encouraged even further by this success, we decided to now incorporate my existing sixth-grade history curriculum with some definite concepts of social justice and devised our unit on racism. We continue to delve deeper into the realms of social justice teaching and allow the students to become inquirers in an environment where it is safe for them to discuss issues candidly and take risks in their thinking and learning.

Monica: Again that is why I think that we believe that whole language and social justice issues are really connected—they give space to one another. Let's think about all that we know about thinking, learning, and language now that we have done these units; I think that we would find that even the multiage collaboration speaks to whole language beliefs about learning. Also as we continue to develop these units and incorporate the action portion with perhaps a partnership with an urban group of children, our students will develop an even stronger awareness of the power of language and their potential as change agents.

References

Anyon, J. (1981). Social class and school knowledge. *Curriculum Inquiry*, 11(1), 3-42.

Edelsky, C. (Ed.) (1999). *Making justice our project: Critical whole language practice.* Urbana, IL: National Council for Teachers of English.

Freire, P. & Macedo, D. (1987). *Literacy: Reading the word and the world.* South Hadley, MA: Bergin & Garvey Publishers, Inc.

Greene, M. (1978). *Landscapes of learning.* New York: Teachers College Press.

Short, K. G., Harste, J. C. with C. Burke. (Eds.). (1996). *Creating classrooms for authors and inquirers.* Portsmouth, NH: Heinemann.

Stock, P. L. (1995). *The dialogic curriculum: Teaching and learning in a multicultural society.* Portsmouth, NH: Heinemann.

Vygotsky, L. S. (1978). *Mind in society.* Cambridge, MA: Harvard University Press.

CHAPTER SIX

All I Remember Is That It Was Fun

M. TAMZIN SAWYER

Interview with Hector: September 5, 2002

Tamzin: Ok, so I just want you to tell me a little bit about what we did at the end of last year. Remember that project that we did?

Hector: Which one?

Tamzin: The one where you did Egypt?

Hector: Oh that one! That was fun!

Tamzin: Why?

Hector: Actually I don't know. It was just fun doing the writing.

Tamzin: Doing the writing? What did you have to do for that project?

Hector: Let's see. I had to read a lot of books, which was fun. I had to get some ideas down on paper and I had to write it down sloppy copy. And then I had to write it on the computer.

Tamzin: What else did we do?

Hector: I forgot the names of the things but we did a lot of things.

Tamzin: What did you learn from doing that?

Hector: A lot. I learned about Egypt.

Tamzin: What did you learn about Egypt?

Hector: I learned about the hieroglyphics in Ms Smits' class and I learned about just plain old Egypt here. Because I did a report on the modern Egypt in Ms Smits' class.

Tamzin: Now didn't you bring in something to show me the other day? What was that?

Hector: A statue of Anubis.

Tamzin: Oh, what did you learn about Anubis?

Hector: He was the God of Embalming.

Tamzin: So do you think other kids would like this project?

Hector: If they like to write and read, it would be a good thing for them.

Tamzin: How did you pick your topic?

Hector: I was wondering about it.

Tamzin: I didn't tell you what to pick?

Hector: No.

Tamzin: What do you think about that?

Hector: I thought it was pretty good. I did reports in first grade.

Tamzin: Did you get to pick?

Hector: Yeah, we just had to have the right topic. I had dolphins. After we didn't pick the teachers picked for us.

Tamzin: So what do you think? Which do you think is better?

Hector: To pick for yourself.

Tamzin: How come?

Hector: Because it's actually funner.

Tamzin: What else would you say about this project? Anything else that you remember about it?

Hector: All I remember is that it was fun.

Tamzin: What did we do at the end?

Hector: What did we do? We had a big party.

Tamzin: What was that like?

Hector: It was fun. Seeing all their different work.

Tamzin: Did you have to do anything at the party?

Hector: Tell people about my project.

Tamzin: And what was that like?

Hector: It was cool.

Tamzin: And who came to watch? Anyone?

Hector: No. Not from my family. But yeah, other people's families.

Tamzin: Did anybody from our school come?

Hector: Yeah, Tania [special education teacher].

Tamzin: And who did she bring?

Hector: Her two daughters.

Tamzin: So, do you think I should do this again?

Hector: Yeah. It's actually pretty fun.

Tamzin: Should I change anything from last year?

Hector: Nuh-uh. It wouldn't make the right report.

Figure 1. A Celebration of Learning

In May of 2002, parents, grandparents, siblings, our principal, special education teacher, and librarian crowded into room 311, our third-grade classroom at Carrillo Intermediate Magnet School in Tucson, Arizona. Many brought refreshments, dressed up, and took time off from work for our "celebration of learning." They listened expectantly over the sound of the air conditioning working overtime as each child or group delivered short oral reports on the topics they had chosen. After the oral reports the students took their places by their displays (which included a poster, computer-generated banner, and written report) to answer questions about their topics. Finally we had a wonderful reception with refreshments, which we of course let our guests enjoy first.

Listening to comments made during the reception it was obvious that our audience was extremely impressed and believed that everyone did a fantastic job. I too couldn't believe how much my students and I had learned in the process. For example, we all learned that Egyptians once pulled the organs of their dead out through their noses using a special tool to preserve them in their tombs, and that pandas can eat 83 pounds of bamboo a day. Indeed in the past month I had learned more about the state of Nevada, The Leaning Tower of Pisa, and tigers than I ever thought I would need to know.

More importantly, from this process my students learned they could do research. They could take a topic they found interesting, learn about it in depth, and then impress their peers and adults with their knowledge. Furthermore, students who spent the year reading short, simple, "easy reader" books produced reports as rich with information as did students who spent the year reading Harry Potter. Indeed, it was a celebration.

Learning to Trust My Students

Obviously this experience was a profound one for me especially. Ken Goodman (1986) in *What's Whole in Whole Language?* emphasizes the need to empower children and to encourage them to take an active role in their own learning. He says to make language easy it should be interesting, relevant, and accessible. By allowing my students to take charge of their learning for a month, I observed a marked change in their attitudes. While researching they were excited, enthusiastic, and eager to share their findings with anyone who would listen. They became so immersed in what they were doing I think they forgot they were in "school." Although they were all a bit nervous getting ready for their oral presentations (as was I!), no one protested. That day they all arrived at school prepared and eager for our guests to arrive.

Perhaps the most important thing I learned was how to step aside which, as a teacher, is often hard to do. And despite my wonderful experiences with whole language in the past, it wasn't until this point that I realized I had truly done something that closely resembled whole language, which, coincidentally, is the teaching I am most proud of to date. It wasn't *that* easy, of course. In response to state standards, we had quickly covered the entire math book (testing came early that year). We had also finished our curricular unit studying the desert. The previous year I had let the class vote on our next unit; the girls worked as a team and voted in their choice, leaving half a class of very disappointed, unenthusiastic kids. So, I decided it was time to try something different. Why not just let everyone pick any topic they want and let them choose to work with a partner or without, I thought. It will be crazy, but it just may prove amazing. It was both.

Earlier in the year during our desert unit each student had written a report. The librarian and I first modeled how nonfiction books are used; namely, that unlike a fiction book you do not need to read a nonfiction book sequentially. We gave the students four questions to research about their desert animal and showed them how to use a table of contents to find the information to answer each question. The questions were: 1) What does the animal look like?; 2) What does the animal eat?; 3) Where does the animal live?; and 4) What are the animals' babies like? Then we modeled how to take notes and how to use those notes to write a report. Each student then selected a desert animal and wrote a five-paragraph report.

The second time around it would have been a lot easier had they all wanted to research similar topics, such as countries. That way I could have developed the same questions for all of them. But, again, I really wanted them to have the freedom to research anything they wanted. Most of my students chose to have a partner, selecting topics ranging from The Leaning Tower of Pisa to tigers. (It's amazing how much you can learn about your students just from observing what they choose to study and asking why.) Again the school librarian assisted our class in doing our research. First we talked about good questions to research; questions that can be answered with yes, no, or an otherwise simple answer do not provide enough information for an entire paragraph. Then we talked about how to formulate questions that would provide more information for the reader of their reports. I think, in fact, that a critical part in this process was both choosing questions to investigate and realizing that some questions were not easily answered.

Together with the students we designed a rubric, determining what would be required to get a score of four, three, two, or one for the project. They had high expectations for themselves, and made getting a four attainable only by writing seven paragraphs (more than the five I had required for their first report). Students could receive a 1 for one to two paragraphs, a 2 for three or four paragraphs, a 3 for five or six paragraphs, and a 4 for 7 or more paragraphs.

For the next month the students read books and researched on the Internet. Some students indeed had challenges finding information to answer their questions. Fortunately we had countless helpers, from the curriculum specialist—who spent hours helping students find websites with good information—to my friend at the University of Arizona who found international students from China and Italy who, although they were having final exams, generously came to our class to be interviewed.

During this process I know the students learned a lot about their topics, but they also learned about themselves as learners and members of a classroom community. I had originally wavered between wanting them to work alone or with a partner but had decided to allow them to choose for themselves what they wanted to do. I think working in a group presents a unique set of challenges. One group struggled throughout their research time, finishing nearly last. They argued with each other about nearly everything, slowing down their progress considerably.

After giving their oral reports I asked each student or group to share one thing they had learned about doing research. The group that struggled with each other said they would choose next time to work alone. Another group learned during their researching that their initial goal of writing ten paragraphs was too high, and that they needed to decrease it to seven. By standing back and letting my students discover these things on their own, I think they gained decision-making skills even more valuable than the information they learned about their topics. I also think that "real life" presents many more situations where adults are required to collaborate (rather than fill in the bubbles of a standardized test), and children need more practice than ever learning to work together towards a common goal. I was curious to see how many students would put forth the extra effort to write the seven paragraphs they had required for a four grade. To my surprise, nearly everyone earned a four. Again, when the students were given control, they rose to meet their own challenge. I doubt I would have received the same results had I selected topics for them and presented them with an identical rubric. That was my fourth year teaching, and it took me a long time to get to the point of trusting my students as much as I had to during that project.

My Own Whole Language History

I began my teacher training in a whole language methods block. I was extremely fortunate to have had some wonderful whole language experiences as a preservice teacher. In fact the idea for the inquiry-based research I tried with my students in the spring of 2002 probably rooted itself in my head in 1996, when I enrolled as a "post-baccalaureate" student at the University of Arizona. In my second semester I began the required methods block, in the whole language section led by Yetta Goodman, who has written professionally about whole language. Our group was placed at Borton Primary Magnet School, a school community that included constructivists and whole language teachers, under the leadership of Bob Wortman. For a few hours a week we observed in a classroom. I was assigned to the Saguaro Room, a first-grade classroom.

In that class the students were doing a similar project, researching a topic of their own choosing in small groups. Each group had several books on their topic that they were using to answer their research questions. It was so unlike anything I either remembered from my own experiences in elementary school or had even witnessed since then. I was especially curious about the books they were using to do their research. One group, for example, was researching World War II. How could there possibly be books on the first-grade level about World War II? Indeed the books and encyclopedias they were using were intended for an audience reading at a higher level than a typical six-year-old. There were only two adults in the room, the teacher and her assistant, and they were obviously not able to be with each group all the time. So some of those first graders were working alone, just the kids with the books which I thought might be too hard for them. I remember thinking the entire situation was chaotic and wondering how any of the kids could possibly be learning anything.

Fortunately during this time we were required to keep a journal of our thoughts about the classes we were observing. On February 6, 1997 I wrote, "I find myself wondering how Borton students learn to read without 'formal' instruction." I think I was not alone amongst my fellow preservice teachers in thinking that students can only learn how to read when they are sitting in a group with a teacher, taking turns reading from a textbook, as many of us likely did when we were learning how to read. The Borton School was indeed devoid of textbooks, workbooks, worksheets, and the like. The study group that was researching World War II did not have a social studies book with a chapter on WWII to summarize or required videos to watch with corresponding worksheets. In spite of that (or should I say because of that?) they learned a lot about WWII.

I was interested to see how the kids dealt with those "too hard" books. The teacher, teacher's assistant, or parent volunteers read aloud to them some of the time, and the students read to each other as well. Mrs. Walker, the teacher, went from group to group, asking questions like, "What did you learn?" and "What was interesting to you?" In the end I decided the reason the kids were able to get information from their higher level books was because of their great interest in their topic. It didn't matter how hard or easy the books were. The kids wanted to learn about WWII, so they did.

What I think made the greatest impression on me was the mood of the classroom during research time. No one was complaining, uninvolved, or bored. Every child in that room was actively engaged in what was going on. Everyone was reading, writing, discussing, and learning.

Every few weeks Yetta or one of her graduate student assistants read and responded to our journal entries. My journal partner, Steve Bialostok, addressed my joys, doubts, and concerns throughout the semester. Rereading my journal entries and responses now after four years of teaching, I remembered what it was like to begin my education becoming a professional in a whole language setting. At first I was dubious, asking, "How do you get a child to figure out a word if s/he doesn't sound it out?" I kept looking for a formula; the book that tells you exactly how to teach kids how to read. My colleagues and I wondered what the students in the other, "traditional" methods block were doing. What were we missing? Did their required reading include this enigmatic "teach them how to read in five easy steps" book? Of course later we found out the other block students were just as lost as we were and certainly didn't have any sort of five-step plan.

Throughout the semester I included in my journal only a fraction of the discussions the Saguaro Room teacher had with her students about literacy. The students interacted with written text all day long, through shared reading, independent reading, journal writing, shared writing, and calendar activities. They talked about the beginning sounds in words, the ending sounds in words, and the common patterns found in words, all of which stemmed from real-life situations. Reading the lunch menu with the word *ranch* brought on a conversation about what other words have the "ch" sound and whether that sound came at the beginning or ending of the word.

And indeed the Saguaro Room kids did have "formal reading time" with their teacher on a regular basis. During this time every group was given a choice of what they wanted to read together, so stories were selected on the basis of interest. Mrs. Walker mainly chose stories with a moral or a lesson as opposed to nonsense stories because "kids can get more meaning out of them." During this time she wanted kids to have an idea of what the story was going to be about, to be able to think about what they were reading, and to imagine what was going on.

Mrs. Walker also instilled in me the importance of exposing children to literature as much and as often as possible. She encouraged us to read aloud six times a day to the students and to be open to reading favorite stories again and again. Through my interactions with Steve Bialostok in our journaling I came to realize that in fact some children's first and most important experiences reading a book independently may stem from just this type of experience. After a child hears the same story repeatedly, even to the point of memorizing it, s/he may then pick that book up and read it on their own, gaining confidence next to try a book they perhaps have not heard before. Later on in my journal I wrote, "So is reading something that just 'clicks,' eventually, for kids?" Now I know that it does seem to click with so many varied, rich, and relevant experiences, because children are constructing new schema about written language as they read.

At the end of the semester, for my final journal entry I had to write an entry entitled "My Teaching Philosophy." Actually, nearly every education class I took has had this same activity as the final project, and each time it was a bit different as my views continued to change. In 1997, wanting to reach each and every child, I wrote, "I believe to be a successful teacher, I must be able to foster interest in students in what they will be studying. I would like my students to have a voice in their classroom as far as helping direct me in terms of what they already know, and what subjects they would like to study in greater depth." That statement was clearly based on a whole language philosophy. Never did I think about the long, frustrating hours first-year teachers put in and the struggles I would have leaving my teaching at school instead of bringing it home every night. Nor did I consider that being a whole language teacher is a *lot* harder than it looks. Everyone can follow a teacher's edition, assigning the corresponding workbook pages, but listening to your students and being innovative are certainly much more. Steve had in fact commented, "I want you to remember that the wonderful points you make are things to strive for. They don't come in the first, second, or even third year. But they will if you keep plugging away and don't get frustrated when your class falls apart and you feel like a failure."

My First Four Years of Teaching

It's especially interesting for me to look back on this exchange and then at my first year of teaching. I was very fortunate to be hired at another magnet school in Tucson, Carrillo Intermediate Magnet, where many Borton magnet students went to continue their education after second grade. No two magnet schools in our school district can have the same focus. Borton School had a whole language focus, while the Carrillo School's focus is in the areas of social studies and science. So the reading programs between the two schools differed quite a bit. When I arrived at Carrillo a reading program was already in place. Students had formal reading instruction 45 minutes a day, four days a week. This time was sacred and could not be used for anything other than teaching reading. The system was in some ways ideal. The actual reading time spanned an hour and a half. For the first 45 minutes half of my class of 20 went to a specialist (music or physical education) leaving me with only half my class. For the next 45 minutes the groups switched, so all students saw specialists and received their reading instruction. It was wonderful to conduct reading groups with such a small number of students in the classroom at a time.

When I arrived I was shown the leveled Houghton Mifflin textbooks, teacher's manuals, and workbooks. We were to use these materials at least three out of the four days a week. Dutifully I took four sets of materials (my students actually tested into reading levels spanning from emerging to extending readers, but four groups seemed like the most manageable number I could tolerate) and taught reading. We "did" a story a week, including reading the story itself several times and doing the corresponding workbook pages. In our workbooks we learned skills such as how to identify the four types of sentences and how to punctuate them, to cut and paste synonyms, and to color in naming words (nouns). At the end of each unit the students took a multiple-choice skills test, which we sent home. I realized what I was doing differed vastly from what I had learned, observed, and admired during the whole language block, but it seemed, at that point, easiest to follow the procedures being used in other classrooms.

Indeed things were going along fine until one of my groups hit the workbook page dealing with the difference between the sounds that "oo" makes in words like *moon* and *book*. On this particular page, students were to write the "oo" words in the correct place (depending on the sound the "oo" made) under the word "book" or under the word "moon." I remember my assistant and I walking from desk to desk, trying to figure out which word went where. I watched the students working alone and saw them mouthing the "oo" words, exaggerating each word and still looking frustrated. I couldn't imagine how listening for such subtle differences in sounds of words the kids already knew could possibly help them become better readers. "Let's just skip this page," I ended up telling them.

Despite having the teacher's manuals, workbooks, and textbooks I was overwhelmed. Planning for four groups every day was exhausting, as were keeping up with grading and recording the workbook pages. And honestly, during those first two years of teaching neither my students nor I had much choice in what we studied. I ended up spending a lot of time trying to figure out what third graders needed to know (I had always dreamed I would teach first grade). Additionally, I had both district and national assessments to worry about.

Integrating My Teaching with Professional Development

My third year teaching I started graduate school with Yetta Goodman as my advisor. Slowly I rediscovered many of the aspects of teaching I had admired from the whole language block but had never quite put into practice. I was also introduced to the work of several influential educators. Theodore Clymer's (1996) article reviewing the utility of phonic generalizations reaffirmed for me the futility of teaching traditional phonics rules. Many children learned to read without these rules, and often we learn the rules from reading (Smith, as cited by Krashen, 2002). Indeed, in line with whole language, we learn to read by reading, not by doing "oo" phonics worksheets. I was also introduced to the work of Sharon Taberski (2000), and the idea of reading conferences, which I integrated into our reading time. Most importantly, though, I rediscovered what it was I had learned during my whole language methods block, namely to allow reading and writing instruction to permeate everything we did, not just happen during reading block.

Indeed, reading and writing began to filter into other parts of our day, especially into our school's focus. In 1999 the Carrillo School was one of the first in our district to participate in the D.E.S.E.R.T. project, a district-run program funded by a five-million-dollar grant from the National Science Foundation. Grants were given to school districts with an effective science education program already in place. During the summers and throughout the year we went to training workshops led by current and former teachers, and had a liaison who came into our school to observe and offer suggestions.

One summer's institute focused on inquiry-based learning. We were taught how to turn the science experiments included in the curriculum over to our students, and have them, not the worksheets, ask the questions. And so we stopped doing many of the worksheets and created blank science notebooks with graph paper instead. Our science time went from half an hour to an hour-and-a-half, integrating science, reading, and writing. Students made predictions, drew diagrams, and wrote conclusions.

That year I also incorporated different kinds of reading activities into our reading time. In a class taught by Bob Wortman (who by that time was an adjunct professor at the University of Arizona) I read Don Holdaway's *The Foundations of Literacy* (1979) and rediscovered Big Books (large books with pictures for read-alouds are well known literacy tools). At that same time I had been reading aloud the Arizona Young Children's book nominees. My class overwhelmingly decided *What! Cried Granny: An almost bedtime story* (Lum, 1998) was their favorite, so I suggested we make our own big book based on the story. I copied the text onto large sheets of chart paper and we made our own book, each child making an illustration for a page. With Bob's encouragement I let the kids discuss what to do next, and they decided they wanted to read their book to an audience. I had planned that we would invite their parents, our librarian, and the principal. I thought that half the class would work on one invitation with my assistant, while the other half would work with me on the other. Then they could each write one invitation to their families, and we'd still be done in time to do math before the end of the day. What about the playground monitor, they asked, and the crossing guard? And I realized that by deciding for them who to invite I had taken control away from them. So, acting as their note-taker instead of as the organizer, the students devised an invitation list with me, choosing the people most important to them including our librarian, principal, playground monitors, and our beloved 80-year-old crossing guard. In preparation the kids practiced reading their page of the book aloud, as we would do for the actual performance. I was concerned about my struggling readers, wondering if they would be able to read on their own or if I should give them a partner. Instead they each rose to the occasion and did superbly.

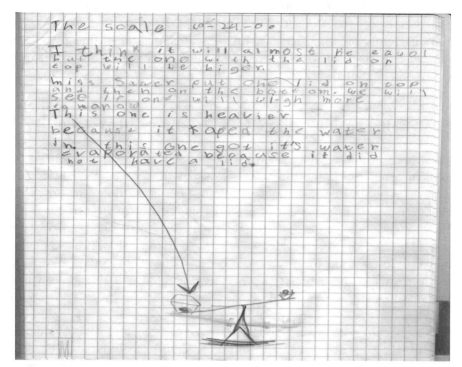

Figure 2. Inquiry-Based Science Notebooks

This first experience I had with inviting students' family members to school for an event focused on reading was a powerful one for my students, their parents, and me. I learned that such people as parents, grandparents, *tias*, or *tios* love to come to school to see their children perform. Most importantly I learned you don't need to put on a fancy play with costumes, music, and fanfare (although refreshments do help!). And actually, families were shown how powerful literacy can be by seeing their children get so excited about a book that they have created.

By allowing my students to take control and responsibility for what happened with our book they were able to take ownership of their learning. They wanted to show off what they had done instead of moving blindly on to their next assignment. Later on that year I remember assigning my students the task of writing directions on how to complete a task. I demonstrated the process by asking for their help in describing how to make a peanut butter and jelly sandwich. Then they chose their own topics to write their "how to" paragraphs. When they were writing their paragraphs one of my students asked me why we were bothering if no one was ever going to read it. I suggested we put all the stories into a class book, which satisfied him enough to want to finish. He taught an important lesson: to make writing meaningful, kids need a purpose. They need to know why they are writing and who will benefit from what they have written. By helping *them* find their own purposes, reading and writing take on meaning, which gives them their own motivation to want to succeed.

School-Wide Changes in Reading and Writing

Our school went through a transformation during that time in our thoughts on how to teach reading. As a staff we began to have conversations and workshops about reading and how to improve our instruction. One important change was the development of a school book-room for use by teachers. Book sets were pooled together from all over the school, and teachers were invited to select book sets which were ordered from catalogues as well. The books were arranged by levels, with an easy check-out system. We were allowed to use these books and/or the Houghton Mifflin books while teaching reading. It was wonderful to be able to select from a variety of books, and to have so many available.

One faculty meeting our principal arrived carrying a large, heavy duffel bag, to talk to us about reading. He told us until recently he hadn't read a book since high school because he never had anything he wanted to read. Then he opened up his bag and began unloading books he had read within the last year. He took out each one, showing us the titles. The books piled up and nearly toppled over on the floor. All it took, he told us, was finding what he liked to read. Our principal's purpose in bringing in the duffel bag was to talk to us about SSR or Sustained Silent Reading. He felt it was important for our students to have opportunities to read independently for pleasure. Some of the classrooms in our school had some type of SSR program, but we didn't have a school-wide SSR commitment. Inspired by our principal we decided to implement one.

We argued quite a bit over the structure of SSR. We argued over how students would choose the books they read. We argued over how to hold them accountable for what they read, and we argued over what type of reward system to implement. Finally we all agreed to have SSR for half an hour every day, a sacred time which would not be disturbed. Everyone in the school would read during this time. The role of the teacher during SSR differed in each classroom, but generally some days we had students read with us individually, while other days we modeled reading by reading our own books for pleasure.

In the beginning the students in our class used mini-book report sheets and recorded the number of pages they had read each day. Everyone *was* reading, but I noticed a few major problems. With such a wide range of abilities in one classroom some students were reading chapter books while others were reading simpler picture books. Unfortunately the students reading shorter books were filling out book report papers much more often, and spending less time reading. They were reading books to complete worksheets, essentially. Some were actually spending more time filling out these pages than reading books! (At the same time they were creating mountains of paperwork for my assistant and me.) I also found that it was time consuming for my third graders to count up all the pages they had read, especially when the books had unnumbered pages. Finally, I still wasn't sure how to incorporate our SSR program into the school's reward system. Somehow, in an effort to give children independent reading time, everything had become very complicated.

In the end, instead of counting pages and filling out papers I asked my students only to record the names of three (or less if they were reading longer books) of the books they had read each day. If they participated in SSR and recorded what they had read they got a sticker for the day. After a certain number of stickers they were allowed to participate in the school-wide reward system, which was to select a free book. Finally, this way everyone had equal access to the free book giveaway.

I also thought a lot about my role during SSR. Following Taberski's *On Solid Ground* (2000) model I began checking in with my students individually about once a week. During this time we would review what they had read, what they liked about the books they chose, and what book they thought they would like to read next. Sometimes I asked students to read aloud to me, and we would discuss the qualities of a "just right" book and if they thought they were indeed reading one. Sometimes I would go with a student to our classroom library in search of new books. Based on a child's interest level I was able to pull out some possibilities from which the student made the final selection. Other than that roughly once-a-week contact, I did not interfere during SSR. Students were allowed to choose the books they wanted to read, and read on their own. Several times a week I pulled out a book I was reading and joined in by sitting at a desk and reading with them.

I think a lot of the debate we had about SSR was based on issues of trust. Teachers often find it is hard to let go. How can we be sure our students are choosing appropriate books? How can we be sure they understand what they are reading? When I looked at SSR more closely, I realized that my real goals were for my students to actively participate in SSR. I wanted them to have an opportunity to practice reading independently and to learn to enjoy reading as much as I do. I wanted them to become independent readers. And to accomplish that I needed to trust them.

More Changes: What Could We Do to Avoid the District's Interference?

In my fourth year of teaching we had a new principal, and our school began a reading block. There were concerns that our school would soon be declared a "STAR" school and be placed on a regimented schedule, requiring all teachers on the same grade level to teach the same Performance Objective (PO) on the same day, and it was thought that implementing the reading block could help improve our scores, avoiding a bad designation. So, each child in the school was placed in a reading group based on their Diagnostic Reading Assessment (DRA) level. This program was considered a group effort; all certified staff (including our art teacher, music teacher, physical education teacher, and librarian) in the building had a reading group during reading block time, which occurred for an hour, four days a week. I had a group of third, fourth, and fifth graders all reading at DRA levels 12-18 (roughly first-grade level). It is of interest to note that this type of program has been implemented in other schools around the country as well in attempts to raise reading levels (Rimer, 2002).

We all had concerns with doing this type of reading block. After all, sending your students to other teachers required us to trust each other immensely, just as I had felt I needed to trust my own students. My students went to more than ten different classrooms during reading block time, and I had little idea what they were learning in the other settings. I was unable to follow through on what they had learned during our SSR conferences and I did not know what to tell their parents about what they did during their reading block time during conferences. Conversely I was unable to follow through with the third, fourth, and fifth graders I had in my reading group throughout the rest of the day.

Simultaneously in graduate school I was learning about miscue analysis and retrospective miscue analysis. Again, I had been exposed to miscue analysis quite a bit during my whole language block, but I think having teaching experience helped me bring an entirely different perspective to my learning. Fortunately my group of first-grade-level readers consisted of only thirteen students (a positive aspect of the program). That year I really started to think about teaching reading strategies and how to guide my students into being more independent. I realized that so many students have only one strategy to use when they read "sound it out." I have read with many students whose reliance on this strategy results in their reading being so halting that they end up having no idea what they have read when they are finished. I decided to provide my students with a wider repertoire of strategies to use when they encounter unfamiliar words.

My reading group became reading detectives and followed Debra Goodman's *The Reading Detective Club* (1999). They worked together on cloze activities, wrote reflections on their own reading, and discussed what they were doing when they read. By the end of the year they had many reading strategies to use. But most importantly, they learned to make sure what they read made sense to them. And finally, by the end of the year when a student made a miscue they were able to remind their peer that making mistakes helps us to learn.

More than just our reading program changed that year. Whereas previously we could write the skill being addressed for each lesson, we now were required to label each skill taught with a six-digit code in our lesson plan books using our state standards notebook. Again, in compliance with the district we began having periodic professional development sessions teaching us how to look up test scores on the district's website. From that information we were to develop "power standards"; standards which, based on the test scores, we needed to spend more time addressing in the classroom. I question how much my students gained from the training I received and the time I spent coding my lesson plans instead of hunting down books they would have enjoyed reading and developing innovative, interesting lessons. We could have also spent time sharing ideas with one another or learning about ways to make reading come alive. There is only so much time you can spend, after all, analyzing data before you *do* something with that data.

I don't have a problem being accountable for teaching what third graders need to know. I think teachers should be required to teach what third graders need to know, but I regret that our motivations stem from raising test scores and not on what teachers, the people who interact the most with students, think their individual students need. During this time, I felt that the trust I had so hesitantly began to give to my students needed to be taken back.

Teaching and District Demands

Honestly, it's a scary time to be a teacher. Accountability is high (as it should be), but unfortunately teachers and students are being held accountable for test scores instead of helping children to be inquisitive and self-directed learners. In 2000 Arizona developed the first AIMS test (Arizona Instrument to Measure Standards). Students in third, fifth, eighth, and twelfth grades were required to take the test; they were told that elementary and junior-high students would not be able to pass on to the next grade, and that high-school students would not be able to graduate, if they failed this test. So starting in 2000 my students spent two weeks testing, one week for the AIMS and one week for the Stanford 9. Testing is not a fun time for anyone. I hate watching my students agonize over passages they can barely read, much less relate.

In the fall of 2002 our worst fears were realized, as our school was listed as one of 22 schools with a designation of "underperforming." As a result of this designation, our school was required to send a letter to every household in our area indicating this designation, as a warning that property values may decrease. It makes me sad and indeed sickens me that something as far removed as property values can decrease as a result of how well a child performs on a test.

That fall several teachers, our curriculum specialist, and our brand new principal attended several days of training on the PDCA (Plan Do Check Act) Model, the model last year's STAR schools are using. After a series of meetings the PDCA team returned to share with us what they had learned. They were also to share with us how our school was now required to change our schedule. The first step was to cut lunchtime by ten minutes and rearrange our specialists' schedules. Music, art, and physical education were all cut by half-an-hour a week and put only in the afternoons so as to not disturb our morning arts and math blocks. Math now begins the moment students walk in the room (causing us to lose our chance to talk about the day or do a read-aloud before getting started). After 75 minutes of math, language arts class begins (cutting out our all-important snack and break time). Eight of my 22 students (who scored the highest on the DRA assessment) leave the room and go to another teacher for these 90 minutes. With my remaining 14 students I teach reading and writing. At 11:15 we have math tutorials. All third-grade students are given an identical assessment (designed by the third-grade teachers) on Thursdays to cover that week's skills. Students are then placed in groups depending on their score from the assessment. For the remaining half hour before lunch students head off to a "tutorial," "maintaining," or "excelling" math group, taught by either a teacher or teacher's assistant. These groups generally contain from 10 to 15 students. The afternoons are comprised of music, physical education, and art. Teachers who work with bilingual students or English language learners (those who did not score high enough on the English assessment, who are in SEI Standard English Immersion classes where nothing but English is spoken) spend most of their remaining time working on language. Fortunately, being in a 'traditional' classroom, I have a bit more unscheduled time to use than the bilingual and SEI teachers do.

After adjusting our schedule, we began the arduous task of scheduling the Performance Objectives for the year. Armed with blank calendars, an ordered list indicating which specific skills the test results showed our students had most poorly mastered, and the number of how many school days remained until the tests, we schedule. We now each have posted by our doors, in our lesson plan books, and posted in our classrooms in 'kid-friendly' language, three calendars, for reading, writing, and math. On any given day we are all required to teach the same PO's, at the same time.

I can't begin to explain how upsetting these changes have been. It is also remarkable how much extra time is required to keep up with the unending paperwork that comes with the PDCA Model. Perhaps now would be a good time to mention also how much paperwork this plan requires, what with typing up the extra lesson plans, schedules, and weekly assessments. The assessments alone are extremely time-consuming. Every Thursday the third-grade teachers meet after school. We bring our students' weekly math assessments and categorize them into the three groups (each week the groups change, based on the student's scores). We then agree who will write the lesson plan for each group, type up the lessons, and distribute them to the other teachers on our team. Although students are not required to go to special tutorial sessions during the school day in reading or writing, they are still assessed weekly on the skills taught. All students take the identical assessments (again, designed by the third-grade teachers). Week after week students who struggle to read simple texts are given these third-grade assessments, and week after week they fail them.

A plan like this takes power away from children. It takes away from the community aspect of the elementary school classroom when children are taken away for sometimes four hours at a time and sent to other classrooms. It assumes teachers are incapable of determining how to teach based on the students they have. Kathy Hibbert (2002) states, "When teachers adhere rigidly to a program under threat of this type of accountability, they lose the 'self' that teaches. Instead of being thoughtful decision makers, teachers of programs are reduced to managers, and their thinking limited to functionalist implementation of a preconceived structure." I highly doubt that classrooms on regimented plans have the same sense of wonder that I experienced in the Saguaro Room at the Borton School. I highly doubt those students come to school excited to learn. I feel for the ones who do not master the PO's fast enough and are sent elsewhere to relearn them. I wonder about their self-esteem. I wonder if we are doing what is best for our kids.

The Future of Whole Language

This is clearly a very important time to look at whole language and its place in this test frenzy trend. In a recent interview with Bob Wortman I asked him what he recommended for teachers trying to use whole language while on a plan such as the PDCA. He suggested I take a look at my current situation and ask if I feel I could adapt to do the PDCA model yet still keep kids engaged. Indeed, despite our rigid schedule, I still feel I have the freedom to teach using the methods I know would most benefit my students (as opposed to some schools which use scripted reading programs with specific texts the students must read). While I may be required to teach cause-and-effect on Monday of next week, I can do so using whatever story I choose. I feel I am able to give my students options for what they would like to read, and some afternoons are available to us for independent research projects and the like. Bob also gave me some advice on how to cope with these rigid standards: Do what you can do where you are planted. And I think that advice was what I needed to hear. I know when I go into work tomorrow my schedules will still be there, complete with PO's and assessments. But I do know that I love to teach, I love the kids I teach, and I love the school where I teach. As one teacher at my school shared with me, "Our school is more than underachieving and I'm proud to be here. I'll do what I need to do to take the ugly label away."

When Hector stood by the poster of Anubis that he drew and answered questions about Egypt, he was having fun. He had read informational books about Egypt, researched on the Internet, taken notes, and written a lengthy report. But in fact, all he remembered was that it was fun. When I asked a fellow teacher about the PDCA model she told me, "It's too structured. The children are not enjoying it. The teacher assistants are not enjoying it. I don't even think our principal is enjoying it. I don't know who is enjoying it. It's being handed down from above, and takes the trust away from the teacher."

I have to say I agree with my fellow teachers. I feel like much of the trust I should have, as a professional, has been taken away. I fear that the school day will become even more rigid, and I hope that doesn't happen. Teaching and learning *can* be fun. Hector told us that himself. Devoting day after day to this project was fun. Students were engaged and learning. By allowing my students choice and control they rose to the challenge and exceeded all my expectations. And the only reason they did was because, again, they were having fun.

I guess, in a way, not only being a student but also being a teacher is a matter of trust. We've looked at the data, we know what we need to do, and we know what is best for kids. We don't need to spend any more time coding lesson plan books for hours each week, making hundreds of copies of assessments, learning how to look up test scores on the computer and analyzing them fifty different ways complete with color graphs. Just trust us.

References

Clymer, T. (1996). The utility of phonic generalizations in the primary grades. *The Reading Teacher, 50* (3), 182-188.

Goodman, D. (1999). *The reading detective club: Solving mysteries of reading.* Portsmouth, NH: Heinemann.

Goodman, K. (1986). *What's whole in whole language?* Portsmouth, NH: Heinemann.

Hibbert, K. (2002). Don't steal the struggle! The commercialization of literacy and its impact on teachers. *Talking Points, 13* (2), 2-6.

Holdaway, D. (1979). *The foundations of literacy.* Sydney: Scholastic.

Krashen, S. D. (2002). Defending whole language: The limits of phonics instruction and the efficacy of whole language instruction. *Reading Improvement 31* (1), 32-42.

Lum, K. (1998). *What! Cried Granny: An almost bedtime story.* New York: Dial Books for Young Readers.

Rimer, S. (2002, Dec. 3). Failing and frustrated, school tries even F's: A push to improve reading in Philadelphia. *New York Times.*

Taberski, S. (2000). *On solid ground: Strategies for teaching reading.* Portsmouth, NH: Heinemann.

Walker, Paula. (personal communication, 2002).

Wortman, Robert (personal communication, 2002).

CHAPTER SEVEN

Whole Language in Taiwan

LIAN-JU LEE AND WEN-YUN LIN

L
ike many educational theories and practices, the development of whole language in Taiwan is a complex and dynamic process, involving many different factors inside as well as outside the educational community. Inevitably it has been shaped by actions taken among interested individuals and groups within the context of a society. Looking closely into the process, we found that our society is made up of cultural, historical, social, and political influences as well as input from the academic fields. In Taiwan, considering whole language as a theory and then accepting it as an educational practice has been a socialization of knowledge through the sharing of concepts and experiences, clarification in discourse and dialogue, and action and adjustment. We are still going through this process as we write this chapter.

Some Educational Realities

To better understand the path of change and the significant influences that whole language has had on classrooms and education, it is necessary to first present a brief description of some of the related educational practices at the time when whole language was introduced to Taiwan.

Much like in the United States, test-directed teaching and learning have been the major obstacles slowing the progress of our education in Taiwan in the past several decades. Tests, including regular examinations used to evaluate students' learning outcomes and entry examinations for the next stage, have played a crucial role in instruction and curriculum at the elementary and secondary school levels. Most teachers, administrators, parents, and even students take test results as the major and sometimes only evidence representing learning outcomes and use it as the primary indicator of a student's ability. From this perspective, performing well on a test is the major if not the only concern of teachers, students, and others involved. Teachers therefore serve as watchdogs to maintain high performance on examinations. And as a result, in most cases teaching solely for testing, relying exclusively on textbooks, becomes the major job of teachers.

Another related fact is the issue of unification. Prior to 1996, the government strictly endorsed a unified policy of curriculum. Curriculum and textbooks used in elementary and junior high schools were centrally controlled. Teachers in all grade levels were mandated at the minimum to completely teach the standardized textbooks written by the Central Textbook Committees under the Ministry of Education. All learning evaluations were based on the content in these textbooks. Teachers had little opportunity and time to bring in content or materials beyond the textbook. To most teachers, teaching meant teaching from the textbooks. The emphasis on test results as the major measure of learning added more weight to textbook teaching and textbook-based evaluation. From 1996 to the present, our textbook choices have been broadened to include private publishers. However, textbook-based teaching and evaluation is still the main emphasis in elementary and secondary schools due to the school culture. Teachers who later adopted whole language have mostly had these types of experiences.

Development of Whole Language

Whole language was first introduced to the educational community in Taiwan through a series of speeches and articles on whole language theory given to teacher educators and teachers in early childhood education in the early 1990s. Whole language teaching was developed, however, through implementation and research in various early childhood and elementary classrooms later on. Workshops, conferences, and published research reports and articles in the following years provided opportunities for further dialogue and negotiation which resulted in the continuing reconstruction of whole language theory and practice beyond personal interpretations in Taiwan. Taking the time line as a frame, we will present the major elements involved in this process to sketch the developmental passage of whole language in this country. These elements include: speeches, conferences and workshops, research, classroom practices, related publications, ongoing discourse and dialogue, and teachers' groups.

A Seed Is Sown: Knowing About Whole Language (1990-1994)

The term "whole language" first appeared in Taiwan in late 1990 in a speech given at a teacher's college entitled "Whole language: Its theory and practice" by Lian-Ju Lee. Later at three successive Annual Conferences in Educational Research in Taiwan, Lian-Ju presented her research in early literacy development from a whole language perspective. A year later, another scholar, Han-Hwa Chao (1994), presented her paper on the theoretical background of whole language, which was the first academic paper presented in Taiwan using the term "whole language" (although its Chinese translation was different from previous and later translations). These were the earliest introductions of whole language to the academic community in this country.

The early introduction of whole language to practitioners took place around 1993. In March and April of that year, there were two workshops focusing on whole language for early childhood teachers held at Tainan Teachers College, where Lian-Ju taught. In September, another workshop was provided, again at the same site, to teaching consultants who were senior teachers from across the nation. These teachers were expected to bring whole language seeds back to various schools in several areas of the nation after the workshops. At that time, a more common name, which was later accepted as the formal Chinese translation of whole language— "chyun-yu-ying"—was used.

Another handful of significant seeds, which later had fruitful results in elementary classrooms, was planted in 1992-1996. Upon looking for some alternatives in language education, the Ministry of Education appointed a curriculum research team, which involved Wen-Yun Lin, at the Taiwan Provincial Institute for Elementary School Teachers' In-Service Education (IEST) to develop a new language arts curriculum for elementary schools, followed by a series of research endeavors. A set of research-oriented curricula and learning materials in language arts thus were developed in 1992. This set was intended to reflect whole language principles and was funded by the government. When the old language arts curriculum policy was in effect, this set of learning materials brought teachers and later textbook publishers a new vision of language learning and teaching and evoked a different way of thinking. It also functioned as a bridge between the old tradition and new national curriculum guidelines, which were developed six years later. Once the new materials were published, regular teacher training programs featuring whole language theory and practice were provided to teachers and principals, including those who participated in this nationwide research, since 1992. These programs and workshops provided opportunities for participating teachers to reflect on their own teaching in the past. Some found that they were partially applying whole language principles without realizing it. Others were inspired by the ways in which whole language embraced love and passion for children and teaching. More seeds were spread out to different parts of the country.

As teachers in the field learned about whole language teaching, preservice programs in some of the teachers' colleges provided whole language related courses to students who were becoming kindergarten or elementary school teachers. Such courses have been developed at the National Taipei Teachers' College, the Municipal Taipei Teachers' College, and the Tainan Teachers' College (where Lian-Ju worked). These programs act as seedbeds that later have the potential to yield a deep cultivation of whole language when these future teachers enter the field.

Deep Cultivation: Implementation and Research in the Classroom (1994 to present)

The research conducted by the team at IEST mentioned above was one of the foundations on which whole language teaching was built in this country. Programs and research in whole language practice in other educational settings and by other researchers along with the IEST team together cultivated a whole language field on a deeper level.

From 1994 on, there have been several research-oriented programs conducted in various kindergartens, including private and public, in the southern parts of Taiwan. Teachers applying whole language in their classrooms are still continuing to do so, with this trend growing stronger today in this part of the country. In 1997-1998, Lian-Ju participated and documented the process of curriculum reform in a public kindergarten. This yearlong research documented how children benefited from the program in several ways (for more details, see Lee, 2000a). This program and its developmental process provided useful references to kindergarten teachers who were interested in becoming whole language teachers.

Besides in the early childhood setting, whole language curriculum development and related research have been conducted in some elementary classrooms in different areas. Research in third- and fifth-grade classrooms by Tien-Jun Shen in 1996-1997 was one of these projects. Shen (1997) indicated in his research report that students developed higher abilities and interests and a better attitude in language after being immersed in whole language programs.

Whole language attracted the interests of educators in the field of Teaching English as a Foreign Language (EFL) as well. Programs in EFL applying whole language principles in various classrooms were developed. Researchers in different settings in 1996-1999 also conducted research. Yueh-Hung Tseng (2000) documented the process of applying whole language in EFL programs in elementary and kindergarten classrooms. Since 1998 EFL has been mandated from the fifth grade up, making whole language more prevalent.

A Milestone: The Beginning of a New Trend (1996)

1996 was a milestone year for the development of whole language in Taiwan. In January of 1996 Drs. Ken and Yetta Goodman, and Debra Goodman, an experienced whole language teacher at that time, were invited to visit. A series of workshops for teachers and educators were held at two of the major cities in Taiwan, Taipei and Tainan. Their visit and workshops attracted great attention among scholars and researchers in education and classroom teachers in this country. Related news reports and articles were also published around that time. Later in 1996 the first whole language teachers group was formed at one of the workshop sites, Tainan, inspired by the Goodmans and the information that they provided in the workshops.

Evidence showed how whole language caught the attention of academics and practitioners in education from that year forward. First, more in-service training programs and workshops in whole language, funded by individual departments of education on the local level, were held in different parts of the country. Second, more publications related to the whole language philosophy were available, including books, articles, research reports, and masters' theses. The first master's thesis in whole language was completed in 1997 (Hung, 1997). Over 20 masters' theses investigating whole language theory and practice in this country were completed by the year of 2002. Third, more studies related to the application of whole language in classrooms were conducted and reported, including studies in the areas of early childhood, elementary, and secondary education, EFL education, science and environmental education, after school programs, programs for learners with special needs, and teacher education. Finally, whole language became a theme or topic in several nationwide or international conferences funded by either the universities or the government. It also has been a popular theme of workshops in Chinese as well as in English language arts offered by publishers or private organizations. These discussions expanded the pool of whole language and added multiple views. They also encouraged more dialogue among interested individuals and groups in the community of education.

A Flowing Trend: Inspiration for Educational Reform (1997-present)

The period from 1997 to the present was important to elementary and secondary education in this country. Major educational reforms, which were historically significant, took place within this period of time. Administrators and educators searched for curricula that were more learner centered and relevant to students. Ideas such as school-based curriculum, integrated curriculum, and connections between elementary and secondary curriculum were discussed and later became national policies. Some administrators and policy makers began to encourage teachers to construct their own curriculum. During this period in time, the whole language philosophy and instructional principles inspired some educators who participated in the process of reform and influenced new curriculum development. For example, some members of the Development of the Nine-Year Curriculum Guideline for Language Arts Committee who had participated in the IEST research team mentioned in an earlier section were inspired by whole language and brought its principles into the new curriculum. In early childhood education, a new national Kindergarten Curriculum Guideline also was developed in 2000 to replace the old one issued in 1976. Lian-Ju was appointed by the government as the chair of the Language Arts Committee and centrally applied the whole language principles to the curriculum. Following the new curriculum policies, teacher training became part of the follow-up process. In some places, whole language was taken into training programs to help teachers think about teaching in different ways. It was expected that whole language would bring these teachers different views of learning, teaching, curriculum, and education.

Classroom Case Studies

To demonstrate how whole language was implemented in this country, some kindergarten and elementary classrooms will be presented as case studies in the following section. It should be noted that they were not typical or atypical but were some of the observed classrooms in which the teachers were considered to be applying whole language.

The first case study was taken from a kindergarten classroom. It was a class of five- and six-year-old children. Yuen and Mei were the two teachers. The following describes how this class usually looks and functions.

Yuen and Mei's Kindergarten Class

It was free time after lunch in Yuen and Mei's class. The children who finished lunch gradually came back to the room. Two girls were at the sign-in table. One was checking whether everyone had signed in, in order to notify those who hadn't. The other one was standing next to the sign-in sheet taking a large piece of paper and carefully copying all the names onto her own sheet. When she saw this, Yuen, the teacher, asked: "What are you doing this for?" The girl replied: "Then I would know how to write their names the next time I want to send a gift to someone." At the library center, groups of children were reading books that they had selected on their own. Some were in pairs reading together, and some were reading silently. There was one child reading to a group of three, and another one was tape recording her own reading. At the other side of the room in the writing center, another teacher, Mei, was helping a couple of children writing their journals. One child was dictating his sentences to the teacher, and the other was writing by herself and coming to check the conventional form of certain characters with the teacher once in a while. Another group of children was collaboratively building a block construction using different kinds of blocks, miniature figures, and toys. They also added printed signs on certain parts of their construction. At the same time one of the group members was drawing a picture, along with labels, of the construction to document the design.

Yuen was then talking to three children who came to report something to her that excited them; they had discovered a colorful insect on the potted plant in the yard eating the leaves of the plant. Yuen asked them what they thought they wanted to do about it. Ideas were shared, and at the same time questions were raised. It did not take long for them to reach an agreement—they wanted to know more about this little figure. Yuen referred one of the children to an insect encyclopedia in the classroom library to look up the insect. The child promised to bring this discovery to a discussion in the class. Later in the first afternoon session, the teachers and the children discussed the incident and how they could learn more from it. Two study plans emerged: to look for more information from different resources and observe and document the habits and changes of this insect. Some children signed up to look at books that they had at home or with their parents and to bring in the information if available. An observation plan was developed with the guidance of the teacher, which included the frequency of observations, the volunteer who would do the observations, and the way of note taking. This emergent curriculum lasted for a few weeks.

Incidents such as these were common in this classroom. The emergent curricular ideas might come from incidents that interested children, events that happened among children or their families, unexpected results from planned learning activities, or books that they read. The following incident better describes the learning process in the emergent curriculum observed in this classroom.

In the middle of reading the book *My Mama Says There Aren't Any Zombies, Ghosts, Vampires, Creatures, Demons, Monsters, Fiends, Goblins, or Things* by Judith Viorst, a girl, Yi, expressed that she didn't want to listen to the book anymore because it was scary. Mei stopped as requested and put the book back on the shelf. Many other children, however, who were interested went back to read the book themselves later during free time. Observing this, Mei decided to go back to the subject a couple of weeks after the first reading to discuss the emotional reaction that the children had to the text. During one reading session, Mei asked the children who had read the book to share what they thought and how they felt about the book. Surprisingly to the teacher, many of them indicated that it was not scary at all and in fact the ghost stuff in the story was not real but just the main character's imagination or made up by the character's mother. With Yi's agreement, Mei reread the book and let the class talk about the creatures in the book and the children's own similar experiences. In this discussion, some children indicated that there are a few other children's books that had a similar theme or plot. Mei decided to further explore this issue in order to expand the children's learning experiences. During the following days, she brought in and read a series of children's books which dealt with different kinds of fear. After reading most of the books, they came to a session and talked about the kinds of fear that the characters in these books had and developed a chart that showed the titles of the books, the main characters in each book, what they were afraid of, and the possible solutions. Mei also arranged a session for the children to talk about their real-life fears. A survey form was then developed with the focus generated from the previous discussions for everyone to interview one another and their family members. Surveys were conducted and then brought to class to share.

It was unexpected but appreciated that at the end of the discussion one of the girls in the class indicated that she had an idea of how to take away the fears of all of the class members. She suggested that everyone write down on a small piece of paper whatever he or she was afraid of and then give it to her. She then asked for a box from the teacher, decorated it, and put a label called "Taking-fear-away Box" on its outside panel. The next day when all the children had their sheets written and turned in, the girl and her helpers tossed all the sheets into the box in front of everyone, sealed it thoroughly, put the box away in a secure place to which everyone agreed, and then announced "Now your fears are trapped in the box so they cannot harm you any more."

What a valuable learning experience for the children! The activities were mostly initiated and implemented by children and revolved around what they were concerned about, one of the most intimate aspects of a child's personal world. The children themselves, rather than the teachers, owned their learning process. Many different kinds of learning had been involved during the process. They spoke and listened to each other for opinions and comments, read for pleasure as well as for fulfilling curiosity and obtaining information, and wrote to accomplish work related to their investigation. They learned many more strategies, adding ways of reading and writing used in daily life to their repertoires. They learned how to be good listeners, speakers, readers, and writers, and how to collaboratively work together to solve problems. They comforted each other and helped each other find solutions. It was a learning experience that promoted emotional, affective, and social as well as cognitive development in each individual child. It was relevant, meaningful, and functional to this group of children.

Curriculum in Change

Mei and Yuen had been kindergarten teachers for several years before they learned about and decided to do whole language. After learning about whole language at in-service workshops, they had an opportunity to consult with Lian-Ju about the possibility of implementing whole language in their classroom. The availability of one-on-one professional development later turned out to be one of the supports in their process of becoming whole language teachers.

Their implementation of whole language was a continual process that involved gradual changes in the following aspects: (a) Their perspectives of and attitudes to children, learning, and teaching; (b) Organizing the classroom into a literate environment; (c) Organizing curriculum to be more open, flexible, and child centered; (d) Building routines to facilitate children's literacy development; (e) Incorporating children's literature into the curriculum; and (f) Incorporating reading and writing in their daily lives and theme investigations. These changes also revealed their grasp of functional and authentic whole language principles and the use of various authentic materials for reading and writing.

Their Pedagogical Framework

The way Yuen and Mei organized their class and the activities revealed several pedagogical components of a whole language framework. Two of the major principles will be discussed with the following activity examples.

Functional use of language. Yuen and Mei facilitated and encouraged children's spontaneous reading and writing. Functional reading and writing could be observed in different parts of the children's daily lives: during work, in centers, in personal business, and in social interaction. The following are some of the examples of functional uses of language: signing up for use of the equipment or participation in an activity; documenting one's work; writing hospital signs, prescriptions, restaurant menus, recipes, or taking orders during dramatic play; developing observational notes; filling in worksheets when necessary in the science center; making memos or lists as reminders; exchanging cards or letters between class members; and making books for certain people as gifts. Signing and giving blessings on friends' "Memory Books" during the graduation season used to be one of the most popular child-initiated literacy activities.

Children learn literacy as a powerful tool to facilitate activities in theme investigation and their learning. In the process of their inquiry, children often read or write to fulfill their purposes. Reading and writing are part of the inquiry process themselves, rather than something to be learned. The following are some examples of the use of literacy through inquiry: writing a letter to a manager in order to get permission to visit a convenience store; completing a personal profile of family members while exploring the theme of "my family;" and reading story books and developing character charts for further discussion when doing an author study. Children would read or write to get information, to organize an activity, and to participate in each other's work.

Authentic learning with real purposes. In considering the authenticity of reading materials, Yuen and Mei abandoned the publisher's packaged teaching materials that the whole kindergarten used to use. They used various authentic materials for reading and writing, including a great amount of children's literature. They actually incorporated literature into the curriculum. Children's books were used to support learning in subject areas and for theme investigations. They purposefully used strategies to promote the children's love of books, through such means as special displays or introductions of new books, popular book elections, audio recordings of stories, dramatizing stories from children's books, and allowing books to be checked out for home reading. They also provided opportunities for the class to explore literature in depth, by examining story elements, the author, the illustrator, and the process of writing stories. With the facilitation and encouragement of teachers, activities emerged naturally from the students' engagement with the literature. One example of authentic learning was a popularity survey of several of Anthony Browne's books conducted by two girls emerging from their lunch table conversations about Browne's work. The rich literate environment in their room provided the children with different kinds of reading and writing experiences for real-life purposes.

A Young Authors' Conference

The second case study was taken from a variety of elementary classrooms. Five first-grade teachers Pei, Huan, Fong, Yi, and Chio have been involved in a collaborative research project with Wen-Yun, (who is a whole language teacher educator). The following was taken from a young authors' conference in which second-grade authors from Su's class, a second-grade teacher at another school, came to visit the first graders.

"Would you please read a little louder? I cannot hear you."

"Slow down a little bit so that I can follow you."

"How many days did it take you to finish the story?"

"I like the title you gave your story. How did you come up with that title?"

These were some of the comments and questions that the first graders had for the second-grade authors who came to read and share their writing at the young authors' conference. Some of these questions were prepared beforehand and written on a memo whereas others emerged during the conference.

The authors' conference began with the children getting into small reading groups. Each group proceeded differently. In some groups, the author read; in other groups, all members read together; in still other groups, the children took turns reading. How each group proceeded was up to the children. The process was not prescribed by the teachers.

After the questions, many first graders lined up and waited patiently for the authors' autographs. The proud authors carefully designed the signatures that they had practiced over and over again during the past month. All that the teachers did in this scene was to beam at the children with excitement and pride.

Behind the Scene

The idea for the young authors' conference began when Su's second graders said to her, "We want to read our books to a larger audience, not just to our classmates." Su mentioned this to her friend Pei. A few days later, Su's class received 175 invitations from five first-grade classes in Pei's school to read at an authors' conference. It was the teachable moment for which the teachers had been waiting.

For two months, teachers and students prepared for the conference. They also had follow-up activities after the conference. The following table lists some of the activities.

	Second Graders	**First Graders**
Before the conference	Wrote stories and recipes Responded to the invitation Became pen pals with the audience Learned from strategy lessons: how to read aloud, how to respond to questions, how to answer clearly	Wrote invitations Became pen pals with the authors Learned from strategy lessons: how to listen, how to ask

		questions, how to interview Prepared a memo with a list of potential questions for the authors Prepared welcome posters, name cards, signs, a school map, and conference scheduling
After the conference	Wrote thank-you letters Talked about the conference Wrote reflections about the conference Continued pen pal writing	Wrote thank-you letters Talked about the conference Wrote reflections about the conference Read the books made by the second graders Wrote responses to the second graders' books Continued pen pal writing

The Pedagogical Framework

The steps that teachers and students took in the process of the young authors' conference revealed some of the pedagogical frameworks that these teachers utilized. The major ones are presented below.

Authentic learning with real purposes. Keeping learning meaningful and relevant was a major concern for the teachers as were reading and writing for different audiences and purposes. In their classes, the children had been writing stories and letters, posters and signs, but many of these activities were still forced and make-believe rather than real. The young authors' conference offered a multitude of real purposes and related learning activities. Some examples of this: the invitation, pen pals, audience, and feedback were authentic; the memos were practical; and the autographs were formal and very grown-up.

Signing autographs was not originally on the program, but Su's keen kidwatching revealed that the second graders felt that their audience might ask for autographs and had also noticed that signing their names was different from writing their names. They began to practice making their signatures look cool. The hint was passed along to the first graders who loved the idea and the autograph session was added to the conference schedule. This episode demonstrated that the authenticity of the situation was a critical motivation to explore penmanship and was applied to other aspects of their learning as well.

Becoming independent learners by learning how to learn. While preparing for the conference, the first graders made many posters to help them make use of their literacy learning. These posters were the results of strategy lessons on "how to listen," "how to interview a person," and "how to talk in a small group." The posters helped them become independent learners by reminding them of what they needed to do. They only needed to look at the posters to remember, so the posters freed them from the teacher. Gradually, children learned to take notes as reminders. The memos on what questions to ask the young authors were like posters that they could carry around with them. Gradually, the children's teachers changed from people to posters to memos to an internal reminder within themselves, and the children became their own teachers.

Learning in a learning community. At the conference, children learned from each other. The second graders wrote for a specific audience, read to them, and received feedback. The children learned not from writing conferences with their teachers but from each other and from children in other learning communities. The teachers did not need to check their work. The other learners did it.

The first graders learned how to be real listeners. "Please keep your voice at the proper volume while we all speak at the same time," a first grader suddenly said to remind the community that as many small groups began to read aloud, the conference room was getting noisy. This was how children became teachers for one other.

Teachers as kidwatchers and facilitators. The conference itself was very much the children's. The teachers were there as facilitators. They simply stayed on the sidelines to assist with equipment and time control and sometimes sat beside a shy student who needed support speaking to strangers.

The conference preparation and participation provided rich data for kidwatchers. The autograph signing was a result of kidwatching during the action research process. Another example was the miscue analysis opportunities. Normally, teachers asked children to read to them in order to analyze and assist children in their reading development. The conference allowed teachers to gather information about each child's oral reading, evaluate her potential when highly motivated to perform for an audience and her actual performance under public scrutiny. In Fong's words: "The children are our informants. After we saw them in action, we didn't follow the textbook any more; instead, we began to teach by following our children."

Changing Curriculum

The young authors' conference was an indicator of how far the teachers had come from their traditional mode of teaching through action research. It showed up in their use of instructional resources, their teaching methods for reading and writing, and the way they interacted with their children. They made such comments as: "A critical aspect of our changing curriculum is that we see children differently from how we used to see them." "Whole language helps us see our students." "I have changed not only as a teacher, but as a mother." These quotes were drawn from conversations recorded in the teachers' meetings. The following table gives some examples of the changes in their literacy curriculum.

Former Curriculum	Present Curriculum
The textbook was the major teaching resource.	The textbook was only one kind of learning resource along with trade books and other authentic texts.
The teacher closely followed the teacher's manual step-by-step without making connections with students' experiences.	The teacher taught by following the students' lead instead of the textbook.
Students practiced listening, speaking, reading, and writing for instructional purposes, focusing on mechanisms of language.	Students listened, spoke, read, and wrote for communication, focusing on meaning construction.
The teacher directed the discussion by asking factual recall questions.	The teacher facilitated discussion by encouraging students to explore their thoughts.
The teacher was the only audience for students' writing. She gave grades and corrected mechanical errors.	There were various kinds of audiences for students' writing. The audience responded to meaning.
The teacher was an authoritarian.	The teacher was a kidwatcher and facilitator.

From the above two illustrations, along with data from other classrooms, we have traced some common phenomena among teachers and children in many classrooms in which the teachers tried whole language teaching.

The Teachers' Development

To many teachers, becoming a whole language teacher was a continuous process of professional development involving the pursuit of knowledge, self-reflection, kidwatching, sharing, decision making, and readjusting. Their first decision to try whole language teaching often resulted from reflecting about their teaching over the years. For example, Yuen and Mei in the previous kindergarten case study reflected after several years of teaching:

> We are getting to a point where teaching has become routine. We feel we are doing the same thing over again each year. Nothing is exciting any more. It seems that we could better facilitate children's learning than we're doing. But we are not sure what and how to do it.

First grade teachers Fong and Huan reflected on their teaching and stated:

> We knew the way we taught, following mandated textbooks and teacher's manuals, did not fit our students' needs, but we just did not feel secure enough to stray from the mandated curriculum.

Their dissatisfaction and high self-expectation turned into strong drives to seek something more fulfilling for both themselves and the children with whom they worked. To teachers like Yuen, Mei, Fong, and Huan, whole language thus became a choice after they first learned about it. Whole language helped these teachers to see their ability to learn and to teach. They no longer were limited to the textbook and did not solely follow the teacher's manual to teach. Instead, they saw their work as a profession with which they made decisions necessary to facilitate children's learning. Fong and Huan stated:

> Whole language helped us to value ourselves as teachers and to value the professional knowledge we had. Now we know how to make instructional decisions through kidwatching, reflecting, and learning with our students.

Another motivation that drove them to continue to be whole language teachers was their observations of the ways in which their students changed over time. Whole language teachers learned to be kidwatchers who had lenses that captured the children's needs and strengths. They understood children better. It was often the children's change in their learning attitudes, abilities, and sometimes of their whole beings that convinced these teachers that whole language was helpful to children.

Upon deciding to do whole language teaching, teachers needed to face several realities which could be also sources of problems, including: (a) professional preparation and adequacy, (b) the administration, (c) peers, and (d) parents.

Most teachers who devoted themselves to whole language teaching strongly desired to be better equipped with more whole-language-related knowledge and teaching strategies. In Yuen and Mei's story, they were concerned at one time or another about their inadequacy when organizing an activity. This awareness led them to more professional book reading and discussion. A challenge or obstacle often turned out to be a motivation or a force for self-education and growth that pushed their professional development.

Problems also arose from the administration when a teacher implemented whole language. Curriculum consistency throughout all of the grades or classes was a policy in most schools. Requiring teachers to teach the same textbooks created more difficulties in terms of time and energy for both students and teachers who wanted to facilitate more student-centered learning. High expectations on test performance added more pressure. Teacher autonomy was not favored yet in many school cultures.

Another source of pressure came from peers. Peer pressure was reflected in some of the school culture. Issues such as comparison, competition, reluctance to change, or sometimes fear arose among the teachers. In many schools whole language teachers performed a different kind of teaching which demanded more commitment from teachers and, on the other hand, more professional autonomy. To their peers whole language teaching could be seen as a risk that some would want to take. Resistance also came from the fear of some teachers that they might be asked to live up to the standards of the whole language teachers. In Yuen and Mei's case, their director decided to have all of the kindergarten classes shift to whole language in the interest of consistency. Under this policy, Yuen and Mei felt pressured by some of their peers. A few teachers complained about not having enough resources for teaching in an unfamiliar way and about terminating the use of packaged teaching materials. Some of the frustration turned into a negative force against the new curriculum.

To solve the problems from the administration and their peers, whole language teachers needed to be more open to share their thinking as well as their work. Presenting what they did with students and how students reacted to their colleagues at different grade levels helped to ease tensions among them. Yuen and Mei's devotion to sharing with administrators and peers later helped their school to become a more whole-language-oriented kindergarten.

Those first-grade teachers decided to work collaboratively with other non-whole-language teachers with the hopes of coming to an agreement.

Parents usually were considered the major source of problems in most curriculum-related change in the past because they were concerned with their children's skill and test performances. Many teachers presumed that they had to worry about the parents and how to negotiate with them since the students would demonstrate their learning in very different ways when they first began learning in a whole language classroom. Contrary to what they anticipated, whole language teachers received support from the parents rather than objection to their new way of teaching after they explained their changing beliefs. Ongoing communication between teacher and parent was essential.

In the past, most parents were quite demanding about their children's literacy skill performances before whole language was applied. Most teachers maintained close communication with parents. In their kindergarten, Yuen and Mei planned a year-round parent education and involvement program when they started to do whole language in order to minimize problems from the parents. Their plan included ongoing communication in various forms with parents about what was happening in the class and what could be expected from their children. They provided parents many references and children's work samples to show growth. They also involved parents in helping their children read and write at home. With the information that the teachers provided and after seeing the evidence of their children's growth and love of schooling, parents were convinced that the new program was better for their children. They were generous in expressing their confidence in the new program and actually gave support to teachers, administrators, and other parents.

Change in the Children

Many whole language teachers indicated that one of the most important strengths that kept them insisting on whole language was their awareness of change in the children. Yuen and Mei found their children changed over time in many different ways. At the early stage they developed (a) a better attitude toward schooling; (b) more confidence in themselves as learners, readers, and writers; (c) overall better language abilities; and (d) a love of books. By the middle of the school year, these children demonstrated that they (a) were independent and active learners and risk-takers; (b) had high interest in learning and actively participated in classroom activities; (c) developed a willingness and a capability to cooperate with others in work; and (d) were emotionally more stable. As Yuen and Mei looked back on the children's overall performance by the end of school year, they found, in addition to the above changes, that these children developed better control of themselves and over their relationship with others. They also concluded that children actually learned more in that year than when they were taught in years past (Lee, 2000c). Similar findings were also true in the other teachers' experiences. All were fascinated with how much children gained when the power of learning was handed to them. With autonomy over their own learning, along with the teachers' facilitation of material and opportunity, the children took control of their own learning and were highly motivated. They appeared to be masters of their own learning. Yuen's understanding of the children demonstrated how well whole language facilitated the children's learning:

> To me whole language means that everyone has an equal opportunity to learn. All can have a sense of achievement. Everyone can have an individual learning opportunity and equal opportunity to succeed. With these opportunities children know how to express their thinking freely. All children learn what they want to learn in a natural and spontaneous way. They really can get it!

Su in the second-grade case study also documented how learners who struggle learned with confidence in a whole language classroom. She stated:

> I found my slow learners learned very well with support from their peers. They soon developed confidence in their learning. Whole language nurtures a safe and trustworthy environment for every child. It enables both students and teachers to see the strength of everyone and that is what we treasure the most.

Notes from the Teachers

Becoming whole language teachers is a long-term learning process that is never-ending. It is also a process of taking charge of one's own learning and development. Through this process, teachers learn more about their students and how they learn, their own role as supporters, and what good teaching is about. They also recognize their role in their own professional development and learn how to take initiative in different aspects in their career to defend their good teaching on behalf of children. Mei and other teachers in the previous case studies appreciate being whole language teachers. Mei commended her own teaching after doing whole language for a year:

> This is a BIG step in my professional development as an early childhood teacher! Teaching is no longer only a job. It's a creative endeavor and an attitude. I have wanted to change for several years but just didn't know how. Now, I don't have to change the curriculum completely, I don't have to completely change what I was doing, and I can see all these changes in children and in my classroom. I feel great about myself and about my teaching. Now I always want to try something new out in my class. I get excited often and can't wait to come to school to be with my kids. I greatly enjoy watching them grow. I see only good things among them now.

This passion for teaching was what encouraged Mei to be a whole language teacher. This was true for many others who devoted themselves to helping children and themselves become true learners.

The TAWL Group

As mentioned earlier, 1996 was a milestone year for the development of whole language in Taiwan. In January of 1996, a series of workshops given by international scholars of whole language was held at Taipei and Tainan. Through these workshops, Dr. Goodman and other local educators provided an in-depth knowledge base as well as practical experiences to participants. Through these workshops, whole language was formally introduced to people in the field of education in this country. Responses from the audience and readers were tremendous. Interest from different parts of the country greatly increased for further understanding of the whole language theoretical base and for whole language teaching support. Educators who were interested in whole language started to get together to share their ideas.

Organization

The first teachers' group was formed in June of 1996, five months after the workshop, at one of the workshop sites, Tainan. Organized by Lian-Ju, it was entitled "Teachers Applying Whole Language, Southern Taiwan." Teachers (mostly in early childhood education), educators from universities, and researchers from research institutions gathered to pursue their interests in whole language. Initially, there were approximately 40 teachers and educators in the group. They gathered to read professional books, to discuss and share their thinking about whole language teaching, to address and discuss their concerns about curriculum and teaching, and to share their teaching ideas and experiences. They met three times each semester in order to prepare for, reflect on, reorganize, and evaluate their own teaching.

The organization of this TAWL group played an important role in the professional development of the participating teachers. It provided an opportunity for teachers to have input on and to shape their professional knowledge, through participating in lectures and workshops, sharing reading, and discussion. It was also an opportunity for them to reflect on their own teaching, as well as to gain support from each other.

The number of members grew as time passed. As a Tainan-based local group, the number of teachers this group served was limited. Upon greater demand for a broader service, TAWL of Southern Taiwan proceeded to become a nationwide organization.

In September 2000, TAWL of Southern Taiwan officially registered with and was approved by the government as a nationwide educational association. Its Chinese title was then changed to "The Association for the Study and Development of Whole Language Education, Republic of China." This meant that it served members from all over the nation and was organizationally and fiscally under the supervision of the government. However, its English title—TAWL, ROC—was partially reserved to represent the unchanged nature of this group. Regardless of these organizational changes, the group functioned in a similar way for teachers, except the number of members grew. In the first year of reorganization, there were around 120 registered members. At the point of this writing, there are over 200 registered members.

The growing number of members indicated two facts about whole language in this country: more educators and teachers were interested in whole language, and the whole language teachers' group had gained recognition to a certain degree in the community of education. The recognition was accumulated via various paths: presentations by members of the association in different workshops at different places and the exchange of information in formal and informal teachers' gathering. Recognition was given not only to the group but to individual members as well. Some of the teachers in the group earned a reputation for being good teachers and took on lead roles in whole language teaching. They played important roles in modeling and promoting whole language to teachers in different settings.

Service

In the last several years, either prior to or after the reorganization, TAWL provided teachers services in many different ways, through regular meetings, study groups, conferences, and publications. Regular meetings, three times each semester, have been established from the beginning. Various study groups were also formed and reorganized each year, focusing on topics selected by the teachers.

As old members grew more experienced and new members continued to join, the way teachers supported each other progressed. Three new services were developed a few years later: a published journal, a mobile library, and a formal annual conference. In the fall of 2001, the first edition of a semiannual journal was published, titled *Whole Language*. The journal was intended to reflect how the TAWL group functioned. It included articles in whole language theory and teaching practice, reviews of children's books and professional books, and responses to professional books. It also included a column to respond to questions about whole language or issues in education. As a benefit to members, it documented each regular meeting and provided avenues for announcing TAWL affairs.

The mobile library was established to facilitate teachers' self-growth in professional knowledge. A bibliography of books and articles related to whole language theory and practice and audio and videotapes released from workshops in language curriculum and instruction were collected. A thoroughly annotated electronic database of published children's books was established. These references were provided for members to check out.

The annual conference was a formal way in which teachers could systematically present their growth or accomplishments in whole language teaching. It was also an effective way to share with others and to help new teachers grow. The first annual conference took place in September of 2002 at the TAWL headquarters in Tainan. Volunteer teachers signed up to present examples of their teaching practice at the conference. There were keynote speeches, workshops, and sessions with different subjects and themes. This conference was funded in part by the Ministry of Education and opened to the public for free. TAWL hosted a maximum number of participants on the conference day and received much positive feedback from participants.

Since 1996, TAWL has influenced teachers and classroom practice, especially early childhood classrooms in southern Taiwan. There are now great numbers of whole language teachers participating in TAWL. Through participating in TAWL activities as well as informal sharing on other occasions, these teachers demonstrate what good teaching is about and how to create a community of support. Their commitment and achievements have gained recognition and respect. They develop and, as a result, also model whole language teaching to some degree. To many other teachers, whole language no longer is just a kind of theory and applying whole language into practice is no more just an educational ideal that is hard if not impossible to achieve. It can become a true story in real schools if the teachers are willing.

Whole Language and Educational Reform

From an educational and sociological point of view, educational reform goes hand in hand with social revolution. For the past 20 years, Taiwan's political, economical and social situations have been changing rapidly. Following the withdrawal of martial law in 1987, the country has been moving toward a more open and democratic society. The educational system was fortunately not an exception to this trend.

New Policies

The current educational reform emerged from a bottom-up movement, the "April 10th (# 410) Educational Reform Demonstration" in 1994. The central government responded to 410 as well as public voices with many policy changes. In 1994, the Teacher Education Act opened up preservice teacher education to all universities. Before 1994, only graduates of the three normal universities and nine teachers colleges could be certified teachers. This brought greater diversity, new perspectives, and alternative voices into the teaching profession. In 1995, the Teachers Act allowed teachers to form unions to raise issues of their rights and privileges. This act brought democracy to schools and campuses; the changes in elementary and secondary schools have been especially important. In 1996, legislation allowed the public sector to write and publish textbooks for elementary schools. Teachers and parents can now choose textbooks for their children. Before this, the entire country used the same set of textbooks, written by government-appointed committees. In 1998, the announcement of the new Nine-Year Curriculum Guidelines gave further decentralization and deregulation of power in education.

The Ministry of Education and local governments have been promoting policies such as open education, small classes, small schools, school-based curricula, and promoting integration of learning and learning-centered curricula. Integrated and multiple forms of evaluation that emphasize flexibility and multiplicity are also promoted.

In general, the new educational policy strongly advocates the empowerment of teachers as instructors and curriculum designers to create meaningful and functional curricula and learning experiences. It also emphasizes the empowerment of students as capable learners, ideas compatible with the philosophy of whole language education.

New Practices

With the rapid growth of international communication, parents have been pushing local governments to start teaching English at the primary school instead of the secondary school. Since Teaching English as a Foreign Language (EFL) to young children is new territory in Taiwan, no limits are set to new approaches. Whole language, therefore, has become the new pedagogy favored by teachers.

Whole language is not only studied in most of the programs for EFL preservice and in-service teachers; it is also shared in programs for early childhood teachers. Moreover, it is often a hot topic in non-governmentally organized teachers' workshops.

With the publication of the Chinese version of *What's Whole in Whole Language?* (Goodman, 1986) translated by Lian-Ju in 1998, whole language has made an impact on the curriculum, influencing teaching and learning in various fields and at different levels. For example, there have been over 20 masters' theses with whole language in the title, as indicated in an earlier section. In addition, many papers and articles have been published about practicing whole language in Taiwan.

Although there are misunderstandings about whole language—for example, whole language has been equated to teaching with trade books and with using an integrative curriculum—most teachers know that whole language is a philosophy, a pedagogy of constructivism that focuses on meaningful learning, child-centered curriculums, and print-rich environments. It is a good sign that whole language seems to be an ideal pedagogy about which many teachers dream.

It is quite obvious that educational reform in Taiwan is progressing at breakneck speed. Whenever there is rapid reform, theory and practice cannot keep up with the change. Although the solid theory of whole language education is not yet clearly understood by most of the educators in Taiwan, with the cries of educational reforms in the air, the trend of teacher action research, and the encouragement to teach flexibly, we see hope for whole language in Taiwan.

The Future of Whole Language in Taiwan

Whole language in Taiwan has not yet become the mainstream in either early childhood or elementary education in the past 13 years. However, its influences to the field of education can be observed and will continue.

To many teachers, whole language has opened new ideas of learning, teaching, parent-teacher relationship, curriculum, and professional development. As whole language teachers continue to apply whole language principles in their teaching, they open windows to good teaching. They demonstrate to other teachers, parents, and administrators that a more learner-centered curriculum facilitates learning and at the same time can produce successful learning outcomes. Many whole language teachers present successful cases of developing teacher-student, parent-teacher, and teacher-peer partnerships.

Another observed influence extends to curriculum development, textbook publication, and staff development programs. Some well-trained whole language teachers bring their whole language views of curriculum and teaching to their work when they are involved in developing curriculum, writing textbooks, or in-service teacher training for the government or publishers. As a result, the whole language philosophy is more visible and influential to a broader domain and to more users and recipients.

As in other parts of the world, to many teachers in this country whole language is a professional choice. This choice operates, however, in different ways. For teachers who are not bound by mandated curriculum, such as most kindergarten teachers, whole language can be a free choice in their professions. For elementary school teachers who are convinced by the whole language philosophy but are obliged to teach the mandated curriculum, applying some of its principles when possible is their way to announce their educational beliefs. Furthermore, some teachers try and are successful in convincing their administrators and parents to put off textbook bondage. They are able to use trade books as well as various authentic texts to replace mandated textbooks. These whole language teachers earned support from their principals and parents with their professional knowledge and, convincingly, their students' learning performances.

Although whole language as a curriculum policy nationwide may have a long way to go at this point, whole language as a choice by teachers is a fact in many different educational settings and is expected to be the choice of more teachers in the future.

The change of social environment could also create positive conditions for whole language to be more broadly accepted in Taiwan. This includes changes on the micro level—that is, change within school context—as well as on the macro level, that being change beyond the school context in the educational system. As with all educational reforms in the past, the development of whole language in Taiwan is up against a major obstacle: testing- and textbook-led teaching and learning as described in the first section of this chapter. The narrow view of teaching and evaluation has stopped many elementary and secondary teachers from trying anything beyond textbooks and test content in their classrooms. They don't want their students and themselves to fail tests, causing possible pressure from administrators and parents. Changing this narrow view toward teaching and learning is still one of the major tasks for teachers and teacher educators who want whole language to be the choice of more teachers. Continual communication between teachers, administrators, and parents is necessary at places where teachers hesitate to take actions.

Change within school, however, is interrelated to change in the larger socioeducational context in which school is embedded. If teachers need to fight with the system outside of the classroom, attention and energy are taken away from teaching. Teachers need support within and by the system when they move towards change. From this point of view, whole language seems to have a chance of being rooted at this time. While new educational policies are announced, as indicated in the above section, a more open and empowering environment is gradually forming where teachers have more autonomy over their work. They have more options concerning their teaching. With necessary changes beginning to take place and the system becoming more supportive for teachers, the last question then would turn back to the teacher. Whether or not teachers are willing to commit themselves to support true learning in their classrooms becomes the most crucial factor for implementing whole language or other pedagogical improvements. And this is only up to teachers.

References

Chao, H. H. (1994, May). *Whole language education: A possible alternative*. Paper presented at the Annual Conference on Education for Teacher's Colleges and Normal Universities in Taiwan, National Tainan Teachers College, Taiwan.

Goodman, K. (1986). *What's whole in whole language?* Portsmouth, NH: Heinemann.

Hung, G. R. (1997). *Whole language in USA elementary school.* Unpublished masters thesis, National Taiwan Normal University, Taipei, Taiwan.

Lee, L. J. (2000a, July). *A program reform to facilitate literacy and learning among kindergarten children.* Paper presented at the 18th World Congress on Reading, Auckland, New Zealand.

— (2000b, November). *The history of the development of whole language in Taiwan: Looking back and looking forward.* Paper presented at the Conference of Language in Learning and Teaching of Science and Math: Whole Language Perspective, National Chang-Hwua Normal University, Taiwan.

— (2000c, June). *Whole language and whole language kindergarten: A case study of a kindergarten becoming whole language kindergarten.* Paper presented at the International Conference of K-12 Language Education and Integrated Curriculum, National Taitung Teachers College, Taiwan.

Shen, T. J. (1997, October). *The influence of whole language to writing attitude and ability among fifth graders.* Paper presented at the Conference of Teaching Strategy and Practice on Chinese Language Arts, Laboratory School of National Chiayi Teachers College, Taiwan.

Tseng, Y. H. (2000). *English language arts for children: Whole language perspective.* Taipei,Taiwan:Wu-Nan.

CHAPTER EIGHT

The Politics and Passion
of How Johnny Should Read

DENNY TAYLOR

O n April 23, 1997 James Collins of *Time Magazine* interviewed Ken and Yetta Goodman. During the interview Ken and Yetta Goodman answered questions that focused on [1] their personal and professional lives; [2] the epistemological foundations of their miscue research and their research on reading as a transactional, socio-psycholinguistic process; and [3] the roles they played in the development of the whole language movement. The Goodmans also provided critical understandings from their own perspective of the differences that exist—ideological, epistemological, theoretical, and pedagogical—between researchers and teachers who are holistic in their pedagogy and researchers and teachers who focus more on a skills approach to early reading instruction.

The interview provides insights into the contribution of the media to right-wing policy changes of the current administration through federal and state laws and policies that undermine the participatory emancipating principles that many of us expect to frame reading instruction in America's schools. It also sheds light on the complexities of the political shift that is taking place. My own analysis of the interview, as an ethnographer and social theorist who supports whole language but is not a whole language teacher, is presented in a fictional interview that takes place in 2027. It is written to be provocative as well as informative, to encourage discussion and other imaginings of the future of our struggle for a participatory democracy as well as the ways in which we teach and children learn to read and write. In the car park on the way to lunch Jim Collins said that in a good article there had to be sides, and that he was interested in reading because it was a case study in politics and passion. He said a story must touch the emotions but he never talked about fair representation, or accuracy, or truth. Based on his recommendations for the construction of a story this chapter is presented as a case study in politics and passion that will touch the emotions, but I have also tried to ensure fair representation, accuracy, and truth. Of course, the second interview is fictional but the information contained in the interview is at least a version of the truth. Jim Collins gave his permission for me to audio record the interview which lasted approximately eight hours. Excerpts from the transcript are presented without commentary. In my representation of the interview I have focused on semantic authenticity. I have kept to a minimum the imposition of syntactical structure and inserted punctuation. Now it's time to go to the University of Arizona, take the elevator to the fifth floor to Ken's office where the interview takes place.

Jim Collins: We're doing a story about reading. [It's] shaping up to be a fairly big story. A big story. We're focusing. Right now we have some other reporter going around Texas. Seems to me politically there's a lot of activity. We've got reporters in California. Some other places but we're trying to find one case study or local where politics and passions come together. Texas seems like the place.

Yetta: California's like that too. They are both diverse states and they are both very large.

Jim Collins: Yes. Well, California seems to us to have gone through this process a little bit. But it's not over obviously.

Yetta: California has already passed their laws. They're just passing [them] now.

Jim Collins: That's why we're interested in Texas. I think that what I'd like to talk about. First of all I'd like to get a little bit about whole language history. And origins. And this pervasiveness. I know you have strong feelings about that. [Laughs] But first who you are?

Yetta: I did a history of whole language a number of years ago and Ken did something on the research of whole language because people kept saying that there was no research on whole language. So, those are two pieces that might be helpful to you.

Ken: And then there's something else we did fairly recently on miscue.

Jim Collins: Oh, okay.

Ken: We need to talk about miscue analysis with you.

Jim Collins: Oh yes. Sure. I read about it. And one of the questions I want to ask you actually is where the research is?

Yetta: There's no question that miscue analysis was Ken's invention; I worked with him probably from the beginning, although we weren't working together. I sort of bootlegged working with Ken.

Jim Collins: And when did you get married?

Yetta: '52.

Jim Collins: '52? [Collins sounds surprised.]

Ken: We're going to celebrate our 45th wedding anniversary next week.

Jim Collins: And just some personal stuff. How did you meet?

Yetta: We met at day camps. We were both working with children in Jewish day camps in Los Angeles. I was 18. 17. Ken was 21. And we both worked in Jewish day camps for about 15 years. In Los Angeles.

Jim Collins: Is that where you're both from?

Yetta: No.

Ken: Well, we grew up in the Midwest. I grew up in Detroit and Yetta grew up in Cleveland.

Yetta: And we both moved to California and we found each other there at day camps. And we both taught in LA County and LA city schools from 1950. [Yetta looks at Ken] You started in '51?

Ken: 1950.

Yetta: Our histories are different at this point. I taught for ten years in LA schools and Ken moved into social work for a period of time before he went back to teaching.

Jim Collins: What grade did you teach?

Yetta: I taught junior high. And I went *up* to elementary school.

Ken: We both worked with kids in a wide range of levels.

Yetta: In day camps we worked with kids of all ages. Then we were both day-camp directors. In many ways I believe that holistic teaching was informed by the kinds of things that social work does. Where you're concerned with kids' growth and their social relationships as much as you are about their academic growth. That doesn't mean that academic growth is secondary. It just means you're concerned about both.

Ken: My doctorate was from UCLA. And Yetta's doctorate was '67.

Yetta: At Wayne State University. Where Ken was a professor. My dissertation was the first dissertation done on miscue analysis. There have been hundreds and hundreds of them since. But mine was the first. Ken was *not* on my committee.

Jim Collins: [laughs]

Ken: One of the things about being at Wayne State in Detroit in the early '60's, at the time when the Civil Rights Movement was strong, and in a place where there was a heavy interest in urban education and minority education.

Yetta: And dialects.

Ken: And we did research in urban schools in Detroit and in Highland Park, Michigan. I don't know if you know the Detroit area but Highland Park is an urban suburb. It's surrounded by the city and we worked from the very beginning with interracial populations. Partly because we wanted to try and understand the reading process from the point of view of a full range of kids. Not just kids who had difficulty or didn't have difficulty.

Yetta: And that's why Ken really was so interested in kids that people would say had difficulty reading. And, because of our backgrounds in camps, and because of our own working-class backgrounds both Ken and I felt that we couldn't just say that poor kids, or Black kids, or working-class kids can't read. We wanted to understand why. What were the issues? And so, Ken started miscue analysis trying to answer that question.

Ken: In trying to answer the question we didn't start with what I would call intervention kinds of research. What we were studying was the actual process of how kids read. I was developing a background in linguistics and psycholinguistics to try to understand reading as a language process. And so we did very extensive in-depth kinds of studies of kids reading material they hadn't seen before. And we tried to describe the process.

Yetta: Most of the tests that are done on kids reading are done on passages, and because of Ken's work the passages are longer today than ever before. The passages may be three or four paragraphs, but miscue analysis has always been done on a complete text, a complete story, a complete article. So that we could see what happens to a reader as the reader engages a text across a whole piece. And that is what is so unique about miscue analysis, and still to this day nobody else has done this kind of work.

Ken: There are two major camps now on reading. From the beginning the mainstream research on reading was done by psychologists, who used experimental designs, who needed to control very carefully what it was that [kids] were responding to. That kind of research focused on words. They devised various experiments looking at how kids recognized words. By using a much more holistic view I was looking at how kids read text and made sense of it as well as recognize words. We get very different findings from very different kinds of research. And it's still true. There's the kind of research that Marilyn Adams (1990) in her book that is all focused on the word as the unit. So you have two very different views emerging of reading as a process, of making sense of print, and their view of studying reading as recognizing words. Marilyn Adams says this at the beginning of her book, that reading is about recognizing words that caused her to dismiss not only our research but a large body of reading research.

Yetta: She does quote my early literacy research but she never quotes any miscue research.

Ken: So we have a body of research that went on for some time and there were several major funding grants. One grant was the study of second-to tenth-grade readers and then we had another major grant.

Jim Collins: When was that?

Ken: They were both in the '70's. The two reports were published in '72 and '78.

Jim Collins: The federal government?

Yetta: Yes, were from NIE. National Institute of Education at that time.

Ken: And in the second one we used eight different populations and four second-language groups. We had Navajo, Samoan kids and Spanish-speaking kids in Texas.

Yetta: Arabic kids in Detroit.

Ken: Then four different dialect groups. Rural Black, Down East Maine, Appalachian, and Pigeon speakers in Hawaii.

Yetta: And Samoan kids. Did you consider those second language?

Ken: Yes. So there was a very broad base of research. And then Yetta's research began to look at kids learning to read, not being taught to read, but learning to read. In a sense, how did kids begin to read growing up in a literate society with print all around them? How did they begin to respond to that and her research paralleled research that was going on in other parts of the world.

Yetta: One of the really interesting things, an interesting research phenomenon, is that when you start a research project that you think is sort of unique and you look around you find other people are doing similar things. It's almost as if the question is such a big one that everybody's asking the same question. So Marie Clay (1987, 1991) was doing similar research. You know Marie Clay? She was doing similar research to Ken's work in New Zealand that Ken was doing here. And then I began to do early print research working with kids as young as two, three, four, and five, walking out in the streets with them and taking them to the supermarket and then cutting out pieces from newspapers and magazine pieces and asking what do they see when they see McDonalds?

Ken: How they respond to print.

Yetta: Is literacy something you learn in school or is literacy a history of becoming literate? Of course, that's our position, that literacy is a social cultural phenomenon, and it doesn't start in school. The school extends it, supports it, or doesn't support it. Some teaching is negative. Then there are researchers doing similar kinds of things. There's a researcher, she's actually Argentinean but she lives in Mexico City, by the name of Emilia Ferreiro (1982).

Jim Collins: How do you spell her name?

Yetta: F-e-r-r-e-i-r-o. Emilia Ferreiro's work is so important and none of the researchers related to phonics reference her at all. She has a group of researchers who work with her, who live in Brazil, Argentina, Italy, Switzerland, France, Israel, and Spain. All of their research supports our research and helps us understand that children learn to make sense out of the world.

Ken: And because they are maturing in a literate society.

Jim Collins: And Adams?

Yetta: I don't see her talking about what kids learn. I see her talking about how to teach kids.

Ken: Basically she's summarizing research on instructional strategies and experiments.

Jim Collins: Let me just go back a minute. In the '70's you were doing miscue analysis research. What was that system? What was the typical? You know?

Ken: Of miscue analysis?

Jim Collins: Well, I guess I have a sense of it reading your studies.

Ken: Let me take you back through a little bit of history. The research we were doing was to look at the reading process. So over a period of several studies we developed a very complex taxonomy to analyze the miscues.

Yetta: Ken, do you want to back up? Do you want to know how we collected the data itself?

Jim Collins: Well, I just, well, I do, I do, I have a sense about this research.

Yetta: Right. Generally we sit down with one kid. We're in a school. We've selected stories. The kid reads from the actual text and we tape it. It can be a basal reader. It can be a storybook.

Ken: We would go back over and over the tape until we were sure that we have a reasonably accurate transcription of everything that went on.

Yetta: We've used newspaper articles. We've used magazine articles. I have a *Time* article that we used.

Jim Collins: What grade level? (Laughs) No, don't tell me.

Yetta: High school. No, I've used a *Time* article.

Jim Collins: *Time Magazine* is so horribly low. [Laughs]

Yetta: So we sit and the kid is reading in the book and we're taping the child. Then we make a printed transcript of the text. Then we listen to the tape recording of the kid reading and jot down the kid's miscues.

Ken: Miscues are anything unexpected that the reader does.

Yetta: And we've been avoiding saying that a miscue is a mistake, or that a kid makes a mistake in the text, because it's not simply a mistake. It's the child's, the reader's construction of the text. People say it's a deviation from the text and it's not just a deviation. We make a thing about that. Then when the kid goes back to their classroom we take the miscue data back to our research offices. As Ken said before we listen to the tape over and over again and we try to understand what the kid does. We ask what does a reader have to know to make the kinds of miscue they make. And I say readers because we haven't just done this research with children. On the research bibliography you'll see we have research on senior citizens, people who *are* considered good readers, or poor readers, or average readers. There are studies that have been done on miscue analysis in many other languages now around the world.

Ken: There is an interim point here. We were looking at the reading process. So as we did miscue analysis, I was developing the theory of reading. What I was trying to do was understand from the point of view of the reader the way a text works and how a reader is transacting with the text. How meaning is constructed. As we were doing this kids were surprising us because there were things that they were doing that we hadn't expected.

Jim Collins: And the fundamental lesson of the mistakes that readers make, if I were to say what we learn is that they do not need all the visual information.

Ken: That's one of the primary things. Right. It's not any different than what you do when you understand speech, because you can't possibly process all the information. What you do is sample from what you learned, what is the most useful information. You construct meaning as you do it and that leads to very efficient and effective strategies for making sense. So reading is never an issue of recognizing some serial sense of the word. It's always focusing on how you get to the meaning. You have a sense, as you do with hearing, that you've heard the details but we can demonstrate very easily that you don't. I wrote a paragraph that I used where I had six errors.

Yetta: Did you see that paragraph?

Jim Collins: Yes.

Yetta: We believe that readers are constantly interpreting when they read. You don't read and then interpret and comprehend. You are constantly interpreting while you are reading.

Ken: You're making sense. Constructing meaning. Interpreting.

Jim Collins: But again how would you characterize Adams' view?

Ken: I call it scientific word recognition. Adams (1990) and Stanovich (1988). She says it very clear. Reading is a matter of seeing every letter in every word.

Yetta: They believe that readers see every letter in every word. We just don't find that in miscue analysis data. Readers tend to look like they're very accurate, but they are accurate because they are such good readers, not because they are seeing every letter in every word.

Ken: It also is the issue I mentioned before of whether you consider reading to be the analysis of words, recognizing words, or the analysis is of a whole text. Those are very different kinds of things.

Yetta: And when Ken uses the word "text" he's not talking about textbooks. Do you understand the concept of a text?

Jim Collins: Stories?

Yetta: It's a linguistic term.

Ken: Articles. Stories. Anything that's an authentic text which has some meaning.

Yetta: Some linguists even use "text" now to mean oral language discourse. In a sense what we are doing here as we talk to each other is building text.

Jim Collins: Miscue analysis led you to the conclusion that people don't use all the visual information. You said that was one of the big findings. So maybe I should ask what are the other major findings?

Ken: I describe proficient reading as having two aspects to it. One is that it has to be effective. That means you have to be able to make sense of what you are reading. And that's my definition of effectiveness. But it also has to be efficient, and efficiency is using only as much information as you need to be effective. That's where the issue of how much visual information do you need becomes important.

Yetta: Efficiency is related to the visual information. How much you need to make sense. Effectiveness is related to how much knowledge you have. This is what other people in reading call "background knowledge." How much knowledge do you have so that you can read text and understand it? That's being effective as you read.

Ken: And how well you're able to integrate all the information that you're reading.

Yetta: Prediction becomes a very important part of Ken's model. That's another thing that's very important, being able to predict as you read. But, of course, that's because we know that prediction causes miscues. The reader is predicting because it's the author's text. And the thing that Ken has helped us all understand is that the reader is as creative in reading a text as the writer is in writing a text. That's a very hard thing for people to understand because historically reading has been looked at as a receptive process.

Ken: High-school teachers have taught kids that you are supposed to understand the authors' meaning, and what they don't understand is that the kids are constructing their own meaning.

Jim Collins: Okay.

Yetta: If you remember in high school or junior high school, how teachers told you that you have to revere every word that an author wrote because the author spent so much time deciding on that word? No. I don't argue with that. I think the author does spend a lot of time, but that doesn't mean that it has to captivate the reader.

Ken: An important thing in helping people understand literature is the knowledge that each of us has our own response, that's based on our experiences, our values, as well as those of the writer.

Jim Collins: Okay. Going back to the question of miscue analysis that led you to the conclusion that with predictions readers don't need the individual information.

Ken: They don't *use* all the information.

Jim Collins: Don't *use* all the individual information to confirm their prediction. Other than miscue analysis are there other methods of exploring that subject that you feel drawn to?

Yetta: Reader response theory and that's Louise Rosenblatt (1992). There are also some language philosophers. Eco (1976) and Bahktin (1983). We feel the kinds of things that we do are supported by their work.

Ken: And Emilia Ferreiro.

Yetta: Emilia Ferriero's work is so powerful in South America. She talks about interpreting reading.

Ken: The constructive view. Constructing meaning in terms of the research of reading. It's very similar to the research on writing. The research of Don Graves (1982) and Lucy Calkins (1994).

Jim Collins: Where is he?

Yetta: Don Graves was at the University of New Hampshire.

Jim Collins: Oh, that's right.

Yetta: There are lots of people in NCTE who are into writing.

Ken: James Britton (1993) in England.

Yetta: James Britton for England. In fact I was just reading a piece. I just found it yesterday. There's a piece that just came out. In England they are going through a similar problem. They call it the "Real Book Approach." They don't use "Whole Language." So they develop the term Real Book Approach to reading instruction. There are plenty of people in England who have been constructivists. James Britton. Harold Rosen. Margaret Meek (1992). John Dixon. Oh yes, and Nigel Hall.

Ken: There's a lot of work in Australia.

Yetta: Australia. New Zealand.

Ken: There's a lot of different people who have an interest in reading as a process.

Jim Collins: But have you found that people who use other methods of reading analysis. Are there people who say we've done something else with a kid's reading?

Yetta: Marie Clay's (1987, 1991) research is the closest. There is also a whole group of people who are studying the social and cultural contexts in which people read.

Ken: Denny Taylor (1983, 1988, 1998) has done work.

Yetta: Judith Green at Santa Barbara. David Bloome at Vanderbilt.

Ken: A lot of ethnographic studies. They're interested in how literacy is used in cultures and societies. There's a British group. Brian Street (1995) is the most noticeable among them. There is a whole group of people who are going into homes and looking at how literacy is used and how what happens in homes relates to what happens in schools.

Yetta: David Barton (1998).

Ken: David Barton. These are ethnographers. Some of the ethnographers are working in the classrooms like David Bloome. They get involved in teaching and writing situations. Some of them now are looking at literacy and societal kinds of things.

Jim Collins: A quick couple of questions. Let's get back to what the research was like. Going to the kid. Having the kid read. The various studies. Doing this with different kids. Different times. That's pretty much the data collection system?

Ken: The data collection in miscue analysis. We wanted an understanding of what the kid has understood from the story, and very early on we rejected the notion that we could get that through asking specific questions. So we asked the kid to retell the story and asked a very open-ended question so we had as much as we can of a retelling of a story. We kind of pioneered that, but that's become very popular in many other kinds of research, not just miscue research.

Yetta: When I did my research study I researched six kids for seven years, from first grade to the seventh grade. My committee told me not to use the word "retelling" because it wasn't a specific enough term. They wanted me to use the word "recall" because that's more specific. Now everybody uses retelling. It's those kinds of things that have changed.

Ken: We got in a sense what the reader has understood. I differentiate between comprehension, which is what people know, and comprehending, which is the process of making sense.

Yetta: One of the reasons that retelling is so important is that we have data on kids who make very few miscues and cannot retell. Then we have kids who make more miscues than anybody would think possible and they reconstruct the story in a way that seems to be very close to the original text. What the author had in mind. So the retelling is always part of miscue analysis.

Ken: There's a great deal of quantitative data, but what's most interesting is not numbers, it's the qualities of the miscues that are happening and the kinds of profiles we get. And that's where the relationship with theory came in and what we understand about the reading process and what that means for teaching reading. You can't plug a concept out and then plug it in. It's one of the objections we've had to what's been happening with word-centered research. But because we're looking at real kids reading real texts teachers can replicate the kinds of things we're doing in classroom situations. They don't have to take our word for it. They can listen to kids reading. They can use that as a procedure for deciding what kind of instruction to give kids and they can do their own classroom research which uses some of the ideas. One of the things for instance that's come out of the model and out of miscue analysis is a whole genre of children's books called predictable books. Predictable books build on the concept that prediction itself is a powerful part of reading, and to the extent that books are predictable they're easier to read.

Yetta: Interestingly, predictable books have been around for centuries. *This Is the House That Jack Built* was a marvelous example of a predictable book. This is when we begin to understand the power our intuitive knowledge as human beings. Great authors have always known that predictability is important.

Ken: Another thing for us has been this emergence or resurgence of teacher research. Teachers are doing sometimes very important research.

Jim Collins: Why do you find that exciting?

Ken: What's exciting about it is that teachers are doing research in the classroom. They are doing the research as kids are reading and then using the research to build instruction and curriculum.

Yetta: The most exciting thing about it is how knowledgeable teachers are. I teach a course in miscue analysis every year, and so do other professors, and the feedback we always get from teachers is: "I'll never listen to a child read in the same way again." Once that happens everything that the teacher does is informed by what the child knows about the reading process. So the teacher becomes a knowledgeable professional. This is what we are about in teacher education. We don't tell teachers what to do minute-by-minute in the classroom. This is the whole language philosophy of teacher education. We provide teachers with support so they become knowledgeable themselves. So they can be professionals. We know that's when good teaching happens.

Jim Collins: Can I ask, going back to the question of research. You don't have an alternative method that finds the same results? You can measure the temperature one way. Then use a different method and, you know, measure the phenomenon another way and get the same results.

Ken: Miscue analysis is the theoretical base. Teachers are using it because they understand the process. When they hear a kid read they can understand whether the kid is making sense, whether the kid is making predictions. *The Boat in the Basement* (1996), which I use, that's not miscue analysis, that's a question of predicting how people will respond to a text that has errors in it and it clarifies the process of reading.

Jim Collins: Would you say that teacher research is something that you find also supports your work?

Ken: Very much so. And it's because of the real-world context.

Yetta: Every teacher who does a miscue analysis in my class selects a child in their own classroom. They select their own materials. They do the taping themselves. So, they are constantly validating the experience. Some researchers say that kids don't use context. We never find kids who don't.

Jim Collins: Who are some of those researchers?

Yetta: Well, Stanovich is a major researcher. Jay Samuels, Phil Gough, G-o-u-g-h. He's a big player in Texas. Marilyn Adams. Then there are other researchers involved in some of this too.

Ken: Let me try to explain something from my view of the philosophy of science. I can't dismiss research because I don't like it. I can't dismiss Marilyn Adams' summary of research because I don't like her. But what I can do is explain her findings in terms of my knowledge of the reading process. For instance, what I can't find in Marilyn Adams' book is the word "dialect." She claims to have summarized research over large populations and she makes a lot of pronouncements about the research.

Yetta: On poor kids.

Ken: Inner-city kids. Or, minority kids. I have to say one of the problems with her research is that they didn't consider the issue of dialect, and therefore I suspect some of the findings of her research are biased. If I ignore dialect what I'm doing is creating a biased situation in which some kids are going to look less accurate than others.

Yetta: And also rejecting everything we know about language variation.

Ken: Also, I find that they are working in monosyllables and I have to raise the question, what would have happened if they had used multisyllabic words where you get unaccented syllables, or if they were working in context reading, a word when it's a noun and when it's a function word? Based on this analysis I can begin to say that I don't like her research.

Jim Collins: Okay. Let's for a minute talk about what you said to me which is that it's not really about reading, or what is the best method to teach reading. Actually I have a whole bunch of difficult questions of research. What findings are valid. All that stuff. But anyway. Let's talk about the politics.

Ken: You have to look at it at several levels. Let's start with the most extreme and then work inward from that. When the Christian Coalition or Eagle Forum publishes on phonics it really doesn't have anything to do with reading. I think that it has to do with using politically the fear many parents have, particularly poor people who didn't do well themselves in school, but they may belong to fundamentalist churches and they are worried about what schools are doing to the values and morals of their kids. The thing that really scares these parents is to say that there is some kind of conspiracy to keep your kids from learning how to read.

Yetta: Or to capture their minds.

Ken: Or both. The message is simple. Obviously if the teachers are doing what they ought to be doing they should be teaching phonics and if they did then all the kids would learn to read. The message is that there was some time in the past when that happened. Since teachers are not doing that they're obviously conspiring to keep the kids from learning. So, what we have to do is to take over the school boards and take over the State School Board in the case of Texas and California. There was a kind of intensive campaign and the State School Board reversed the curriculum commission. Fundamentalists have been the driving force behind the laws in different states that are being proposed and they're the ones that are reducing everything to phonics versus whole language.

Jim Collins: Okay. Well. So. In Texas and California. Where else?

Yetta: North Carolina and Michigan.

Jim Collins: If I went out I could actually find people?

Yetta: There's an organization in Michigan called Michigan for Public Education. The person who knows a lot about it is a professor at Western Michigan University by the name of Connie Weaver.

Jim Collins: You said there was an organization called Michigan's for Public?

Yetta: Michigan for Public Education.

Jim Collins: And that is?

Yetta: Connie Weaver.

Jim Collins: That's Connie Weaver. Right. Okay. That's Connie Weaver.

Ken: Let me just say that the far right uses phonics. They need simple contrasts. Phonics works. Anything else is whole language and doesn't work. They need simple labels. One of the dilemmas that our colleagues are having, and I don't mean just whole language colleagues, they are finding themselves pushed into camps. If you're not for the teaching of phonics as a way of teaching reading then you are whole language. And there are messages on email from several people like David Pearson and Richard Allington who are finding themselves defending whole language.

Yetta: And they're *not* whole language people. But the extreme right is pushing them into a situation where they're saying we go into classes all the time and we don't see whole language teachers who are not teaching phonics.

Ken: You have to differentiate between those who have a frankly religious motive like the Christian Coalition and the Eagle Forum. Phyllis Schaffley's group, the Right to Read Foundation. That's Robert Sweet.

Jim Collins: He worked in the Reagan Administration.

Ken: And eventually he was, I think, with the Bush Administration. Now he has this Right to Read Foundation. He's one of the main forces going around to different states like North Carolina and pushing for explicit laws. The essence of the lies is that we're having terrible crises. Kids aren't learning to read. And it is because of whole language and not enough phonics. Therefore we should invent laws that make teachers teach phonics.

Yetta: Then that moves it to the teachers have to know phonics too. So we're now going to have laws and say that colleges of education have to teach courses in phonics to teachers. Teachers who supposedly are literate. I mean, how did they become literate if they don't know phonics? Do you understand? That's an interesting dilemma. I don't think we talk about that much.

Ken: And if you look at the material. There's a very strong home-schooling movement among the religious fundamentalists and the material parents are being sold is almost entirely what I would characterize as very simplistic phonics material.

Yetta: But that's not the whole home-schooling movement.

Ken: No. It's not the whole home-schooling movement. But if you go to a conference on home schooling, and you look at the materials they are only phonics materials.

Jim Collins: Okay. So then you have, maybe, the Mother Sweet types. Is there anyone, are there other people who are kind of in that category in Washington?

Yetta: Do you know Dave Berliner and Bruce Biddle's book *The Manufactured Crisis* (1996)?

Jim Collins: No.

Yetta: That's a very important book. They don't talk about reading. They talk about testing.

Jim Collins: Oh that's right. Yes. Right.

Yetta: And they argue that we've manufactured this crisis and that there are three political groups according to them. And so the fundamentalists—

Ken: Well, it's not the fundamentalists per say. It's the groups that are exploiting the fundamentalists.

Yetta: Right. And, then this group that's very conservative. Then the business group who are conservative business people who really would like not to support public education. And then this third group. I don't know how Berliner and Biddle categorizes them. But they are people who believe in culture with a big C. Like E. D. Hirsch and William Bennett, and what's the woman who's the historian? Ravitch. Diane Ravitch. And, if you look into their writings they don't deal with reading all the time. But whenever they do it's a back-to-basics kind of thing. So you have that group who are anti-multicultural and bilingual education. You see how all these things are all politically interrelated? You see an article on phonics and on bilingual education. You know, "How terrible all the kids are growing up speaking Spanish and nobody is speaking English."

Ken: The thing that I find startling is that relatively liberal people who immediately recognize and reject the tactics that the far right uses, for instance, on teaching evolution in schools, don't seem to recognize when it's being used in a field like reading. So there's a tendency to accept the notion. I think it's a bias against the schools and teachers in general.

Jim Collins: And what is?

Ken: That teachers don't know what they're doing and that teacher educators are stupid.

Yetta: And if we get our way the kids won't really buckle down, learn to take tests, and get to the right schools. That's the group of people that we try and work with a lot because politically we're, we are, I don't even want to use the word. Liberal.

Jim Collins: Oh. [Laughs.]

Yetta: [Laughs] But I don't want to say anything worse.

Ken: Can I try to tie the political paradigms with the research that's going on?

Jim Collins: Well, that's what I want to get to. What good does it do Marilyn Adams to write something?

Ken: Let me give you my perspective.

Yetta: Ken. There's another issue. Do you want to talk about publishing or not? See, one of the things that very few people are raising. Ken did a major research on basal readers.

Ken: With other people.

Yetta: With other people. About how many years ago was the first one?

Ken: It's almost ten years.

Yetta: Ten years ago. Raising a lot of ethical questions.

Ken: Not just ethical questions, but pedagogical questions.

Yetta: But the ethical questions comes back to Marilyn Adams, because the question is, "Why do people like that who have their names on reading programs get involved in research that supports their own kinds of materials?" In Texas there's a lot of use of a basal reading program called "Open Court."

Jim Collins: Right.

Yetta: The Barbara Foreman Study used Open Court. Well, it's interesting who the authors are on the Open Court Series.

Ken: Marilyn Adams.

Yetta: Marilyn Adams is an author and nobody is raising conflict of interest issues.

Ken: It's starting to be raised.

Yetta: In the press? I haven't seen anything.

Ken: And it's not simply who's an author, because that's obviously a definable conflict of interest. But there are other subtle ways that publishers can support researchers. They can support them as consultants. They can support their research. They can supply them with materials.

Yetta: And see, in our field our own colleagues always feel a little vulnerable because many are reading researchers across the country.

Ken: I was a basal author.

Jim Collins: Who is? I'm sorry. Researchers are?

Ken: Vulnerable.

Yetta: Yeah. So they're vulnerable because even if they are on a basal that maybe is more eclectic, or has more literature in it the whole notion of where the conflict of interest is in all of this is very interesting.

Jim Collins: Let me ask a question. I mean you guys. I mean you published whole language books and things. And I'm not saying.

Ken: I make money from people buying my books. I don't want to say I don't. On the other hand I have never let a publisher pay for my presentations at a conference. One of the seductive things that the publishers can do at the local and national conferences. Eight out of ten of the major speakers will be there because the publishers paid.

Yetta: Have you ever been at the International Reading Association convention?

Yetta: Okay. Watch the parties that the publishers present. In San Diego when IRA was there or Anaheim. A publisher will rent a boat for thousands and thousands of teachers.

Ken: New Orleans.

Yetta: New Orleans they rent out the fanciest restaurants.

Ken: In Atlantic City.

Yetta: Oh Atlantic City. Nightclubs. The underground jazz. But if you don't get any invitations call me and I'll tell you where to go because people go around to all the publishers' parties. They won't stop you even if you don't have an invitation, but they do send out invitations.

Ken: One of the things that happened with whole language is that it very much upset the traditional patterns of publishers.

Yetta: Ken has written two books on the analysis of basal readers.

Jim Collins: Right. That's upset the basal publishers.

Yetta: Whole language did too.

Ken: One of the things that got lost in the National Reports in 1992 and 1994 was the huge shift, almost across the board in the United States, toward a mixed use of basal and trade books. Or, just teaching reading without basal at all. You understand what I mean by trade books?

Jim Collins: Yes.

Ken: Our books kind of gave a push to that. But I think teachers simply stopped using them.

Yetta: What's happened to children's literature, supported by whole language teachers is unbelievable.

Ken: Yetta. I want to come back to the issue of the research paradigms. Let me give you my explanation. There are a group of researchers, Marilyn Adams and Keith Stanovich, and a large number of others. When Marilyn Adams came out with her book *Beginning to Read* (1990) it got a tremendous fanfare. It was a government-sponsored book. They had the publishers distribute it to the main organizations IRA, NCTE.

Yetta: They wrote a summary.

Ken: It had zero effect on the teaching of reading, and it was largely because, from our perspective, teachers are too sophisticated to accept as truth what Adams was saying, which is a fairly narrow focus on teaching words, and on pre-teaching certain kinds of things, as if they're essential for teaching reading. Teachers themselves are much too knowledgeable. That left them in a strange position, because if in good faith they've got the truth and nobody is paying attention to it, then they have to ask themselves why. What they are arguing is that although there are nice things about whole language, it treats teachers nicely, and it creates excitement about nice literature, the problem with it is that it has the wrong model on reading. And, there are two things that they explicitly reject. One is that reading and writing are learned like oral language. They're claiming that oral language is innate and isn't learned and that reading has to be taught in a very exclusive way. And the other thing that they are rejecting is that reading is making sense of print rather than recognizing words. So, what they want to do then is to plug that in but everything that they were doing wasn't working. Then along comes this campaign by the far right to reject whole language and attack it, and to substitute phonics, and suddenly they are being courted.

Yetta: By state departments.

Ken: By the far right.

Yetta: Basal-reading companies.

Ken: Marilyn Adams was brought in to hearings in Texas. Jean Osborne who used to work with DISTAR was there. She's at the Center for the Study of Reading. She was in Texas on a per diem basis.

Jim Collins: I'm sorry?

Yetta: Jean Osborne. You know the group in Oregon?

Ken: Then there's a guy named Doug Carnine who works at the University of Oregon. He worked with Zeigfried Engleman on a very old program called DISTAR which is a kind of a stark, fundamentalist, behaviorist reading program. And then he's suddenly the main advisor to the California State Government on reading.

Jim Collins: Sorry his name is?

Yetta: Carnine.

Ken: So what I'm saying is that you have this unusual situation. In fact as one of my students said this is really strange. Usually the far right, particularly the Christian right and science are at odds with each other, but they are working together.

Yetta: There are also scientists who are doing very different research than ours who are bemoaning the fact that we're going back to skills and drills with worksheets and they are unhappy about that.

Jim Collins: Right.

Ken: But you see what's happened is that they've gotten caught in a vortex. I think what these people think is that they're smarter than the far right so they can control them, and they're not.

Yetta: I think that the one thing we've learned, we've been in education as teachers since the 1950s, so I think that people coming in now don't appreciate the complexity of education, the history of education. You know there are so many forces influencing education and in this country they are very complex. The issue isn't just reading. This whole focus on phonics not only narrows the whole discussion of education to reading and literacy, it narrows it to early reading, kindergarten, first and second grade. We've got issues around reading throughout the twelve grades. We have issues around history and social studies. Whole language deals with language, but it also deals with curriculum, with how kids learn, with how kids read, and with how education takes place within a community. It has all these major influences.

Ken: Let me bring in another issue that's political. Besides being researchers, one of the things we have worked hard on in our lives is changing what happens in schools.

Yetta: For kids and for teachers.

Ken: And we've learned a number of lessons. We cannot simply force things on teachers. In fact we have been in situations where administrators have brought us in without sufficiently involving the teachers, and we find that the teachers are defensive, that they're unwilling to participate and listen.

Yetta: The teachers resist things that they don't understand.

Ken: It's insulting to them. That's one of the things that's happening now in Texas and in California. They've fallen into the notion that you can force change on teachers, that you can do it by writing laws, that you can mandate it, that you can threaten administrators and teachers, and it doesn't work. It never has worked. When you write a law in California that requires that all teacher educators have to teach phonics using direct instruction, and you start sending a lot of people to check up on that, what happens is that teachers begin to fight back.

Yetta: Or they close their doors. If there is a reason not to fight teachers we will find a way to get around it.

Ken: If you classify everything that isn't direct instruction of phonics as bad, and whole language as unacceptable, then a broad number of people find themselves under attack. And those people are doing two things. Yetta says they close the doors and they do what they believe in anyway or they begin to fight back, but there's a third alternative and that really worries me, that we're creating situations where some of the best teachers are being pushed out of classrooms because they won't teach under these conditions.

Yetta: They won't teach under these kinds of circumstances. We know teachers who are leaving our local school district because they refuse to move into a system that they believe is hurtful to their kids. This is more than a phonics problem.

Jim Collins: Let me just go over this. The interesting thing about the sort of thing the fundamentalists are arguing is that the right-wingers have taken up phonics, they've gotten control of the school boards, locally, and maybe at the state level, and they have brought in the researchers.

Yetta: Right.

Jim Collins: And the basal? The publishers?

Yetta: That's very complicated. If you go back to the 1970s, the phonics people were attacking the basal people.

Jim Collins: This is a source of confusion for me. Where do basals fit into all of this?

Yetta: Okay. Ken knows more about basals but I just want to go back. There was an article in *Family Circle* in the 1970s that was a pro-phonics article that attacked the ten top basal companies. The basal was too wishy-washy for the phonics people. They have literature and they let kids read.

Ken: And phony phonics is not real phonics.

Yetta: They don't focus on phonics explicitly. Step by step and line by line. And that argument by the way is going to come back now as the basal people who have been shifting to whole language for the last ten years now have to go back to the right. And it's going to be really interesting to watch what happens. Scholastic is interesting to look at. Scholastic never had a phonics program until two years ago.

Ken: A basal program.

Yetta: A basal program till two years ago. Scholastic does so many things with wonderful books for kids everybody kept telling them, so why do you want a basal program? Why? Because it's lucrative. So Dick Robinson, who's the president, went into the basal program. And it's a very interesting basal program. It's very complex. It's got many features. This year they have a phonics book that is part of that program. But as far as the publishers are concerned they are in this to make money. Ken documents this in his book. They're not in this to teach kids. There are good people in the publishing world for kids. I don't want to say that there aren't but even they have to give into the bottom line which is making the dollars. And it's not making a little bit. It's millions. I don't know. I'll let you do the money.

Ken: The other thing that's been happening in publishing in general, that is multinational corporations are owning more and more, is exactly what's been happening in school publishing too. We have two *Whole Language Catalogues* (1991, 1992). Both were with Random House. Random House was independent. They were bought by McGraw-Hill. McGraw-Hill also bought a bunch of others and when they reorganized we were then under SRA, a division of McGraw-Hill. When this happens the decision-making shifts farther away from the editorial level and more into the boardroom level. It's a situation in which decision-making becomes very conservative.

Jim Collins: Let me just ask you a general question. Talking of publishers. They seem to be driving things.

Ken: Exactly. They drove things for a very long time. They drove it with a very simple but very important premise and that's what we say in the *Report Card on Basal Readers* (1988). They have convinced schools and particularly school administrators that in order to teach reading you have to have a sequence-controlled set of readers. And what happened was that teachers discovered that they could teach without basal. What that meant was a revolution.

Yetta: When Ken did the *Report Card on Basal Readers* I think 95 percent of all classrooms were using basal readers. That was nineteen eighty—?

Ken: Seven. '87.

Yetta: Really, that late?

Ken: Yes.

Yetta: The latest we can figure now from the national assessment. What is it about '85?

Ken: 60 percent exclusively using basals.

Yetta: And there are lots of basal companies in the last ten years that put the word whole language into their basal programs. They call themselves whole language basals and that's confused the whole language issue.

Jim Collins: Right.

Yetta: Because we don't believe that there can be a whole language basal. It's not possible. There isn't a whole language anything. Whole language is about the way teachers and kids live together in a classroom. But there are teachers who call themselves whole language teachers because they use a whole language basal.

Jim Collins: So in the past ten years publishers have produced things they call whole language basals. Publishers have also tried to produce whole language packaged literature.

Yetta: Oh yes. All of them. Every publisher I know is trying to pull together a literature series. In fact I know of one literature-based program where people come together and decide what sets of books kids should read and write questions for each book that they had chosen. School districts have teachers getting together during the summer, and the school districts pay teachers to turn trade books into basals. They write worksheets rather than letting kids read the books. One of the things that disturbs me is that teachers were given more choice. Teachers were getting more say in what they used and in the decisions that the districts made. What bothers me now is that there is this strong push to limit choice of literature, limit teacher involvement and control what's happening.

Ken: So it's turned into a political process. Do you want to talk some more about whole language?

Jim Collins: Well, is Adams paid as an advisor to Open Court?

Ken: She's an author.

Yetta: She's an author on the Open Court series as far as I know.

Ken: Well, she's listed.

Jim Collins: Okay. Whole language. You said when we talked about teachers you talked about a teacher who had been working with whole language for 15 years and still wasn't sure what it was.

Ken: No. What I said was that there are teachers who say I'm becoming a whole language teacher.

Jim Collins: Well, I didn't know the exact words.

Ken: At public meetings when teachers get up and try to answer critics, they say it took me many years to make the transition myself. And what they're talking about is that whole language is not something you can impose on other people, that you can reduce to a couple of sentences, that could be part of a mandate. You can't mandate whole language. Not that there haven't been some mistakes made when people tried to push teachers too fast. But it really is a belief system. I like to call it a pedagogy that guides one's teaching. And I find myself, Yetta and I both find ourselves, in a funny kind of position because people use the term "guru" and the press tends to pick up on a kind of notion, that whole language teachers are people who don't think for themselves. One of the things, stated flatly, is that teachers are misled by people like Ken and Yetta Goodman. On one hand it's flattering for people to say that I'm the father of whole language.

Yetta: Grandfather. [Laughs]

Jim Collins: [Laughs]

Ken: [Laughs] Grandfather. But it's wrong in a way that misleads the realities of the things that we are saying in our writing about teaching reading, and curriculum in general. I was coauthor, and Yetta became coauthor for the third edition, of *Language and Thinking in School* (1987). Well, that's a book that was first published in the '60s. We weren't using the term whole language in the first edition of that book, but we've been talking for a very long time about a holistic language-centered curriculum.

Yetta: Our views of teaching, which go beyond reading, come out of progressive education. John Dewey and Lucy Sprague Mitchell, who was the founder of Bank Street College. You know there's nothing faddish about this. This is a philosophy that goes back to the 15th century.

Ken: The big difference in this period compared to other periods is the large number of highly professional, very well-informed teachers that are involved. I wasn't joking when I wrote an article with the title "I Didn't Found Whole Language, Whole Language Found Me" because essentially, as I view it, whole language is one of the most remarkable developments in education, anywhere, because it's a grassroots movement.

Yetta: One of the things that people don't understand about whole language is that teachers have to give up power to become a whole language teacher. You're not the power broker in the classroom. You're negotiating curriculum with kids. You're learning from kids. What do they know? What do they need to know? What do they want to know? And then you are constantly negotiating with the state curriculum, the local curriculum, with your own knowledge as a professional, to allow kids to learn. And to me the main term that comes to mind when I think about that is democracy. What we're trying to do is to support teachers. To help kids live in a democratic community within a classroom. I'm trying to do that in my own college classrooms. So whole language isn't a kindergarten thing. It isn't a reading thing. It's based on what interrelationships we build with our students and how we interact in a classroom, whether their beliefs have a right to exist in our classroom and whether their knowledge base has a right to be a part of what we learn. You understand what I'm talking about?

Jim Collins: Yes. Right.

Yetta: I mean, I think that's so crucial and in a sense the fact that it is democratic is another reason that it's so frightening to some people who are afraid to give up power.

Ken: If you put it into a historical context there have always been these two sides to education. The people who believed in education as a way of helping kids to grow and giving them rich experiences and opening things up, and those who believe in education as a way of transmitting a body of knowledge in a very fixed and narrow kind of way. And obviously, whenever you try to democratize it oversimplifies. You have to go back in history. Dewey (1997) was a curriculum innovator.

Ken: Historically, the kinds of things we're talking about had an influence on education theory and teacher education, but they never had a very broad influence.

Yetta: On public education.

Ken: They had much more influence on higher education. We've reached a period in time where we have a very large number of professional teachers, not just in this country but around the world. We're finding, for instance, that we're spending a tremendous amount of time in South America. Because as countries are beginning to democratize and to focus on education they're not interested in the colonial models that they've had. They want to move forward.

Jim Collins: How depressing do you find it?

Yetta: How depressing? [Laughs]

Jim Collins: How emotionally?

Ken: Sometimes it's very depressing. Yetta and I try not to read our e-mail late at night.

Yetta: If we do we can't sleep all night long.

Ken: We get these horror stories from Texas and what's happening there.

Yetta: One of the things is that I'm not interviewed as much as Ken. He has been on television, in newspapers, on radio probably every week for the last two years. Most of it is bad or negative towards him and whole language. Right?

Ken: In a lot of cases I'm just the voice at the end of the article so that the editor can say they had a little balance in there.

Yetta: And that's very hard. When you've lived your life and you've worked hard and your whole life's work is being questioned.

Jim Collins: For years now there have been questions about what is a newsmagazine. Just this thing. How much would be tied up in the week's events and news. How much would be like a monthly magazine. Coming out every week [laughs] we've been trying to figure this out. Actually [laughs] for a while going back and forth, different directions. But certainly you look at newspapers now, they do so much of the kinds of things that newsmagazines used to do.

Yetta: I don't want you to feel sorry for us. Talking about the press because we do get a lot of highs when we walk into classrooms. And then, of course, the stuff that's going on in South America and Taiwan is really quite remarkable, where the president of the country is there to introduce you at a conference.

Ken: We were in Guatemala for the first National Reading Association Conference and there were 1,700 teachers.

Yetta: These were teachers from public schools.

Ken: And the president and the minister of education were there.

Yetta: And I read a children's book to the president and he sat there and loved it. The other thing that I wanted to put in perspective is whole language in terms of the classroom. My goal in education is to help teachers know enough about language and curriculum and learning and teaching so that they can interact with kids and can know how to discover kids' strengths. I don't think anybody would disagree when you have a great teacher who knows how to support kids' strengths, those kids do well in the classroom. In the end everybody would agree with that, but the people who believe in skills would say, "But we can't have great teachers, that's not possible, so why don't we have a program, so that all teachers can follow the program." By the way this is another major argument that's been that's been around for a hundred years going back to William S. Gray.

Ken: That was the original justification of having basal readers.

Yetta: When Gray started basal readers most of the teachers in this country had finished high school and they went right into a two-year training program and they went into teaching. Now most of the teachers that I meet have master's degrees. In Kentucky 82 percent of all teachers have master's degrees. Shouldn't we be respecting the knowledge base that teachers have? I'm in classrooms with teachers a lot and I marvel at what classroom teachers can do. But if I had to go into a second-grade classroom tomorrow, and I think I am a very knowledgeable experienced teacher, it would take me a year to get to a point where the classroom teacher is now. We have so much disrespect for classroom teachers. When we develop materials for them and then we say, "Now you must follow the materials," that's so disrespectful. Materials should be tools. I'm not anti-materials. I'm not even anti-phonics programs. I'm anti when an administrator or a consultant comes in and says, "You're not following that work page by page." "What page are you on?" Every professional has to know how disrespectful that is.

Ken: Let's go back because you asked us to talk about whole language.

Jim Collins: Right.

Yetta: Does this help? Is this okay?

Jim Collins: Definitely. This is fine. Let's talk a little bit about whole language.

Ken: We tend to talk about what it isn't. A number of things have been happening in language in general, and beyond that in curriculum in general. There is the idea of looking at math holistically, and looking at history, and social studies holistically. These are parallel movements. In fact the math curriculum is being attacked in the same way, and essentially mathematicians are responding by saying we need to stop teaching arithmetic and help kids to understand the concepts of mathematics and the relationships in the real world. And that's what whole language is and why putting it as an alternative to phonics limits understanding. Whole language not only integrates the language processes but does not separate reading and writing or separate oral and written language. It continuously involves kids in using both oral and written language in the processes of learning for the purposes of enjoying the literature, for expressing themselves, and for answering questions.

Yetta: And this is where we get the content and ideas about the world, all content areas.

Ken: One of the things we know about the way kids learn language is that they learn it best, when in a sense they're not paying attention to it, by using it, by using it to discuss, by using it to inquire, by using it to represent to each other their understandings of what they are doing. So by integrating the curriculum, we build the development of literacy into social studies, science, and math, through field studies and themes. So instead of dividing the day into discrete periods, for spelling and handwriting and social studies and science you have themes, and often with the kids participating in deciding on the themes.

Yetta: At the present time that's being called the "inquiry approach."

Ken: Or theme cycles.

Yetta: But that goes back to the late 1800s. It was called the "project method." A guy by the name Cornel Parker who wrote books in the late 1800s and early 1900s on the project method. Dewey talks about that. England and Scotland do incredible things with project approaches. But when did whole language start? More or less the modern whole language period started in 1979. Jerry Hartse at Indiana University and Carolyn Burke.

Jim Collins: Are these names in? [He points to a book Yetta has given him]

Yetta: Right. They wrote an article talking about how teachers have three views of language. A skills view of language, a subskills view of language which is the phonics and the skills and the use the basals, and the whole language view. Parts of that whole language view are two concepts. One is that language is a tool to learn with and not something you pay attention to as the object of your study. Does that make sense to you?

Jim Collins: Yes.

Yetta: Right now you're writing. You're not thinking about nouns and verbs and adjectives. You're just listening to me. You're making meaning of what I'm saying and you're putting notes on paper and all of this is through language. Language is a tool to get our jobs done. That's one major thing about language.

Ken: One of the functions of language. To develop language functions, the wide range of genres that kids use, you do that through the focus on problem solving, inquiry, and developing themes in social studies and science.

Yetta: And the other major term that's very important, and it's been batted around too much, is that we try to make learning as authentic as possible.

Jim Collins: Is there something philosophically, fundamentally incompatible about whole language in a broad sense and also within a specific reading sense, and in directly teaching phonics?

Yetta: No.

Jim Collins: In other words the balance from your point of view at least is it really, though, in fact, I talked to Dr. Gough on the phone, and he said you can't do balance, you have two philosophical systems. You just can't.

Ken: Well, I feel the same way. Where I would agree with him is that it's inconsistent to teach holistically and at the same time pull out something and teach it in a kind of isolated way.

Yetta: But with a kid who is struggling with some issue we would spend three or four minutes with that kid on that issue. I do it in context. If I don't do it in context maybe I'll take him aside and give him some information. But I won't do it for all the kids at the same time. This is where kidwatching becomes so important because the teacher has to be attending to very different kinds of things that kids are doing. One of the things that I am doing now with my research is something that I call retrospective miscue analysis. I'm actually getting kids to analyze their own miscues. I have a kid on tape reading the sentence, "He did not have enough." And I asked him to listen to that sentence because there was a miscue there. And this kid looked at me and says, "I said enough and that can't be enough." And I said, "Why isn't it 'enough'?'" He says, "There's no 'f' at the end of this word." What a wonderful moment to stop and talk to him about the "gh." Now at that particular moment why would I have a lesson for 32 kids on that word "enough"? When the other 31 don't have that problem? They read "enough." They've gotten the notion that "gh" can also have an "f" sound. He sort of knew that too, but then when he saw me questioning it he began to wonder if that was correct or not. To me that's great teaching. That's good kidwatching. Good teachers have been doing this forever.

Ken: I want to back up to the situation where they say, "yes, but where's the phonics?"

Jim Collins: You would say that the phonics is there anyway?

Ken: The phonics is there, but it's there in a way that it's meaningful. That's what I tried to say in *Phonics Phacts* (1994). That there is no single set of sounds, or single set of letter forms in any alphabetic language. So the only way that you can build the relationships is in the context of reading and writing. By that I mean that we build a set of relationships between the sounds of your language, your own personal language and writing systems. That's what invented spelling is all about. My granddaughter Rachel is doing that now. She's at the point where she has invented a phonics system, and her phonics system makes it possible for her to write what she wants to write.

Jim Collins: So?

Ken: What teachers do is build on her invented system and then help her to carry that over into her reading. So she's looking at the way words are spelled and that's going to influence her writing, which will become more conventional. The graphophonic sound system and writing system and the phonics that relates to them. In the context of trying to make sense of print, as Yetta said, sometimes you stop at a key point and you talk about that funny thing, in English spelling, where there are words that sound like they should end in "f" and don't. And in the case you're addressing the only time that happens meaningfully is when kids are really involved in using the system.

Jim Collins: Is that what all this is about?

Yetta: First, it's about allowing kids to express themselves, allowing them to read.

Ken: Encouraging them. Encouraging them to figure out how reading works.

Yetta: Here's a writer. You are a writer. Now let's look at books and see how other authors write and let's share our writing with each other. And then even helping kids understand that there is conventional writing out there. These kids have to learn that there is conventional writing, and of course, we have data, teachers have data in portfolios. I guess you know about portfolio assessment?

Jim Collins: Um.

Yetta: We encourage teachers to keep kids' work. Well, do you have a portfolio? You must have a portfolio of your writing?

Jim Collins: Yes. Sure. I do actually.

Yetta: Well okay, that's exactly what we want kids to have. We want them to keep a portfolio.

Ken: In my daughter's fifth-grade class there was a kid who came in knowing virtually no English. He was from Hong Kong. He kept a portfolio and you could easily follow the development of English as you looked at his writing.

Yetta: It's the greatest assessment tool that we have. Much greater than any standardized test. Standardized test people will tell you that no standardized test can give you any information about an individual learner.

Jim Collins: Right.

Yetta: So what we have to help teachers do is know how to assess their own kids through this kind of knowledge base and that's one of the jobs I do. Miscue does that for reading. Looking at writing samples does that for writing.

Jim Collins: Well, okay. Well, let's see.

Yetta: There's an interesting thing that's happened and it drives me crazy. We've discovered that kids can invent spellings. So now there are people who want to teach kids how to invent spelling. That's ridiculous.

Ken: What it does is miss the point because the way that spelling works in any alphabetic language, particularly in English, is that we conventionalize spelling across a wide range of dialects so there isn't any single match. And the power of invented spelling is that each kid is inventing. Bilingual kids are inventing spellings that reflect their Spanish influences on their English, and kids are creating spellings using the conventions that represent how they hear the sounds of the language in both Spanish and English.

Jim Collins: Okay. What I really don't quite understand is I guess your position. Or your view that by teaching systematic phonics, or teaching letter-sound correspondences this will block or override or prevent each kid from—

Yetta: No. No.

Ken: No. What we're saying really is that you're teaching untruths, that you're teaching a variant system.

Yetta: No. But there is another issue. If teachers taught phonics and let the kids write using their own system that would be fine, but usually the teachers who are teaching phonics are always worried when the kids make any little error so they're always correcting them.

Ken: There's a basic concept here and it's one that's very important to us, that gets misunderstood. There are two forces that are at work with language learning. One is the force of social convention and the power of that is not so much a question of right or wrong, it's that to the extent that language is conventional. It's more accepted and understood, but there is another force that's very important. That's the force of invention. Individuals and societies never lose the power to invent language, so in a real sense language learning is kids inventing the language. That's why we have baby talk; that's why we have invented spelling. But the two forces have to be actively playing against each other. As the kid invents spelling and invents a system of inventing sounds to their writing system, they're also reading and they're encountering conventional spelling and these play against each other. If I say to kids I'm going to tell you what to invent and I'm going to give you the rules of inventing. Or, I'm going to teach you these phonics. There are people now in Texas and California who are saying never let a kid read a book that has words that they haven't learned how to decode. And by that I mean words that don't fit the phonics patterns. Well if they can't read stuff that they can't decode they certainly aren't going to be permitted to write stuff if it deviates from the phonics patterns that they're being introduced to. Well, language doesn't work that way. So you create a kind of impossible situation where the reading materials are so strange that they're unreadable and the kids aren't being permitted to write because they haven't been taught enough.

Jim Collins: I don't quite see why miscue analysis is a way of analyzing reading. Why necessarily it has to be part of whole language?

Ken: Because miscue analysis is a powerful way of getting teachers to revalue language and reading and how they work. There are teachers who use miscue analysis as a regular way of studying to assess their kids' reading. A lot more teachers have used the understandings of it informally, and then there is another group of teachers who understand what we've learned about the reading process in ways that have been informed by miscue but they don't necessarily understand or use miscue analysis. The key thing is that you have professional teachers who have a lot of knowledge and part of that knowledge is either miscue analysis, or an understanding of written language and language development that grows out of it.

Jim Collins: You said that whole language is a philosophy.

Ken: And a pedagogy.

Jim Collins: And a pedagogy. Doesn't it make sense then that it would be attacked on philosophical grounds? Do you understand?

Ken: Sure.

Jim Collins: And philosophically people would come at it that it's not just about, aren't the terms you're putting it all more than just a technique?

Ken: Absolutely. It's the best way to teach reading not because it's a technique but because it has strong roots that are not just with reading research but in how kids learn and how language works. And it's why I object to what I call "one-legged models." If somebody says, "We've got correlational data that shows that phonemic awareness facilitates reading. Therefore we have to build reading programs around phonemic awareness." My response is, "We need to understand how kids learn, and how they learn language from each other, and how teaching relates to learning." We need to look at the issue if phonemic awareness is a reality in reading, then how does it develop? And who develops it? And when? And what will facilitate it? And how it looks under different conditions? And circumstances? That's the whole in whole language that we're trying to pull all of these things together.

Jim Collins: Right. Well. When people, the right-wingers, say, "Look, there's an agenda here to, not just teach, a better way of teaching reading, but there is a sort of philosophical view, that is obligated by all this." They have a point.

Ken: They have a point. Yes. And I'm not going to argue. You know that's one of the things I've said. There are two major bases to whole language. One is the scientific and that has to do with things like how reading works, and how it develops, and we can facilitate it. But the other is a humanistic view, and it's humanistic, in the sense that you start with a view, that schools in a democratic society have a responsibility, not just for teaching skills in isolated ways. We don't want people who can just read. We want people who read and write as citizens in a democratic society. I see it very much related to the whole social welfare issue, because it's the fundamental issue of what's the responsibility of society for education and for health, and for human welfare, and what's the responsibility of the individual. That's the issue we've fought over forever in public education.

Jim Collins: Who else should I talk to?

Ken: From which perspective?

Jim Collins: Well from, if you could tell me, if you could direct me, from your perspective.

Ken: Shelly Harwayne.

Jim Collins: How do you spell her name?

Ken: H-A-R-W-A-Y-N-E. Bobby Fisher. Yetta mentioned her. She's in Boston.

Jim Collins: I'm going to see her.

Ken: Jerome Harste at Indiana University.

Jim Collins: We should be done soon. Well, thanks very much. I have to give you an email address.

Yetta: Don't attack us too bad.

Jim Collins: Okay. Well. [Laughs]

Ken: [Laughs]

Jim Collins: I can't promise you'll like it but I think it will be fair and accurate.

Yetta: I hope we'll see you at IRA.

Jim Collins: Yes. Actually you will.

Yetta: I'm doing a miscue workshop all day Sunday.

Jim Collins: Actually, I've already signed up for that, or whatever. I actually wanted to get some of the others.

Yetta: Marilyn Adams is doing one too.

Jim Collins: Then there's one called "The Radical Middle."

Yetta: Oh yes. That's Dave Pearson. Oh good. Just go into all of them.

Jim Collins: Like Goldilocks. A little hot. A little cold. [Laughs]

Yetta: [Laughs]

The *Time* Article

Six months later Ken Goodman telephoned. "Collins writes that I am 'grandfatherly,' he said, 'with a goatee and longish white hair.'" Ken sounded both angry and disappointed. "He said, 'I'm 'a charismatic leader' and I'm the author of a 'folksy 100-page paperback' on phonics." Ken had been communicating with Collins via email, and a couple of weeks before the article was published Collins had written to tell Ken that someone from *Time* would be calling him to check quotes. "No one called," Ken said, and he expressed concern about the misquotes. Yetta was not mentioned nor quoted in the article.

The article "How Johnny Should Read" that James Collins wrote for *Time Magazine* was out on the newsstands a week before the October 27, 1997 cover date. Publication of the article coincided with the publication of the *Newsweek* article "Why Andy Couldn't Read," and the *US News and World Report* article "The Reading Wars Continue." In the November issue of *Atlantic Monthly*, which was also already on the newsstands, another article, "The Reading Wars," appeared. At the same time, in the *Policy Review*, which is published by the ultraconservative Heritage Foundation, an article entitled "See Dick Flunk" appeared. The publication of all these articles on reading coincided with the Reading Excellence Act, H.R. 2614, being marked up by the House Education and Workforce Committee and being passed out of committee on October 23, 1997, for consideration by the House of Representatives.

The rest, as they say, is history. There was nothing scientific about Collins' piece. He had no authority in the reading field except that he published in *Time*. He had the opportunity to decide what counts as data and what doesn't, what counts as science and what doesn't. He had the power to influence the hearts and minds of the American people and to help shape the teaching of reading and writing in American public schools.

Fast Forward: April 23, 2027

Life as we know it in the United States no longer exists. America has become a totalitarian world power, militaristic and capitalistic. The purging of ERIC that began in the late 1990s led to the mass eradication of any research on language and literacy that was not approved by the federal government. All traces of the 20th-century progressive educational movement have been destroyed. There are no records of the whole language movement of which Ken and Yetta spoke with Jim Collins.

In 2027 as the United States struggles to understand the turbulent times in which we live, an investigative reporter from the state-controlled media finds an obscure reference to whole language and manages to make contact with a retired teacher who is willing to talk with him about the illicit movement. The teacher is old and venerable. She started teaching in the late 1960s, and she is not afraid of violating the censorship laws that control what can be written, read, and said. She is too old to care and she agrees to speak with the young reporter who is eager to find out more about whole language. He knows very little about reading and writing or what happened at the end of the 20th century that led to the federal government's control of who reads and who writes. He knows there's a connection between literacy and democracy but it is difficult for him to figure it out.

Reporter: We're doing a story about reading. It's shaping up to be a fairly big story. We're interested in the demise of public education and the rise of the totalitarian national security state. Of course, we'll have to give it a spin, and we won't be able to publish anything that criticizes the present regime but I found an old article in an ERIC dump about something called "whole language." Can you tell me something about it?

Literacy Teacher: [Smiles.] Whole language was a philosophy and pedagogy that imagined American society as a participatory democracy. The philosophy and classroom practices of the teachers at that time placed the languages of children, both spoken and written, and the languages of their families and their communities at the center of the curriculum.

Reporter: Well, I just. Well. Can you tell me about that?

Teacher: Whole language became a politically unfashionable idea. [Smiles.] Too democratic.

Reporter: I read that researchers thought it was unscientific.

Teacher: The proponents of positivistic science didn't get it. How could they? To consider the scientific basis of whole language they would have had to acknowledge that their own reading research had the potential for seriously damaging the lives of young children. At that time the dominant ideology of pathology was buried deep in their cultural psyche. They found out what was "wrong" with kids and they set about trying to fix it.

Reporter: Fix what?

Teacher: Fix kids. Their arguments were tautological. They really convinced themselves that it was possible to diagnose a reading problem without ever listening to a child read. It happened all the time. Children were given phonics tests and tests of word attack skills and prescribed instruction in phonemic awareness, intensive systematic phonics, and word attack skills and then more batteries of tests. It's worse now but the dominant view of science hasn't changed.

Reporter: Okay. The question of science. Can you tell me about that?

Teacher: Their science was such an orderly process. They never seemed to learn how odd, complex, contradictory, and irrational the processes of scientific discovery can be.

Reporter: Such views of science have long been eradicated.

Teacher: Exactly. It was all about political power, but many whole language teachers were also researchers. They studied the kids in their own classrooms. They had to be stopped. Their research and classroom practices were too participatory. Too democratic. It gave too much power to the people.

Reporter: [Laughs] Do you think it would have made a difference if your positivist scientists studied real kids reading? Is there a possibility it would have changed history?

Teacher: [Laughs] Maybe. There were so many different reasons for what happened. Don't forget profit. I don't think many people made the connection between capitalism and totalitarianism. When researchers pushed their studies on phonemic awareness and word identification skills in the 1990s they made a lot of money. Publishers loved them. All those new workbooks and new basals! Kids represented revenues and profits.

Reporter: Was it really about money?

Teacher: You figure it out. Test makers and test publishers made hundreds of millions of dollars. Billions.

Reporter: But do you really think that the motives of those researchers were anything but honorable?

Teacher: Probably had the best of intentions. Hypotheses. Methodologies. Statistical procedures. All the trappings of the dominant view of science. [The teacher unlocks a drawer in her desk and rummages through some old files. She holds up a faded blue copy of the *Reading Research Quarterly*.] Researchers were outraged when it was suggested that there was anything wrong with their inappropriate use of statistical procedures or their reduction of reading to simplistic interval scales. There's an article in here you might like to read before you leave.

Reporter: Can we go back? You said whole language was too democratic.

Teacher: Yes. I came across an article the other day that was published in *The Nation* in 2002. Remember *The Nation*?

Reporter: I heard about it. Never seen a copy. Long gone. I thought all copies had been destroyed.

Teacher: I have a few that I managed to save. [Again she smiles.] The article was by Tom Hayden and Dick Flacks, the founding members of the Students for Democratic Society and principal drafters of the Port Huron

Statement nearly 70 years ago. Hayden and Flack wrote about Dewey and his definition of a democracy was explicitly participatory.

Reporter: Dewey?

Teacher: Early 20th-century philosopher and pedagogist. Let me read what Hayden and Flack wrote. [Rummages in the files again and pulls out an old copy of *The Nation*.] Here it is. [She reads.] Dewey argued that such participation is necessary both for the general welfare and for the fullest development of individuals, and that such a principle should be applied not only in the political sphere as we understand it but in the spheres of family and child raising, in school, in business, and in religion.

Reporter: Okay? What has that got to do with whole language?

Teacher: That's what whole language was about. In the early 1990s, when U.S. public schools came under attack by the federal government, teachers and researchers were exploring approaches to the development of curriculum that were both participatory and democratic.

Reporter: I don't get it.

Teacher: In the 1980s teachers and researchers in universities and public schools focused on bilingual education, the development of constructivist theory and pedagogical practices, cooperative learning, critical theory and pedagogy, cultural-historical research, and culturally responsive teaching practices. Miscue analysis based on the research of Ken and Yetta Goodman deepened teachers' understandings of the reading process, and they created pedagogical practices which incorporated the use of miscue into the reading and writing curriculum. The writing of Lev Vygotsky influenced both teachers and researchers. Dewey's vision of a participatory democracy was infused into participatory classroom practices and inquiry-based instruction. Teachers were energized. Many saw themselves as intellectuals. There was an emphasis on family, school, and community partnerships, on informal learning environments, and self-directed learning.

Reporter: So what happened?

Teacher: Teachers became activists as well as scholars. They presented their research at national and international conferences as they advocated for their students. Holistic instruction, whole language, inquiry/problem based learning, and portfolio assessment became familiar topics of conversation. Teachers gained recognition, their voices were loud and strong, and there was a shift of power away from elite policy-makers and powerful commercial publishers of textbooks and basal reading programs. Dewey would have found some schools to be remarkable in their vision and interpretation of participatory democratic pedagogical practices. But that time has past. Now, there are no public schools. They are all for-profit and teachers read government-approved scripts. There is no art, no music, no recess, no laughter, just a focus on performance and on tests.

Reporter: You mentioned someone called Dewey and then Ken and Yetta Goodman.

Teacher: [Smiles] I'll send you some of their work. *Democracy and Education* (1997), *On Reading* (1996), *Reading Miscue Inventory* (1987). The United States is forgetful of its history now that there are no written records. It's almost 60 years since Ken Goodman introduced the idea that reading is a language process. He and Yetta Goodman were at the center of the whole language movement. They inspired teachers and built a national community of educators who worked as advocates for children. Some were aware that whole language was a political movement. They got it. They knew that teaching kids to read and write was a political activity. Still is. The commitment was to ensure the rights of all children, children of color, children for whom English was a second language, children whose lives were traumatized by their life experiences, and children who were new to this country, to actively participate and to have the opportunity to become productive members of American society.

Reporter: So where did Dewey come in?

Teacher: The vision began with Dewey. The Goodmans based their pedagogy on his philosophy of participatory democracy. The Goodmans' own childhood experiences, shaped by the political discrimination that they themselves suffered, shaped their work. Their scholarship was fired by an insatiable desire *to know*, tempered by Vygotsky (1978, 1986), Ferreiro, and other emancipatory pedagogists, countered by reductionist theorists and the far right, and shaped by the research of feminist theorists and critical pedagogists, but most of all it was based on their understandings of the meaning-constructing ambiguity of human existence.

Reporter: [Laughs] Say again?

Teacher: [Laughs] Meaning-constructing ambiguity of human existence. To understand the lives of the Goodmans you have to understand, from a particular perspective, the history of the development of reading research and practice in the 20th century. Many reporters interviewed them but none of them got it. Read the article by Jim Collins in *Time* if you want to get a better understanding of the politics of reading.

Reporter: Not available.

Teacher: I have a copy you can read. Collins never got it. He became part of the problem. Maybe you will too. The Goodmans' lives shed light on the different viewpoints that have emerged about what it means to be literate in America and bring into sharp focus the political decisions that are made about who learns to read and write.

Reporter: So. Can you tell me anything about their early lives?

Teacher: Ken and Yetta Goodman were both children of East European Jewish immigrants who arrived in the United States at the beginning of the last century. Ken's father was nine years of age when he arrived from Lithuania, in 1905. He worked in a grocery warehouse, as a taxi driver, but mostly as a salesman. His mother was the first child born in America to Polish Jewish parents. She started work in her parents' store after she had finished eighth grade. Yetta's father immigrated in 1912, leaving her pregnant mother behind in Russia until he was settled and could take care of her. The First World War made it impossible for her to leave Russia and so it was eight years before Yetta's mother and father were able to live together. The experiences of their parents and their early lives as first-generation Jewish Americans are a critical part of the history that Ken and Yetta share, which shaped both their political and philosophical beliefs, and which drove them in both their personal and professional lives to search for humanistic solutions to the educational problems of children and young people, both in America and in the many countries which they visited and worked in around the world.

Reporter: Okay. And their research? I still don't get what was so different about what they did.

Teacher: During the early years, there was an intense sense of intellectual excitement. Both in America and abroad. Researchers interested in language and reading broke with the mechanics of behaviorist stimulus-response traditions and centered their studies on meaning. Inspired by the research of linguists such as Noam Chomsky and energized by the convergence of their own research findings with scholars such as Frank Smith and Roger Shuy, Ken and Yetta continued to push their own thinking. They shared with their students their excitement at the changes that were taking place within the field of education. Especially for those interested in the reading process and in helping children to read. Their research had enormous influence both in the United States and around the world.

Reporter: Hard to believe that they were so well known and we know nothing about them.

Teacher: Censorship, book banning, the purging of electronic files. By the beginning of the 21st century the ERIC files had already been purged.

Reporter: So go back. Talk about their influence here and in other countries.

Teacher: [Smiles] They both became actively involved in professional organizations, attending conferences, participating in committees and steering groups, challenging researchers. Often challenging empiricists who held tight to linear reductionist stage theories of reading acquisition and advocating for a socio-psycholinguistic model of reading in which meaning was central to the process and children were in control of their own learning.

Reporter: And in other countries?

Teacher: During the year that Ken was president of the International Reading Association, he traveled to Argentina, Uruguay, and Chile, and he participated in the creation of the journal *Lectura y Vida*. Then, when Yetta was president of the National Council of Teachers of English, she brought researchers including Marie Clay, Emilia Ferreiro, and Michael Halliday to the United States and provided teachers with the opportunity to meet them. In the years that followed, both Ken and Yetta worked in countries around the world, sharing their research and actively advocating for the rights of teachers and children.

Reporter: You said something about a socio? Socio-psycholinguistic model?

Teacher: Ken's socio-psycholinguistic model of the reading process influenced the reconceptualization of pedagogical practices in many South American countries, in Australia, and to some extent in Britain. Miscue was used around the world. Although not always as it was intended. To assist teachers in understanding the reading process and to enable them to support children as they are learning to read. In this country their work was central to the development of whole language, and it was through their commitment to teachers and their energy to organize that whole language became such a powerful movement for meaning-centered learning.

Reporter: [Laughs] It's going to be hard to leave all this history out.

Teacher: [Laughs] For the few of us who are left it's more than our history. It's still our philosophy and our pedagogy. We are still struggling for a participatory democracy.

Reporter: You've given me a lot to think about.

Teacher: Don't attack me too badly.

Reporter: No I won't. I won't mention you in the article. Too hot. Wouldn't get published.

Concluding Comments

I have taken an extreme position in the second interview, partly because I am convinced it is important that we imagine what could be our future history. The world has changed. It has become a much more dangerous place. The possibility that we are entering a different political era is not far-fetched. "In the worst-case scenario," Richard Rorty (2004) writes, "historians will someday have to explain why the golden age of Western democracy, like the age of the Antonines, lasted only about two hundred years" (p.11).

At a time when the United States is at war, war metaphors are often used to frame the conflict that is taking place between government-employed researchers and teachers on how young children should be taught to read and write. But the "reading wars" are not about whole language or phonics or between Cartesian/positivistic research and post-formal science. No. The reading wars are about the control of language, who reads, who writes, and for what purpose. More control and less freedom are central issues in every sphere of U.S. domestic and foreign policy. All wars begin with words. Before military conflicts take place there are verbal conflicts. Coming under fire is a complex linguistic feat. Arguments are presented, diplomacy is attempted, and threats are made. Within the reading field threats have been made by Reid Lyon (2002) of the National Institute of Child Health and Human Development (NICHD). "You know," Reid Lyon said at a political forum in Washington, "if there was any piece of legislation I could pass, it would be to blow up colleges of education." War metaphors have also been used by the Secretary of Education, Ron Paige, who has referred to teachers as "terrorists."

Clearly, the war of words that is being waged by the current administration and the federal government is *not for* a participatory democracy or for a form of public education which would support such a political system. Instead the purpose of these aggressive initiatives, as Slavoj Zizek argues in his piece "Paranoid Reflections" (2003), might be "the disciplining of the emancipatory excesses in American society." Unfortunately, the second interview is not so far-fetched. "I cannot help thinking that democratic institutions," Rorty writes, "in my country at least, have become pretty fragile," and he refers to Washington as a "military-industrial complex."

The war of words in public education matches the militaristic excesses of our time, and much worse things could happen if we don't participate. Ken Goodman states,

> It's not easy in our personal and professional lives to face reality. There are no magic solutions to our physical, mental, or social problems. The world exists in all its wonder and we are a part of it, subject to its physical laws, limited in the same ways as all living things. We can try to understand the interconnections and do what we can to make them work for us. But we can never disconnect ourselves from those interconnections or make them less complicated by pretending or by wishful thinking. (1999)

This statement represents for me the essence of the intellect and passion that is at the center of the lives and work of Ken and Yetta Goodman. It is the moral, ethical, and philosophical foundation of the work that Ken and Yetta do that Jim Collins did not get. He missed the way in which both their science and their pedagogy recognized the complexity of the ambiguity of human existence and that both complexity and ambiguity are central to the ways in which young children learn to read and write.

If we are to make a difference in the lives of our children, grandchildren, and the children that we teach, then it is essential that we challenge the culture of a government which controls the ways in which literacy is used and the ways in which children are taught and learn to read and write. We have reached a time when teachers are holding the line between the future lives of children and the emergence of an increasingly repressive totalitarian state. Jim Collins was right about one thing. It is a big story about politics and passion and our classrooms, and the ways in which we teach are a part of it.

To live is to teach. At this critical moment in time it is important that teachers and researchers who work with children and their families in schools and communities work together locally, nationally, and internationally to establish working partnerships and collaborative initiatives in the struggle for a participatory democracy.

At a 2001 International Scholars' Forum at Hofstra University, Louise Rosenblatt who was in her 100th year, spoke with the beginning teachers in the audience, "Those who sit back and wait for a backlash from the current damaging reactionary hold on schools are, I believe, ignoring the children who are meanwhile being affected." Louise continued, "We must try to influence what is happening. If we fail, as well we may, we shall at least have spread the ideas and have educated some who will continue the resistance" (Taylor, 2004, p. 351). Ken and Yetta Goodman, who are both in their 70s, dare to imagine a society and a world in which every child has the opportunity to read and write. Louise Rosenblatt who recently passed away did too. She advocated for teachers, children, and their families throughout her life. Margaret Meek Spencer and Maxine Greene are both in their 80s, and they continue to be activists and advocates as well as scholars and teachers. More than ever it is essential that we continue their work and the work of the many other teachers and scholars who have made it possible for children to learn to read and write in classrooms that are both participatory and democratic. "The challenge must be embraced by those of us who are obligated to always carry forth the process of consciousness-raising," Emilia Ferreiro (2003) writes. To teach in this moment in time is both radical and courageous. In a world that has become increasingly opportunistic and militaristic teachers have an essential role to play.

References

Adams, M. (1990). *Beginning to read: Thinking and learning about print.* Cambridge, MA: MIT Press.

Bahktin, M.M. (1983). *The dialogic imagination: Four essays.* Austin, TX: University of

Texas Press.

Barton, D., & Hamilton, M. (1998). *Local literacies: Reading and writing in one community.* New York: Routledge.

Berliner, D. & Biddle, B. (1996). *The manufactured crisis: Myths, fraud, and the attack on American public schools.* New York: Addison-Wesley.

Britton, J. (1993). *Literature in its place.* Portsmouth, NH: Heinemann.

Calkins, L. (1994). *Art of teaching writing.* Portsmouth, NH: Heinemann.

Clay, M. (1987). *Reading begins at home: Preparing children before they go to school.* Portsmouth, NH: Heinemann.

— (1991). *Becoming literate: The construction of inner control.* Portsmouth, NH: Heinemann.

Collins, J. (1997, October 27). How Johnny should read. *Time Magazine,150*(17).

Dewey, J. (1997). *Democracy and education.* New York: Free Press.

Eco, U. (1976). *A theory of semiotics.* Bloomington, IN: Indiana University Press.

Ferreiro, E. (2003). *Pasr and present of the verbs to read and write: Essays on literacy.* Toronto, Ontario: Groundwood Books.

Ferreiro, E., & Teberosky, A. (1982). *Literacy before schooling.* Portsmouth, NH: Heinemann.

Goodman, K. (1994). *Phonics phacts.* Portsmouth, NH: Heinemann.

— (1996). *On reading.* Ontario: Scholastic Canada Ltd.

— (1999) *In defense of good teaching.* International Scholars Forum, Hofstra University, Thursday, March 11, 1999.

Goodman, K., Bird, L., & Goodman, Y. (1991). *The whole language catalog.* Santa Rosa, CA: American School Publishers, SRA div. McGraw-Hill Macmillan.

— (1992). *The whole language catalog: Supplement on authentic assessment.* Santa Rosa, CA: American School Publishers, SRA div. McGraw-Hill Macmillan.

Goodman, K., Brooks Smith, E., Meredith, R., & Goodman, Y. (1987). *Language and thinking in school: A whole-language curriculum.* New York: Richard C. Owen.

Goodman, K., Shannon, P., Freeman, Y., & Murphy, S. (1988). *Report card on basal readers.* Katonah, NY: Richard C. Owen.

Goodman, Y., Watson, D. J., & Burke, C. L. (1987). *Reading miscue inventory: Alternative procedures.* New York: Richard C. Owen.

Graves, D. (1982). *Writing: Teachers and children at work.* Portsmouth, NH: Heinemann.

Lemann, Nicholas. (1997, November). The reading wars. *The Atlantic Monthly,* 128-34.

Lyon, R. (2002). *Rigorous evidence: The key to progress in education? Lessons from medicine, welfare and other fields.* The Council for Excellence in Government, Washington D.C., November 18, 2002.

Meek, M. (1992). *On being literate.* Portsmouth, NH: Heinemann.

Palmaffy, T. (1997, November/December). See Dick flunk. *Policy Review: The Journal of American Citizenship,* 86, 32-40.

Rorty, R. (2004). Post-democracy: Richard Rorty on anti-terrorism and the national security state. *London Review of Books,* 26(7), pp. 10-11.

Rosenblatt, L. (1992). *The Reader, the text, the poem: The transactional theory of the literary work.* Carbondale, IL: Southern Illinois University Press.

Stanovich, K. (1988). *Children's reading and the development of phonological awareness.* Detroit, MI: Wayne State University Press.

Street, B. (1995). *Social literacies: Critical approaches to literacy development, ethnography and education.* Harlow, Essex, England: Pearson Education.

Taylor, D. (1983). *Family literacy: Young children learning to read and write.* Portsmouth, NH: Heinemann.

Taylor, D. (1998). *Beginning to read and the spin doctors of science: The political campaign to change America's mind about how children learn to read.* Urbana, IL: National Council for Teachers of English.

Taylor, D. (2004). Profile: Yetta Goodman, Maxine Greene, Louise Rosenblatt, and Margaret Meek Spencer: Language, literacy, and politics. *Language Arts, 81*(4), 344-351.

Taylor, D., & Dorsey-Gaines, C. (1988). *Growing up literate: Learning from inner-city families.* Portsmouth, NH: Heinemann.

Toch, T. (1997, October 27). The reading wars continue. *U.S. News & World Report, 123*(16), 77.

Vygotsky, L. S. (1978). *Mind in society: The development of higher psychological processes.* M. Cole, V. John-Steiner, S. Scribner & E. Souberman (Eds.). Cambridge, MA: Harvard University Press.

Vygotsky, L. (1986). *Thought and language.* A. Kozulin (Ed.). Cambridge, MA: MIT Press.

Zizek, S. (2003) Paranoid reflections. *The London Review of Books*, Vol. 25, No. 7, April 3, 2005.

CHAPTER NINE

Whole Language: Alive and Well

YETTA AND KEN GOODMAN

For those familiar with whole language, the authors in this volume provide an opportunity to revisit the excitement of the development and influence of the philosophy of whole language on teaching and learning. And it also helps newcomers appreciate what whole language has contributed to education everywhere. In this final chapter, we build on and add our perspective to the insights about whole language documented from different vantage points by the authors.

We choose not to summarize or respond to each chapter; rather we explore the principles that unite the chapters as the authors share their rich experiences with whole language during the latter part of the 20th century. Here are some of the central principles of a whole language philosophy:

1. The dynamic development of language and literacy, whole and in the context of their use.
2. A view of literacy as making sense through written and oral language.
3. Trust between teachers and learners, parents and communities.
4. Life-long learning for teachers and researchers as well as learners.
5. Empowering of teachers and learners.
6. The integration of the development of knowledge with practices designed to promote language and literacy.
7. A seamless connection between the experiences learners have in school and in their homes and communities.
8. A deep and abiding commitment to democracy and social justice and the role of education in achieving both.
9. A commitment to making school a positive, safe, and enjoyable experience for all learners.
10. A respect for differences and acceptance of all learners, and building on the strengths they bring with them to school.

11. High expectations for all learners while recognizing they have different goals, values, cultures and abilities.

Unlike many approaches to curriculum and methodology built on single premises—phonics in reading, controlled vocabulary, individualized instruction, etc., which we have labeled "one-legged models"—whole language has a complete, balanced, and integrated foundation supported by five pillars: learning, teaching, language, curriculum, and social community. These principles and pillars are the themes of the chapters. But characteristic of whole language, neither the principles nor the pillars are discrete from each other. They are always present in all aspects of whole language; that's what makes whole language whole.

Respect for learners and learning is documented throughout this volume, not only in the discussions about children and adolescents but also in the discussions about teachers and teaching, researchers and researching. Teachers and researchers are learners too. Whole language teachers acknowledge their role as learners when they say "I'm still becoming a whole language teacher." Learning is a continuous part of good teaching. In classrooms and other settings teachers expand on understandings about what it means to be a whole language teacher. They even embrace their failures as they reflect on and share experiences with others about ways to be responsive to students and continue to change and grow as teachers. So teaching and learning are reciprocal processes in every respect.

Learning and Teaching in a Whole Language Curriculum

Whole language teachers view teaching as providing a host of problem-solving opportunities to ask questions: Why is this happening? What does this tell me about the intellectual functioning of my students? How does the community of learners contribute to the learning of the individual? What do I see in this environment and in the community to help me continuously plan and organize the experiences that allow for the extension of learning opportunities? Kidwatching, reflective teaching with careful observation and thoughtful interactions with our students, includes the understanding of each learner but also an understanding of how the community of learners works together to explore problems and come to solutions that benefit all the members of the community. In such contexts the teacher follows the lead of the learners, supporting and facilitating by providing appropriate knowledge and at the same time posing probing questions and problems to lead students to their own questions and their own solutions.

In describing teacher Mei's kindergarten class, Lian-Ju Lee and Wen-Yun Lin (Chapter 7) document children's responses to their teachers' reading of a book about scary creatures. One child responded to the book with a great deal of fear. The teacher responded to the child's fears by putting the book away on a shelf but at the same time followed up on the child's fears in a number of ways. With the students, the teacher developed a chart that included titles of related books, the names of the main characters and of what they were afraid. The class developed a survey form to interview each other and their family members about fears they had as they responded to books.

Toward the end of a class discussion about how to get rid of their fears, one child suggested "that everyone write down on a small piece of paper whatever he or she was afraid of and give it to her." She got a box and labeled it "Taking-fear-away Box." With classmates, the girl put the notes into the box. She sealed it, put the box away and announced, "Now your fears are trapped in the box so they can not harm you any more." The authors summarize this sequence: "The activities were mostly initiated and implemented by children, and revolved around what they were concerned about....The children...owned their learning process." The children participated in negotiating the curriculum as the teacher monitored their learning and considered what they needed to know to continue their literacy development. "They spoke and listened to each other for opinions and comments; read for pleasure as well as for fulfilling curiosity and obtaining information and wrote to accomplish work related to their investigation."

In this example as in many others, learners are involved in negotiating the curriculum; ideas fold in on themselves and involve all kinds of literacy practices, and the students are engaged in the extension of learning experiences. Teachers use the tools of literacy as an integral part of the curriculum to involve students at all levels in developing literacy as well as the content of the disciplines (literature, science, the arts). They provide meaningful literacy experiences that connect to the lives of their students. Through students' engagement and search for meaning, teachers become partners with their students in the development of their own learning, building a problem-posing / problem-solving curriculum.

Teachers in such settings are advocates for their students. They facilitate a proactive curriculum that results in action used to better their students' lives and the lives of others. This action-oriented and emerging curriculum is the result of the dynamic nature of teaching and learning that evolves to meet the needs of the learners.

The authors in this book show how they responded to the tensions between state and local (and now national) curricula and a rich whole language curriculum that stimulates and engages learners. They are therefore constructive, composing and inventing curricula to satisfy the objectives of the educational authorities while keeping the learner in the center of how experiences are chosen and organized. Informed teachers know how to demonstrate their students' learning to parents and administrators and at the same time document how each learner achieves the objectives of what is mandated when that is possible. Because they trust that learners respond with their own interests, curriculum does not focus on disembodied bits of knowledge that have little or nothing to do with the world of the learners. They know that students read, write, and learn about their world as part of an engaging curriculum. Therefore spelling, phonics, grammar, and vocabulary are not separate entities but integrated into coming to know about their world. Social conventions are the focus of the curriculum as teachers support students to understand their purposes and appropriate uses in various contexts. Teachers know how to document students' development of the conventions of language in this integrated and dynamic curriculum.

Whole language teachers often need to be courageous to deal with the conventions of a status quo society and to support changes in curriculum that stimulate learners. The classroom curriculum is dual where the teachers monitor their students' knowledge to satisfy district, state, and/or national objectives but allow students to grow in their use of reading and writing as they explore concepts in math, science, and social studies. By answering their own questions through theme cycles that recognize the integration of knowledge with literacy practices, students expand their knowledge of content and their literacy capabilities.

Whole language teachers are willing to take risks in supporting such curriculum because they understand that in a rich learning environment, curriculum involves liberatory practices that transform students to act on behalf of themselves and their communities for the purposes of social justice and their participation in a democratic society.

There is a strong bond between teaching and learning, but it is necessary to be aware that teaching and learning do not have a simple one-to-one correspondence. What is taught is not directly learned. What is taught can be miseducative (Dewey, 1938) as well as transforming. The learner is actively involved in how what is being taught becomes part of his or her schema. Organization and planning are important components of learning and result in how learners explore their environments to continue to develop their capabilities.

Language and Content Knowledge in
the Construction of Curriculum

Teachers know language and the content they teach. They help their students understand the learning process as well as the processes of reading and writing. They converse with their students, exploring what miscues reveal about their language use. They believe that experience grows out of inexperience. They know that growth and development are continuous in learners and a result of challenges, disequilibrium, and hard work in learning about their world.

Both knowledge and language change as a result of a transactional curriculum. Artifacts take on new meaning, concepts develop greater depth, the learner matures and becomes more capable, and the teacher responds to the changes, exploring new ways to engage the changing learners. Language also changes as the students expand their use of language to deal with a variety of new genres and develop the language specific to new fields and levels of understanding. This is Dewey's transaction: the result in the learning community is transformative for the individual as well as for the group, for the teachers as well as the students.

Monica Taylor and Gennifer Otinsky (Chapter 5) provide examples of how preservice teachers use content and language in new ways as they engage in inquiry that "truly meant something to them" in their social justice projects. "Through reading and doing research about race, ethnicity, and the teaching of social justice...they had the opportunity to try out these practices when they entered the classroom and worked side by side with the sixth graders....They were able to grapple with issues of race and social justice teaching in a small group setting...and then they actually...put into practices similar issues with the sixth graders."

Many of the chapters make clear that collaborative learning is not only for students but also for teachers. Social learning is not something that ends as a result of finishing second grade, getting a diploma or a degree or a certification. It continuously builds and extends the learner's language and thoughts.

Knowledge is also dynamic, and curriculum needs to be able to respond to the new knowledge that is accelerating in the information age. Whole language integrates literacy learning with historical information in order to be responsive to the changes in the disciplines that continually take place. The emphasis is often on how to learn, on how to access knowledge and information to involve students in preparing for the inevitable change that takes place as humans continue to explore and understand the world in which we live. Teachers often involve the learners in choosing the specific topics for units of study. As a number of the authors demonstrate, teachers understand that a wide range of concepts can develop within any topic.

Social Community and Participatory Democracy

Building close relations between the classroom and the students' families and members of the community is another important aspect of whole language. This is especially well represented in the description of the development of the Dewey Center by community activists and teachers in renewing an inner-city school. Debra Goodman (Chapters 2 and 3) recounts this history and demonstrates the ways in which parents, students, and teachers come together to develop a vibrant education for children and a rich learning experience for all. It shows how a participatory and democratic curriculum is developed.

Whole language grew, in every venue it developed, as a grassroots movement. Participants came together, in the spirit of mutual respect, to understand how progressive views of teaching and learning contribute to a complete school experience. The respect that each member of the whole language community has for the knowledge and experience of the others is central to the development of whole language. The knowledge of researchers and teacher educators is an important element of growth of understanding, and the experience and knowledge of thoughtful and successful teachers are equally significant. And the community itself provides a rich source of talent, experiences, and funds of knowledge (Moll et al., 1992).

Debra Goodman voices the power of the teacher collective. "We argued, cajoled, laughed and cried together. We responded to administrative and district and national mandates, but we continued because we learned so much—the opportunities of Teacher Applying Whole Language group discussions, conferences, articles, and the Whole Language Umbrella transformed us. We know whole language works and we don't apologize for our zeal and passion."

Tamzin Sawyer (Chapter 6) also describes the excitement of the teachers in her school when they "began to have conversations and workshops about reading and how to improve curriculum." They developed a book room for use by teachers. They pooled sets of books "from all over the school," and teachers were involved in ordering books from catalogs. The faculty implemented a school-wide Sustained Silent Reading Program during which students self-selected books to read independently. "We actually had a lot of debate about how SSR time should look before it went smoothly." Tamzin highlights the issue of trust: "I think a lot of this debate we had over SSR was based on trust. Eventually I learned that I wanted my students to become independent readers. And to accomplish that I needed to trust them."

But Tamzin struggles with how "the system" trusts her as a professional and experienced teacher. In the climate of the late 1990s and early 2000s, the control that Tamzin and her colleagues were developing over their curriculum was challenged once again. She worked with others to sustain her philosophical beliefs about whole language and to adapt to new top–down mandates. She ends her article saying that "not only being a student but also being a teacher is a matter of trust."

The chapters in this book honestly face the constraints of conservative and status quo policies. The authors recognize the need for educators to see their work in a transformative teacher movement as they negotiate curriculum.

Denny Taylor (Chapter 8) makes clear her concerns with the mandates of politicians on schools, teachers, and curriculum development. Her chapter is crafted to "challenge the culture of a government which controls the ways in which literacy is used and the ways in which children are taught to read and write." These controls were established by the passing of the Reading Excellence Act in October of 1997, but at the same time, within a short period, articles with titles such as "How Johnny Should Read," "Why Andy Couldn't Read," "The Reading Wars," and "See Dick Flunk" all critiqued whole language and lauded commercial reading programs as opposed to curriculum developed by experienced and knowledgeable teachers. The intention of these politicians is to take control of curriculum, content, and methodology out of the hands of the professionals and members of the local school community. That would be a terrible loss for the future of American education.

Teachers and Learners—Participants in a Democracy

Action is necessary to regain the momentum and vitality of whole language. As Carole Stice, Nancy Bertrand, and Maryann Manning (Chapter 4) say: "A liberatory pedagogy suggests that education's purpose is to help [all learners] become information-getters and critical thinkers, and that to do their jobs teachers must be more politically savvy and active."

A social and political teachers' movement is needed where teachers work together to discover new ways to interact with the public at large at the same time as they work with their students and their families. Through teacher support groups and conferences, whole language teachers continue their collaborations and discussions. They need to learn to make use of the media and the Internet to make their voices heard. They need to involve parents in understanding educational practices and curriculum development and to help them realize that there is choice in the ways in which schooling happens. The mandates coming from the state and federal government are disguised as school reform, but if anything they bring back the worst aspects of transmission-model teaching. Whole language has never been a defense of the status quo in education. Rather it has provided the means of reaching the original goal of universal public education which is to educate all learners to their fullest potential, recognizing the broad range of individual differences in interests, values, and goals.

One way to achieve change is to make the successes of whole language more clearly visible to parents, administrators, and the general public. The articles in this volume provide many examples, but we need to explore how to make the stories of teachers, administrators, researchers, and teacher educators available to larger audiences. We need to expand on our methods of documentation of what goes on in classrooms, how teachers continuously evaluate their students, how students are engaged in self-evaluation to be accountable to parents and the school community.

Inviting politicians, newspaper reporters, and community members into presentations about the culmination of school projects and thematic units, of hearing about the impact students have in improving community life and listening to the kinds of literacy experiences in which students engage are all ways of documenting what is happening in our classrooms and our schools. Town meetings and school-wide discussions about whole language theories and practices bring the voices of parents into the discussion. In such contexts, teachers need to be specific about what is learned and what teachers and students are doing.

Professional development must be seen as a continuous and lifelong process. Teachers need to build increasing understanding about language learning and teaching. They need to recognize the responses that lead to new learnings and the responses that cut off experimentation and new understandings by their students. In this way teachers come to understand how concepts and knowledge are developed as a result of language use. Respecting learning in all contexts and finding ways to demonstrate what and how students learn in non-school settings help to highlight all kinds of learning opportunities. The role of the knowledge in homes and communities and the influence that plays in students' learning need to be respected. The varied languages and dialects that students use need to be recognized as resources that support learning.

Some critics say that whole language is too optimistic about outcomes and doesn't recognize when results are negative. On the contrary, whole language proponents expect the politics of education, the problems of society, and the struggles with learning to be a dynamic part of the constructive nature of the teaching and learning process. That's why we title this chapter "Whole Language: Alive and Well." Teaching and learning in a democracy will always warrant discussion and debate. There is no utopian ending. The rights to ideas and thoughts must be protected, not as slogans but as opportunities to continue to explore and research the possibilities of education in a democracy. Whole language thrives in such environments.

Whole language is a realistic pedagogy. Advocates know there will be students who struggle in their learning. They know there are problems in education that can't be solved in the classroom but need support and help from a wide range of community participants.

Why Whole Language Came Under Attack

The attack on whole language that misrepresented it as a "touchy, feely" alternate to phonics in reading instruction and blamed it for what Berliner and Biddle (1996) have called the "Manufactured Crisis" in American education, didn't result from inadequacies in whole language or the overzealousness of its proponents. Denny Taylor (Chapter 8) provides insight into the attack as well. We believe it came because as Debra Goodman (Chapter 2) makes clear, whole language is a strong, solidly based and highly effective grassroots movement. Whole language develops a sense of power among teachers and learners. Whole language reached a point where it was producing profound improvements in public education. And precisely for that reason the opponents of universal public education, those who seek to privatize American schools, began their campaign by attacking whole language. The Australians say it's the tall poppies that get cut down, and whole language indeed stood tall.

Ironically, the mandates coming from the federal and national governments read like they have been written to substitute all that is bad in education for all that is good in whole language:

1. phonics-based reading instruction,
2. dull, nonsensical skill-based instructional materials,
3. evaluation based on single tests,
4. unachievable and statistically impossible passing criteria,
5. narrow curriculum with subjects separated and facts to be memorized,
6. rigid grade-level skill specifications,
7. punishment of pupils, teachers, schools, districts and states for failure to achieve,
8. deprofessionalizing teachers.

There is no doubt that whole language will survive and that it still represents the future of education in democratic societies. Whether the term loses the tarnish its enemies have put on it is not very important. The principles of whole language and the productivity it achieved will again become dominant as successful schools continue to be the meeting places of empowered teachers and learners. This book is a documentary of the rich period of whole language. Whole language classrooms still exist in the U.S., Canada, and other English-speaking countries. They are increasingly active in South America and in Asia. And teachers will turn to books like this one to rebuild and carry education forward.

In the current era the authors have provided solid support for teachers everywhere who know what good teaching is, no matter what Congress or their state legislators mandate. We and the authors thank those professional educators for their courage and professionalism.

References

Berliner, D., & Biddle, B. (1996) *Manufactured crisis: Myths, fraud and the attack on America's public schools.* White Plains, NY: Longman.

Dewey, J. (1938). *Experience and education.* New York: Collier Books.

Moll, L.; Amanti, C.; Neff, D, Gonzalez, N. (1992). Funds of knowledge for teaching: A qualitative approach to connect households and classrooms. *Theory into Practice 31*(2), pp. 132-141.

Contributors

Nancy P. Bertrand is a retired professor and former classroom teacher. After receiving her B.S. in Elementary Education at the University of Tennessee, she taught grades 1 through 6 in Georgia, North Carolina, and Tennessee. She earned her Ph.D. in Early and Middle Childhood Education with an emphasis in Reading at The Ohio State University. She spent 22 years in the Department of Elementary and Special Education at Middle Tennessee State University. She maintains membership in NRC, IRA, NCTE and the Whole Language Umbrella. She is currently serving on the editorial boards of *The Reading Teacher* and the *Journal of Research in Childhood Education*. Her passion was helping children author and publish their own books, for which she received the MTSU Distinguished Public Service Award. Over the years she has conducted a number of research projects centered around literacy acquisition and classroom practice. She has co-authored two textbooks, a number of edited chapters, several articles, and has an essay forthcoming in an IRA book about the emergent literacy of beginning teachers.

Debra Goodman is an associate professor in the Literacy Studies Department at Hofstra University. Recent publications address whole language in Detroit, effective beginning readers, dialect and reading, teaching in an unjust world, the social nature of young children becoming literate, and language study in teacher education. She received her Ph.D. in English Education from Michigan State University in 1999. Dr. Goodman taught in the Detroit Public Schools for fifteen years. Dr. Goodman has worked with teachers and teacher educators across the U.S. as well as Taiwan, Mexico, and Guatamala. She is author of *The Reading Detective Club*.

Kenneth S. Goodman is a practical theorist, researcher and teacher educator whose work has changed our understanding of literacy processes, how they are learned, and how best to teach them. His psychosociotransactional theory of the reading process is the most widely cited in the world. This research based theory demonstrates that reading is a unitary process in which readers actively construct meaning, that is they make sense of print. Goodman's theory is a macro view which is solidly built on linguistic, psycholinguistic and sociolinguistic concepts. It is a practical theory because teachers who come to understand this view of reading and the related view of writing can understand what it is that learners are doing as they develop literacy.

Email: kgoodman@u.arizona.edu

URL: www.ed.arizona.edu/kgoodman

Yetta M. Goodman is Regents Professor Emerita at the University of Arizona, College of Education in the Department of Language, Reading and Culture. She consults with education departments and speaks at conferences throughout the United States and in many nations of the world regarding issues of language, teaching and learning with implications for language arts curricula. In addition to her research in early literacy, miscue analysis and the reading and writing processes, she has popularized the term "kidwatching," encouraging teachers to be professional observers of the language and learning development of their students. She is a past president of NCTE, has served on NCTE & IRA Board of Directors and been an active member of commissions and committees. She was a principal force in the development of IRA-NCTE co-sponsored conferences examining the impact of oral and written language development research on the schools. She is a spokesperson for whole language philosophy and in her extensive writing is focused on classrooms, students and teachers.

Email: ygoodman@u.arizona.edu

URL: www.ed.arizona.edu/ygoodman

Lian-Ju Lee is currently an associate professor in the Department of Early Childhood Education at the National University of Tainan in Tawain. She received her Ph.D. at the University of Arizona, with major focuses on literacy development and early childhood curriculum. Before her graduate studies, she taught Language Arts in a junior high school in Taiwan and at the same time worked with preschool children for a number of years. Her research interests and publications have focused on early literacy development and whole language teaching and curriculum development. She has many ideas to share about applying a whole language philosophy to Taiwanese early educational settings and Chinese language teaching. As a teacher educator, Lian-Ju has been working closely with kindergarten teachers in her geographic area. She was one of the founders of the first, as well as the largest at present time, whole language teacher supporting group in Taiwan and has remained active in this group ever since. She is one of the participants as well as witnesses of the development of whole language in Taiwan. She was the president of the Taiwan TAWL for the years of 2000-2002, and 2002-2004.

Wen-Yun Lin is currently teaching at National Taipei University of Education in the Department of Language and Literature Education. She is teaching children's literature, reading and language arts curriculum and instruction. She has been working on action research in terms of alternative curriculum and instruction with teachers across the country for many years. Wen-Yun edited a series of experimental language arts textbooks with the support from the Ministry of Education. She is also active in professional workshops for in-service teachers where she shares research and practice in terms of reading and language arts curriculum and instruction. She studied with Dr. Yetta Goodman and Dr. Kenneth Goodman at the University of Arizona. She is currently the president of Taiwan Teachers Apply Whole Language (Taiwan TAWL).

Maryann Manning is a professor at the University of Alabama at Birmingham. She was a classroom teacher for twelve years before beginning her ivory tower years. She authored and co-authored many books and articles and has served as the reading and writing editor of *Teaching K-8*. She still views herself as a teacher and spends much time helping children read and write.

Gennifer Otinsky is a sixth grade language arts/social studies teacher at Grover Cleveland Middle School in Caldwell, New Jersey. She received her B.A. at James Madison University in middle school education and has a M.A. from Saint Peter's College. She is interested in teaching for social justice, adolescent literature, and the integration of the arts across the curriculum.

M. Tamzin Sawyer is a third grade teacher at the Carrillo Intermediate Magnet School in Tucson Unified School District. She received her B.A. from Smith College in Northampton, M.A., 1994. She then earned her teacher certification from University of Arizona in December 1997. It was there that she participated in the Whole Language Block at Borton Primary Magnet School in TUSD under the guidance of Dr. Yetta Goodman, Steve Bialostok, and others. She received her M.A. from the University of Arizona in Language, Reading, and Culture, 2003 where her advisor was Dr. Yetta Goodman.

Carole E. Stice is a former classroom teacher and teacher educator. She began her career with an undergraduate degree in English, but her first teaching experience was as a reading teacher in an urban Job Corp center in the 1960s. She earned a M.Ed. in secondary reading and taught "remedial" reading in junior high for two years. She earned a Ph.D. in literacy education from Florida State University in 1974 and has taught at the college level ever since. In the early 1980s, she began serving as an editor for the state reading journal. She has been a member of IRA, NCTE, and the Whole Language Umbrella. From 1985 to 2001 she sponsored Middle Tennessee TAWL. She has co-authored several articles, two poems, four books, one set of non-fiction educational materials for middle grade readers called *Book2Web* published by McGraw-Hill /The Wright Group and a set of guided readers titled *Reading for Adults* published by McGraw-Hill/Contemporary. Recently, *Highlights for Children* accepted for publication one of her short stories titled "Stuart, the Lucky Library Cat."

Denny Taylor is Professor and Doctoral Director of Literacy Studies at Hofstra University. She began teaching in 1968 in the East End of London. There were 43 children in her first kindergarten class. She has been continuously engaged in ethnographic literacy research since 1977 and was inducted into the Reading Hall of Fame in 2004. She is the author of nine books including *Family Literacy*, *Growing Up Literate*, *Learning Denied*, and *Learning to Read* and the *Spin Doctors of Science*. She is interested in explorations of the ways in which complimentary and contradictory theories of reading and writing can inform understandings of literacy as mindful social process. For the past six years she has been engaged in ethnographic research in areas of armed conflicts and natural disasters. The focus of this research is on the impact of catastrophic events on the lives of children and the social response of the educational community to mass trauma.

Monica Taylor is an associate professor in the Department of Curriculum and Teaching in the College of Education and Human Services at Montclair State University. She began her career as an urban middle school teacher of Spanish and French in an alternative school in New York City. She has a Ph.D. in language, literacy, and culture from the University of Arizona, where she studied with Ken and Yetta Goodman. Her research and publications revolve around several major themes including middle school literacy and inquiry, teaching for social justice, professional development school partnerships, and methods of self-study such as co/autoethnography.

Index

Studies in the Postmodern Theory of Education

General Editors
Joe L. Kincheloe & Shirley R. Steinberg

Counterpoints publishes the most compelling and imaginative books being
written in education today. Grounded on the theoretical advances in
criticalism, feminism, and postmodernism in the last two decades of the
twentieth century, Counterpoints engages the meaning of these innovations in various forms of educational expression. Committed to the
proposition that theoretical literature should be accessible to a variety of
audiences, the series insists that its authors avoid esoteric and jargonistic
languages that transform educational scholarship into an elite discourse for
the initiated. Scholarly work matters only to the degree it affects
consciousness and practice at multiple sites. Counterpoints' editorial
policy is based on these principles and the ability of scholars to break new
ground, to open new conversations, to go where educators have never
gone before.

For additional information about this series or for the submission of
manuscripts, please contact:

Joe L. Kincheloe & Shirley R. Steinberg
c/o Peter Lang Publishing, Inc.
29 Broadway, 18th floor
New York, New York 10006

To order other books in this series, please contact our Customer Service
Department:

(800) 770-LANG (within the U.S.)
(212) 647-7706 (outside the U.S.)
(212) 647-7707 FAX

Or browse online by series:
www.peterlang.com